15583

QUEEN MARGARET COLLEGE

100 063 096

D1380891

### QUEEN MARGARET COLLEGE

### LIBRARY

Please return book on or before latest date
stamped below

- 3 MAY 1973
11 OCT 1973
29 MAR 1974
11 MAR 1975

2 6 MAR 1981

1 APR 1981
25 FEB 1982
14 DEC 1982
2 JAN 1983

25 MAY 1983

# Acting in the Sixties

Withdrawn from
Queen Margaret University Library

QUEEN MARGARET COLLEGE LIBRARY

# Acting in

Richard Burton
Harry H. Corbett
Albert Finney
John Neville
Eric Porter
Vanessa Redgrave
Maggie Smith
Robert Stephens
Dorothy Tutin

Edited by
Hal Burton

# the Sixties

British Broadcasting
Corporation

Published by the
British Broadcasting Corporation
35 Marylebone High Street
London W1M 4AA

SBN: 563 08576 2
First published 1970
© British Broadcasting Corporation and Authors 1970

Printed in England by The Broadwater Press Ltd
Welwyn Garden City, Herts

# Contents

# Acknowledgements

The BBC wishes to thank Ronald Bryden, theatre critic of *The Observer*, Peter Black, television critic of the *Daily Mail*, and Kenneth Tynan, Literary Consultant to the National Theatre, for writing the introductions. The original television interviews were conducted by Clive Goodwin, Derek Hart and Kenneth Tynan.

Acknowledgement is due to the following for permission to reproduce illustrations:

Chris J. Arthur, p. 208 (top), 209; Associated British Films, 25 (top), 53; BBC, 30, 33, 47, 49, 50, 51, 56, 115, 129, 134, 135, 136, 143 (bottom), 161, 204, 218; Columbia Pictures Corporation Ltd, 14, 15, 28, 29, 175, 176; Compton Cameo, 120; Donald Cooper, 122 (top), 123, 124 (top), 125, 126; Anthony Crickmay, 178; *Daily Mail*, 71; Dominic Photography, 89, 92, 93 (bottom), 147 (bottom), 162, 185, 186, 196 (bottom), 197 (top right), 200, 203 (bottom), 222, 223, 242, 243, 249 (top), 252 (bottom), 256; Friedman-Abeles, 21 (bottom right); Gordon Goode, 130, 148 (bottom), 149, 150, 153 (right, top and bottom), 155, 157, 163, 164, 165, 166, 167, 255; Guy Gravett, 145; George Gutram & Co., 84; Lisel Haas, 139; T. F. Holte, 147 (top), 154; Frank Horvat, 146 (bottom); Allan Hurst, 103, 122 (bottom); Douglas H. Jeffery, 156, 203 (top); London Films, 22 (left); Sandra Loussada, 81, 82, 172, 173, 174; Angus McBean, 17, 19, 20, 21 (top right), 73, 75, 90, 91, 93 (top), 98, 101, 106, 112 (top middle), 116, 140 (bottom), 141, 191 (bottom), 192, 193, 194, 195, 196 (top), 197 (top left and bottom), 207, 208 (bottom), 212, 226, 227 (top), 230, 233, 234, 235, 240, 248, 249 (bottom), 251 (bottom), 254; MGM, 177; Monarch Film Corporation Ltd, 63, 64, 65, 220, 221; Lewis Morley, 77, 78, 188, 224, 225, 229; *Observer* (David Sim), 41; Paramount Pictures Ltd, 24 (bottom), 25 (bottom); Pictorial Press Ltd, 76; Rank Organisation, 60, 96, 97, 180, 181, 244; Houston Rogers, 110, 111, 112 (top left and right), 113, 190, 191 (top), 238, 252 (top); David Sim, 124 (bottom), 146 (top), 148 (top), 179, 198, 199, 216, 217; Lord Snowdon, 117; J. V. Spinner, 34, 35, 36, 37, 39, 40; Syndication International, 158; Thames Television, 58; John Timbers, 182, 202; Desmond Tripp, 114, 142, 143 (top), 153 (top left); Twentieth Century-Fox, 22 (right), 201; United Artists, 79, 80; John Vickers, 16, 239; Warner Brothers, 12, 23, 24 (top); Reg Wilson, 151, 227 (bottom), 228, 246, 247, 250; Roger Wood, 18, 21 (top left), 26, 27, 102, 104, 108, 109, 112 (bottom), 251 (top).

# Preface

THE strident sixties bore witness to so many landmarks in the drama that there appears to be some cause for commemoration. It was a notable period for bold experiment and the realisation of long-term schemes.

After years of debate the abolition of stage censorship became an accomplished fact. The National Theatre, talked about since the beginning of the century, came into being at the Old Vic. The Royal Shakespeare Company was reconstituted, found a second home at the Aldwych Theatre, and set itself up in friendly rivalry. These two houses, together with the English Stage Company at the Royal Court Theatre, made positive contributions to the creative ferment.

All areas of the drama became thoroughly contemporary – a unique event in the history of the English theatre. Playwrights experimented freely, both in form and subject-matter, while directors brought a fresh approach to productions of the classics, which had a special appeal to youthful twentieth-century audiences. The touring theatre came to a halt, but theatre centres have, to a limited extent, taken its place. Nottingham, Manchester, Leicester, to name a few. These together with the long-established repertory theatres at Birmingham and Bristol – all of which receive Arts Council grants – have in many cases been as enterprising as the London theatre; and their best productions have been fed back into the West End. The situation was summed up by Ivor Brown in a tribute to Sir Lewis Casson. He said that the Cassons had fought hard 'to lift theatre out of its small corner in the ramshackle empire of Show Business and to establish it as an honoured necessity of a civilised city and nation'. The fulfilment of that purpose was the great achievement of the 1960s. A partial casualty was the commercial theatre. With rising production costs, the well-made play no longer valid, the subsidised theatres attracting the best of the acting talent, first-rate material was difficult to find.

Across this dramatic field fell the all-embracing shadow of television, which during these ten years grew up to become the majority entertainment. A single statistic throws the magnitude of this shadow into relief: *The Mousetrap* at the Ambassadors Theatre would need to run for a hundred years before its audience could equal in numbers that of a single television play on BBC or ITV. But the effect of this colossal output on the potential audience for the live theatre has not been so harmful as was prophesied. There is some evidence that television has helped to make people aware of the contemporary playwright's vitality and, more especially, of the treasure stored away in our dramatic heritage. The quick growth of the new theatre centre at Nottingham and the youthful audiences who support it, the instant success of the Yvonne Arnaud Theatre at Guildford, the full houses the Chichester Festival has enjoyed since its inception, are a few cases which indicate that there is some truth in this notion.

The American film industry suffered the severest damage from the consequences of television, and the flood of films from Hollywood fell away to a mere trickle; consequently, many cinemas in this country closed down. But not all the effects have been adverse. The number of films made all over the world with English actors and directors – largely financed by American capital – has increased and the quality of the films has greatly appreciated. During the latter part of the decade the number of independent film producers has also increased. They have been willing to take chances on unusual subject matter, actors without big names, and new film directors, some of whom were drawn from the television studios. The fact that American picture corporations have been willing to invest this money outside their own country is a tribute to the strength of the British acting profession and the skill of our directors and technicians.

The actor who works within this complicated and constantly changing framework which goes to make up the entertainment industry is not vastly different from any preceding generation of players. But his material has changed, as has the fashion of the times, and there are now three media instead of two in which he can appear. It is a highly competitive profession, and in addition to any individual talent he may have he needs to be physically well tuned, flexible, and, perhaps, more intelligent than his predecessors if he is going to rise to the top, or even make a steady living.

This decade has not been so star-conscious as the thoroughgoing commercial theatre had to be, when the answer to every vital question was inevitably in the box office. The idea of an ensemble, especially in the subsidised companies, has taken the place of the star system. Stars are still being made, but rarely overnight, in the theatre. (Leonard Rossiter in Brecht's *Arturo Ui* has proved a notable exception.) Young actors can rise to great heights in the classical companies, but it is television or the cinema that provide the escalating charge. There is no set formula for success. Luck still plays a vitally important part in the actor's life – and the longed-for break, if it comes, is nearly always unexpected. Many good actors jog along very nicely without ever getting the big break: most of them are just wondering where their next part is coming from. A British Actors Equity survey carried out in 1966 showed that one in three actresses were out of work for six months of the year or more, and 55 per cent of actresses earned less that £500 a year. For more than six months of the year 25 per cent of the men were out of work and 31 per cent earned less than £500.

The actor's life is now more exacting than it used to be. Rehearsals during the day at the National Theatre and the Royal Shakespeare Company can be of ten weeks' duration for one play, whilst the actor is appearing, possibly every night, in the Company's repertory of plays. This longer rehearsal period helps the director to create an ensemble. By means of improvisation and exchange of parts, during the early stages of a production, the actor becomes fully aware of the meaning, the interpretation of the play and his relationship with the other characters in the cast.

Much thought has been given to the manner in which Shakespeare's lines should be delivered from the stage. The poetry voice has suffered a long decline and is now completely outmoded. Sense has triumphed over sound – and sometimes the pendulum has swung too far in that direction. There have been productions in which the approach to the verse was so cool that the result was a perverse neglect of its music. Young players tend to shy away from lyricism – in fact any kind of sentiment is suspect. As a compensation considerable emphasis is placed on physical movement, which often helps to revitalise and heighten the climax of a dramatic scene, where hitherto the voice had had to provide the sole stimulus.

The theatre of the sixties was definitely a man's theatre. In the classical repertoire, and Shakespeare in particular, parts for men far outweigh those for women, both in quantity and in quality. Unfortunately most contemporary playwrights have followed this pattern – they have written few leading parts for women or young girls, unless they have been specifically commissioned to do so. This applies both to films and theatre. The majority of playwrights are men and therefore they are stronger on male psychology. Most of them are committed people and they choose political or social subjects. Because an element of protest becomes essential they take the male as their protagonist and the field in which he works is almost bound to be predominantly male. But the lack of balance in the distribution of parts is detrimental to the theatre; it can stultify the development of a whole generation of young players and hold back promising leading actresses in mid-career. Television has not been so remiss in this respect. The BBC classic serials have provided substantial parts for actresses in most age groups, while the young have had a number of plays specially written for them.

When the century opened it was an actor's theatre, as opposed to a writer's or a producer's. Pinero, Barrie, Maugham – all good craftsmen – wrote comfortable plays with fat parts for star actors and actresses and they were supported by a faithful middle-class audience. Bernard Shaw was their contemporary and though he was in his fifties before this audience found him respectable, his plays (together with Ibsen's) changed the face of the theatre. He wanted to make the audience think and although he wrote monumental parts for actors they inevitably became the mouthpiece for the author's ideas. A Shaw production also needs a good referee – someone to modulate the orchestration of that elaborate dialogue – and so the authority of the director grew. His position has now become so dominant that we sometimes talk of a director's theatre.

GBS had no disciples and the influence on writers today comes from abroad, from Brecht and Becket. They represent opposite ends of the theatrical scale. Brecht is propaganda and epic; Becket is a dry packet of sparse abstractions with mankind at the end of his tether. Authors such as Pinter, Osborne, Arden, have absorbed what they want from these men and then gone their own ways. The actor is well served by such vigorous writing – and in the best type of theatre he shares the honours with the playwright and the director. The audience which goes to the Drama, with a capital D, can no longer be clearly defined – it is both egalitarian and cosmopolitan.

Although the theatre is now a minority entertainment it is still the actor's seminal training ground, the basic stage (whether it is behind a proscenium arch or an open platform) on which he has absolute control over his performance, while he is acting before a live audience. He hasn't this kind of control in the cinema or television, where the director, with his scissors or electric buttons, has the last word. It is therefore the stage on which his status as an actor will be finally judged. He must receive the overwhelming approval of this live audience in his playing of the great classic roles, like Hamlet, Macbeth, Lear, if ultimately he is going to stand on the same peak as those giants of the past, Garrick, Keen or Irving. It is only in such parts that all the actor's special skills are extended to their utmost limits.

The last few years of the sixties have posed a big question. Is the actor afraid – is mankind afraid – that the machine is going to usurp his natural authority? That may explain the reason why a number of experimental groups have been brought into being (especially in America) where the actors perform improvisations on a naked stage, depending on nothing for effect other than their own powers of self-expression. They wear jeans and a shirt, sometimes less than that – so they are free from the tyranny of the costume designer, the scenic designer, the playwright and, possibly, the director in his usual function. They are certainly free from the sophisticated managerial structure of a subsidised theatre. Once again the actor has become a vagrant, he is often on the move and he is content to live on a meagre salary. But he has proved that the actor can be free, unfettered, entirely his own master if he so wishes. Unfortunately the intention of such acting groups is often misunderstood by people seeking only entertainment from a dramatic performance; they merely take the player's self-expression for self-indulgence. In fact, improvisation is nearly always a means to an end. Only if the audience shares the actor's protest can it become an end in itself.

Trailing a banner title, *Acting in the Sixties*, can be a dangerous pursuit because the assembled company who perform under its aegis may look as if they have been hastily pressed into service without owing any bona fide allegiance to the flag under which they operate, while many whose names are omitted do appear to belong to the cause. The sixties have seen a considerable number of great acting performances – Olivier's Othello, Redgrave's Vanya and Scofield's Lear, to mention only three. Olivier and Redgrave had already discussed these roles in a previous set of television programmes on acting (*Great Acting*, BBC Publications, 1967). Scofield, alas, cannot be persuaded to talk about his work in public, and many other actors think as he does: one respects their feelings with a good grace. This series is devoted to a younger generation of actors than the knights and dames. Richard Burton and Albert Finney were the natural choice to talk about acting for the films; Eric Porter and Harry H. Corbett for television acting, even though their stage work is of equal importance and interest. Maggie Smith and Robert Stephens have both been with the National Theatre company since its inception and have played a variety of parts with great distinction. As a comedienne Maggie Smith is in a class by herself. Dorothy Tutin and Vanessa Redgrave are the two most outstanding younger leading ladies of the English stage – they have individuality, power and range: their several achievements are considerable. John Neville was leading player at the Old Vic for five years and at the time the programme was made he was theatre director of the Nottingham Playhouse, one of the new community drama centres to emerge during the decade, so he speaks for a vital part of the theatre operating outside London.

These nine actors give an interesting portrait of themselves in mid-career. They were all under forty when the programmes were recorded between July 1966 and November 1968. They grew up accepting the cinema, then the established form of mass entertainment, as a matter of course. At no time could they ever have thought of themselves as being solely stage actors, though they all started their careers in the theatre, and they have without exception appeared in seasons of classical plays. Films and television have been responsible for promoting the majority of them to international stardom. Considered as a group their performances are representative of all that is best in English acting during the 1960s.

*February 1970*                                    *Hal Burton*

# Richard Burton

AT the feast of contemporary British acting, Richard Burton's place is the vacant chair: the seat of the lost leader, the great absentee. No one who saw him at Stratford-upon-Avon and the Old Vic in the early fifties can have had much doubt that here was Olivier's natural successor, as Scofield was Gielgud's; the next wearer of the mantle of Edmund Kean. He was the Prince Hal and Hamlet of his generation. He should have gone on to become its Macbeth, Oedipus and Othello – Macbeth is the part he was born for, I suspect. Instead, in the past ten years he has made three stage appearances: in a Broadway musical, a return bout with Hamlet in New York, and an amateur production with some Oxford undergraduates.

He has become one of the superstars of the new, global Hollywood; a member of the international travellers' club who, like oil engineers, opera singers and experts in liquidity problems, jet to work wherever they are wanted from wherever income tax permits them to reside. In the process he has become an excellent film actor, giving some fine performances: as Becket, as the unchurched clergyman in Tennessee Williams' *Night of the Iguana*, as John Le Carré's *Spy who came in from the Cold*. But his quality on the screen seems to come from a baffled power straining against the restraints of the medium; from the suggestion of a force held in reserve, struggling to escape its naturalistic understatement. So do his faults. As Le Carré's spy, he showed that he had learned the cinema's lesson of acting mainly with the eyes. But using only his eyes, in the rigidly expressionless poker face the role demanded, he teetered constantly on the verge of over-playing. Bank it down as he will, too much comes through.

To anyone who saw him in his years of theatrical promise, it is as painful as watching a tennis champion grow competent at ping-pong, an organist of genius work wonders with a concertina. For the theatre is his instrument. It is the scale to which he was trained, accommodating himself instinctively to its frame and acoustic – his medium, as wood or marble become second nature to a sculptor. Opera buffs talk of voices which occur once in a century. Burton's was such a natural gift, an innate expressiveness as fresh, strong and unforced as a head of spring water leaping out of a Welsh mountain. The theatre became the vessel, the bowl in which this natural phenomenon could display itself like a fountain. Its central strength is his voice. Much nonsense is talked about Welsh musicality, but the fact remains that, where Englishmen hum or whistle, Welshmen open their chests, square their shoulders and sing as you can with no sounding-board but the open air. Burton's voice was like that from the beginning, and over the years it has been trained into an instrument as magnificent as the theatre has known in this century.

Yet from the first, his best effects have come from checking this natural expressiveness. The mastery of a wind instrument is knowing how to stop it, but Burton's most characteristic performances start from a wary reserve, as if reluctant to let his enormous transparency give him away. As the lover in Christopher Fry's *The Lady's Not for Burning* he hovered pale and constrained, almost shunning the lines' eloquence; much of the play's spring magic came from the thawing of this icy, amazingly handsome boy. His Prince Hal at Stratford was equally withdrawn: no madcap but a brooding future monarch observing the world in order to learn mastery of it. His Hamlet's principal torture seemed to be his inability to hide or dissemble his feelings; the excellence of his Iago, the ability to combine bluff fluency with total self-concealment.

Is this why he has denied his gift? Does he feel that it exposes him too vulnerably? Or is it that, because it is natural, he feels that it is less valuable, less his own, than the inhibitions of it which reflect his will? Whatever the reason, he has kept it from the theatre too long. The last time that tolling organ-voice was heard, it was before a student audience in an undergraduate production of Marlowe's *Dr Faustus* for the Oxford University Dramatic Society in 1965. Kenneth Tynan's interview with him was recorded just after he filmed this production in Italy.

*Ronald Bryden*

1967 Faustus, *Dr Faustus* (film)

Faustus

KENNETH TYNAN: *A few years ago you appeared in an OUDS production of Marlowe's* Dr Faustus *at Oxford and now you are making a
film of the play. I believe you have always wanted to play Faustus ever since
you were a tiny child.*

RICHARD BURTON: I was actually about twelve years old when I
first read and realised that I understood, or at least I thought I
understood, this particular play of Marlowe's and particularly, of
course, the last speech which dominated and does still dominate my
imagination. Whether we've realised it correctly I don't know.

*Can you tell me what were the differences between doing it on stage and on
film. What were the advantages of filming it?*

Well, there's no substitute, of course, for doing it on the stage. The
immediate reaction of the audience will teach you how to act – they
are the greatest teachers in the world. On film it's very difficult
because your only audience is a black box. However, we tried it and
we used every possible effect; we hope it will be successful.

*Now could we go back to 1944 when you made your first success at Oxford
as Angelo in the production of* Measure for Measure. *How did you get the
part?*

I was fairly ruthless when I arrived at Oxford, fresh from South Wales with a powerful Welsh accent, and determined to play the leading part in whatever OUDS production was coming up. During the war, as you know, the OUDS didn't exist; but there was a substitute company, called 'the Friends of the OUDS', which was dominated, and has been dominated for many years, by Professor Nevill Coghill. I went to see him and said, 'I'm an actor and I want to play Angelo in your present production.' And he said, 'I'm afraid it's already cast.' And I said, 'Well, I'll speak some poetry for you,' and he said, 'Do, go ahead.' And I said, 'Would you like to hear "To be or not to be"?' So he said, 'All right.' And I spoke 'To be or not to be' and at the end of it he said, 'You can't play Angelo, but is it all right if you understudy Angelo?' Eventually the man playing Angelo was so impressed by my earnestness that he said I should play half the performances and he would play the other half. And then he became ill, nothing to do with me, nothing to do with the Welsh and wizardry – he became ill and I played the whole thing, all the time. That's how I began. I was assured a future from it by Binkie Beaumont, Hugh Beaumont of H. M. Tennant, who saw it, and I think John Gielgud also saw it.

*But long before that you must have decided you wanted to act. How did that happen?*

An advertisement appeared in the Welsh papers which said that Emlyn Williams was looking for a Welshman who could act, who was twenty-two and who could speak Welsh. Although I was only sixteen, or whatever it was at the time, I said, 'Well, I can speak Welsh, but I don't know whether I can act.' Anyway, I got the part in this play called *The Druid's Rest*, which I played for ten weeks on tour. Then we came into London and nobody took the slightest notice of me except one man, a certain James Redfern, writing I think in the *New Statesman*. He didn't think the play was very good, and he didn't think the production was very good or anything like that. But the very last line of his notice said, 'However, in a wretched part, Master Richard Burton' – Master, you can imagine how much I loathed being called Master at that time – 'Master Richard Burton showed remarkable ability.' And that was it, James Redfern changed my life.

*After the war you had a great success in two plays by Christopher Fry,* The Lady's Not for Burning *and* The Boy with a Cart. *John Gielgud directed them both. He must have been a great help to you at this stage in your career?*

Oh, of enormous help. In fact I could never repay the debt I owe him. First of all he cast me in *The Lady's Not for Burning* and then in the course of the play, in which I made something of a success, he took me out of that play and put me into another play, *The Boy*

1944 Glan, *The Druid's Rest*, Royal Court, Liverpool

1949 Richard, *The Lady's Not for Burning*, Globe, with Pamela Brown (Jennet Jourdemayne) and John Gielgud (Thomas Mendip)

1950 Cuthman, *The Boy with a Cart*, Lyric, Hammersmith, with Mary Jerrold (Cuthman's Mother)

*with a Cart*, which again he directed himself. Indeed, he made me into what is casually known as a leading man.

*I once described Gielgud, in print, as the greatest living actor from the neck up, by which I meant that his most powerful attributes were his face and his voice. I've often thought the same could be said of you.*

No, I think it's not from the neck up, but from the brain down. (*Indicates area from hair line down to mouth.*) I think that most of my capacity lies in my voice.

*On stage, I've often thought that you seem apart from other actors, isolated, in a world of your own. Do you feel that yourself?*

I've been told that by you and other critics, but nevertheless I do feel that on stage it's virtually every man for himself. I don't think that anyone wants to help you particularly; despite the agonies of a first night, and the nervousness and so on, you really have to look after yourself. I think that particular loneliness, solitude, the idea of carrying on your own private room, is not unique to actors; though all actors have it. I have it perhaps, or sometimes have it, a little more than most. When I go out there on the stage I'm battling the world, I have to be the best as far as I can.

*After* The Boy with a Cart *you had a very successful season at Stratford-on-Avon, in the course of which you played Prince Hal in* Henry IV, *parts 1 and 2. What do you remember of those opening nights?*

Nothing very much except that I was nearly fired from *Henry IV, part 1*, because in rehearsals they didn't think that I was going to be very good as Prince Hal. I tried to explain to the various people involved what I was trying to do, which was to be exactly what you described; that is to be solitary, removed, cold and certainly not the thigh-slapping, stamping, roaring-with-laughter Prince Hal that we'd all been accustomed to. But I'm not sure that many people understood that until the opening night. I thought maybe I'd be fired after the opening night, but it so turned out that it was a great success for me.

*Do you feel happiest when you are playing that kind of part? A man among men?*

I am the son of a Welsh miner and one would expect me to be at my happiest playing peasants, people of the earth; but in actual fact I'm much happier playing princes and kings. Now whether this is a kind of sublimation of what I would like to be, or something like that, I don't know, but certainly I'm never really very comfortable playing people from the working class.

*You once said that Ferdinand in* The Tempest *was your greatest failure. Now was that because it was purely a romantic role?*

Prince Hal at the Old Vic and Stratford.
Below, Old Vic 1955 Henry V, with Zena Walk (Katherine)
Opposite, Stratford 1951 Prince Hal, *1 & 2* Henry I with Alan Badel (Poins) and Anthony Quayle (Falsta

It's an unplayable role. If you happen to be rather shortish as I am, tottering about, with nothing to say of any real moment, bloodless, liverless, kidneyless, a useless member of the human race – well, I found myself incapable of playing such a role.

*What I really meant was, in* Henry IV, *the part was a man who led an army, a leader of men. As Ferdinand you had to play a lyrical part with a girl. It seemed to me there might be something in your temperament that went for the one, rather than the other.*

I can't play with girls. I'm not a romantic actor in that sense. It's perfectly all right. I think I'm recognised as a sort of sexual actor in some senses of the word, but Romeo, for instance, I've never played; it's beyond my capacity. Because the urge, the acting urge to kiss somebody on the stage, is beyond me, I can't do it, I can't bear to be touched, physically touched, on the stage or on the screen; it has to be very carefully arranged. And I very rarely allow myself to touch other people, physically touch them I mean.

*Why is this?*

I don't know. But certainly it is something that doesn't apply to me. When I have to kiss a woman on the stage or on the screen, horrors start up. That is why I prefer to act with my wife more than any other woman in the world.

*I suppose Hamlet is the great untouchable part of all time. You played it first at the Old Vic in 1953. Then you repeated it, or you gave another Hamlet in 1964 in New York, directed by John Gielgud. Did your performance or your interpretation differ?*

Oh, enormously, yes. I think the first time I played it as if I would like to be John Gielgud. The second time, I played it absolutely as myself. In actual fact, I asked John Gielgud to direct it, because I thought that despite his enormous influence on my life, since his personality and diction and speech patterns and behaviour were so entirely different from mine, they couldn't possibly affect my particular thoughts about Hamlet, on that occasion.

*Suppose there had been a commanding theatrical institution like the National Theatre when you began on the stage; would you have joined it, on a long-term basis?*

Oh, good God, yes, of course I would. Yes, if they gave me enough money to keep me alive. After all, the fundamental basis of being an actor is not the desire to be the curate's son, if you remember that quotation, but simply to make money. And therefore if anybody had asked me then, or indeed even now, to play in a theatre which offered me a suitable arrangement of roles, I would unquestionably do it.

1951 Ferdinand, *The Tempest*, Stratford

*What are your feelings about directors? What kind of director do you like working with?*

The old cliché that the French theatre is a writer's theatre, the British theatre is an actor's theatre and the American theatre is a director's theatre – I don't believe any of them. The theatre is essentially a writer's theatre and directors are relatively unimportant. They're no more than jumped-up stage managers. In films it's a different matter. Though a director should tell you vaguely, roughly, the place on the stage where you will be best seen and then assumedly leave the rest to you. John Gielgud was the best director I've ever worked with on the stage, certainly; he was marvellously instructive about *Hamlet*, but he certainly didn't dominate in the sense that he said, 'You must do this or you must do that. Or you must go there . . .', because there were certain stern rules that I had for myself: such as don't come near me, leave me alone;

Hamlet. 1953 Old Vic, with William Squire (Horatio) and Fay Compton (Gertrude), and 1964 New York

which he understood. I think he thinks that I'm a very undisciplined actor; for that very reason I have to have a lot of space on the stage, a lot of space that I can move about in, without being bothered by too many people. Well, John says I'm very undisciplined and he's probably right. But then I wouldn't want to be disciplined, I wouldn't want to be that kind of actor who goes on the stage and gives the same cadence to the same speech every night for days and days and days on end. I would prefer to be free so that I'm invited to be bad some nights if I happen to be bad that night.

*Let's go back to 1948, when you made your first film,* The Last Days of Dolwyn. *Now we've just shown you some sequences from that film. After all these years, what do you think of yourself?*

Oh, heavens above, I would say a lamentable thing. Thank God I never have to live through that again, to live through those terrible years of puerility, of idiocy, . . . I wouldn't like to go through that time again.

Gareth in *The Last Days of Dolwyn* (1948) and *Antony Cleopatra* (1963)

*Is there a phrase you'd use to sum up your performance?*

Febrile.

*What do you think of the films that you made for Fox? Films like* My Cousin Rachel, Desert Rat, The Robe, *etc.*

My career with 20th Century Fox was somewhat chequered. I did some films that I enjoyed and wanted to do, and a lot of films that I didn't want to do. There was no way of my persuading anybody

22

that I wasn't right for them, or that the scripts weren't good, or that the set-up wasn't right, or whatever. Not the most interesting period of my life from the artistic point of view.

*A great many of the films were rather harshly criticised, but how self-critical are you, as an actor?*

I have no self-criticism at all. I firmly believe that if people would pay money to see me in the theatre or in films it's their responsibility not mine. If they stopped seeing me, if my box office ratio went down, or something like that, I'd be perfectly content to stop working. I do it because I rather like being famous, I rather like being given the best seat in the plane, the best seat in the restaurant, the best food in that particular restaurant.

*But if a film is a success with the public, do you criticise your own performance in it?*

Well, it's very difficult, because I rarely see any performance that I've been in. I did see *Who's Afraid of Virginia Woolf?* recently and came out, as we say in Welsh, in a tare. That is to say, I wanted to kill myself because I thought I was so indifferent. Not bad, indifferent in the part. But I was assured by everybody else, including the critics, that I was all right. So I've been solaced by that kind of thing. I don't think that it's a very good idea to see oneself in pictures.

*Antony, in the film* Cleopatra, *is essentially a defeated, passive anti-hero, especially in the second part of the picture. Do you think that kind of role suits you?*

Yes, I think the only kind of interesting parts to play are defeated men. That's why the great tragedies are so attractive to actors. One must always play a defeated man. The hero, the one who succeeds, is always faintly boring. Hamlet is a defeated man, Macbeth is a

1966 George, *Who's Afraid of Virginia Woolf*, with Elizabeth Taylor (Martha)

defeated man, Lear is a defeated man, they're all defeated men. Othello is, Iago is; Antony fascinated me for that particular reason.

*You played Jimmy Porter in the film of* Look Back in Anger, *your first real anti-hero part. I remember you saying that you enjoyed it. Now, could that be because it was so different from the other parts you played, the heroic parts?*

Up to that time, as you know, I'd only played princes, heroes, kings – dressed eternally in togas or whatever. It was fascinating to find a man who came presumably from my sort of class, who actually could talk the way that I would like to talk.

*You once said that you'd learnt a great deal about acting in the cinema from Elizabeth Taylor. Now, what did she teach you?*

I think the chief word is economy. A spareness of voice, of movement, of gesture, of agony, whatever the word is. She taught me that, I think.

*Control?*

Well, control – no, because that implies discipline – no, that's not right. It's something very careful. As she explained to me, when your face is going to be thirty-eight feet high, depending on the size of your face, thirty feet wide, you've got to be very careful how massively you register any emotion of laughter, of idiocy, of delight, of tragedy, whatever it is. She is, of course, the best film actress in the world; I think you may disagree. I may be prejudiced, but she certainly seems to fire, all the time, on all of the many cylinders.

*Do you think that sort of reticence in acting hampers you as a stage actor?*

I think it's the reverse: I think that on the stage, because I have an enormous voice, a very big voice, that is, it is marvellous to be able to give free play to that particular organ. But on the screen I find it extremely difficult to try and control it.

*In your recent films, I mean* Becket, The Spy who came in from the Cold, Who's Afraid of Virginia Woolf? *the scripts were much better than the earlier films you made. Is this an accident or is it because you've become more powerful as a determining force in the building of the film?*

I think it's a combination of both. As a result of my marriage to Elizabeth I became a far more important actor than I was before, though it's not very easy for me to say that, and I think Elizabeth became a far more powerful actress. As a result of all that – that stupid and splendid publicity – it did mean that we could choose, absolutely, what we did. Now there were some things that we chose badly, but for the most part we chose well. For instance, I think that were it not for the fact that Elizabeth and I were married

24

1966 George, *Who's Afraid of Virgina Woolf*

959 Jimmy Porter, *Look Back in Anger*, with Edith Evans (Ma Tanner)

eft, as Thomas Becket in the film *Becket* (1965); right, Leamas, *The Spy who came in from the Cold*, with Michael Mordern (1965)

Old Vic. 1956 Iago, *Othello*, with
Richard Wordsworth (Roderigo) and
Wendy Hiller (Emilia).

Opposite, 1954 Coriolanus, with
**Fay Compton** (Volumnia)

1966 Petruchio, *The Taming of the Shrew*, with Elizabeth Taylor (Katharina)

and are, perhaps, notorious or famous, *Virginia Woolf* would have been virtually unplayable on film. Nobody would have attempted to do it.

*Do you think you were miscast as the very neurotic, henpecked, downtrodden husband in* Virginia Woolf?

Oh yes, essentially miscast. In fact I wasn't asked to play it until the last second. Because quite clearly it should have been an American, an intellectual American, somewhere from the eastern states of America; and obviously I wasn't right.

*Since 1960 you've only appeared on the stage three times. Do you miss that contact with a live audience?*

I don't. The only thing I feel is that one of these days I have to go back and face that live audience; I don't want to do it, but I must do it. Because I'm naturally a frightened man. I must go back to face the audience because I'm frightened of facing the audience. Therefore I must face them. It's one of those silly perverse things.

*Is there any great classical role you still long to appear in on the stage?*

Yes. Only one.

*Which one?*

Lear.

*And how soon do you think you'll be ready for Lear?*

I think I'm already too old, but with a bit of luck, maybe in five years; if I'm controlled and kept under control.

*Is there any great playwright whose work has never tempted you?*

Brecht.

*Why not Brecht?*

Loathsome, vulgar, petty, little, nothing.

*Large, poetic, universal, everything.*

That's what you say.

*Is there anything in the background of Wales, the cultural background, that has specifically influenced your acting?*

We had no actors. No actors, you know, for about forty years. I suddenly realised why we'd never had any actors. It was because all the actors went into the pulpit, the greatest stage in the world. It dominated a village in a chapel. You stood hovering like a great bird of prey over the people in the village; you said, 'I will tell you what is wrong with you, and let me examine your soul.' The greatest pulpit in the world. And suddenly that particular kind of belief went out. They were no longer stars, the great preachers of my childhood. They went out, and the first man in Wales to stop being a preacher and start becoming an actor was Emlyn Williams. It was remarkable for all of us, you know. There was this strange man, who had suddenly decided not to be a preacher, but to become an actor. And what a preacher Emlyn Williams would have made – a preacher in another sense.

*Would it be true to say that the thing that drew you to the stage was rhetoric?*

Oh yes, unquestionably. I think we have a word in Welsh, misused I believe by you lot, called *hwyl*; nobody can ever translate it. But it's a kind of longing for something, a kind of idiotic, marvellous, ridiculous longing.

Petruchio

# Harry H. Corbett

WITH Harry H. Corbett and *Steptoe and Son*, the lovable chump comedy, one of the most enduring of British strains, flowered into dramatic art. In this series the writers, Alan Simpson and Ray Galton, shook off the last trace of 'conscious gag' comedy. They were now presenting the most difficult comedy to write and the widest and deepest in appeal, that which has a universally recognised emotional truth running through it.

Corbett has described what he brings to Harold as 'emotion memory'. After his mother died he was brought up by a widowed aunt in a bleak Manchester slum. A visit to the Opera House to see Leslie Henson awoke a wish to become an actor, but it was not until after the war and a succession of jobs that led nowhere that he got his first engagement with the Chorlton Repertory Company. He stayed with them four years and became aware of his power to hold an audience.

In 1952 he met Joan Littlewood. He had grown increasingly discontented with the stereotyped class characters in the Chorlton Rep.'s standby plays. In Joan Littlewood he recognised a liberating and exhilarating originality of mind. With a group of like-minded actors they began the hand-to-mouth tour which was to settle in London as the Theatre Workshop in Stratford East.

He swam into my orbit with a bunch of performances for Armchair Theatre. He established himself as a character, more than dependable. You never got a generalisation, a cliché from him. It was acting not from the neck up, but from total engagement of body and brain. This was the style he'd worked at with Joan Littlewood and brought, in 1961, to Steptoe and Son. The physical detail – the rakish cap, the scarf, the weighing hook on the belt, the boots and flapping overcoat – came from observation. The understanding came from emotion memory.

The comedy comes out of the soaring and deflation, basic to Galton and Simpson's style. It is the comedy of exaggeration, un-

1964 Harold, *Steptoe and Son*, BBC TV, with Wilfrid Brambell (Albert)

expectedness and incongruity; funny and sad in the way that a home-made *In Memoriam* poem is irresistibly funny and an expression of grief.

Corbett uses the reality and absurdity without letting go of either. His control of timing of the ingredients is in fact a masterpiece. He is the big spender, wine and food expert, connoisseur of birds. He rages and despairs against his father and the bars of his cage. The control of rages, the timing of the moment when that marvellously articulate face allows resignation and acceptance to venture on to its surface, has a precision that is only possible on television.

The emotional truth, coming from deep inside the part, runs consistently between the lines. His grasp on Harold began at a point far back in his past.

*Peter Black*

CLIVE GOODWIN: *One of your early television performances was as a show-biz agent in an experimental production, set up by the BBC and produced by the Langham Group. The play was an adaptation of Turgenev's* The Torrents of Spring. *Can you tell us something about it?*

HARRY H. CORBETT: It was a long time ago, about eight or ten years. It was only experimental in the sense that it was attacking a certain hardness that had come into television; most television directors wanted basically to be cinema directors. They rooted you to a spot, they shot through your earhole, they shot up your nose, they shot everywhere possible to shoot; and intercut so much that you got a disjointed effect. So this experiment aimed at being absolutely the opposite of the cinema, returning to the pure days of early television when the artist moved round with the camera, was in complete rapport with the camera. The only really basic experimental thing you can get out of this one-camera technique is that if a scene needs to flow and every nuance needs to be observed from every character's point of view, you don't interrupt it with a close-up here, and a close-up cut there, or a line off camera that might lose import, or the look lose its import. A good example in this production was a busy scene outside a stage door which flowed with movement as in natural life; whereas by the normal method the three of us would have been stuck in the stage door and there'd be camera one, camera two, camera three, and the director would have cut backward and forward, and interrupted what was, I think, a good flow of dialogue.

1959 Benny, *The Torrents of Spring*, BBC TV, with Sandra Dorne (The Princess)

*So the experiment was mainly concerned with the technique, not with the content?*

Yes, absolutely concerned with the technique. I wasn't interested in the content in those early days. It was the technique of keeping the actor related to the total entertainment value of the play.

*But what kind of script did you start with for* Torrents of Spring?

The nineteenth-century novel by Turgenev. We started basically with that and the idea of translating the story into contemporary life. Then we said, here's something that's usually done in a serial over a long period of time. But we wished to do it in a single play, get the essence of it. We'll call this the new television we wish to go for. So we more or less got hold of the content and bones of the thing, threw it away; then we got everybody together in the room, improvised it, and we taped it. This experiment was carried out by Tony Pelissier who was responsible for the unit known as the Langham Group, helped by this marvellous man Mervyn, who was fantastic. He built a sort of mock-up camera so that we could work for the first time on the floor of the rehearsal room with a mock-up camera. We'd never heard of it before; we still don't get it today; we just have directors moving this way and that way: they do the

C

best they can. But we actually got the feeling of moving with a camera, you see. It was the beginning of what I believe I'm known for, working with cameras.

*You were for many years a member of an experimental theatre group, Theatre Workshop, which is now something of a legend. I know it's a big subject, but could you say what Theatre Workshop meant to you as an actor?*

It was one of those fortunate coincidences that can happen in any life. It coincided with my beginnings as an artist. I have to make this difference because when you first become an actor you're thrilled that you're on that stage, you're having a go at all the things you wanted to have a go at, you're all the dreams you wanted to be, you're really enjoying it. Sometimes they're some of the dreams you don't want to be, but what does it matter; what the hell, you're having a great time getting out there and playing. Then you suddenly discover that the audience believes you. They believe you really feel the thing you're playing. You represent it. For example, I found myself at one period in repertory playing a working-class man with red spotted handkerchiefs, big old Bill moustaches, and all the maids had adenoids. This was in that sophisticated kind of play with french windows, you know, and the fish tank down left, the tea and drinks trolley over on the right. Then suddenly I realised that I was playing to people who were of the same origin as myself and that they firmly believed that this was the way working-class people should be portrayed on the stage, even though they themselves could see the evidence all around them that it was wrong and a lie. I wanted to get out of this completely. So I searched around for somebody else who reflected my point of view. Joan Littlewood was just starting Theatre Workshop and she held the same kind of views as I did.

Joxer, *Juno and the Paycock*, Theatre Workshop

*Where was that?*

That was in Manchester.

*Did you go to see her or did she come to see you?*

Joan never goes to see anybody. There are all sorts of devious ambassadors and ambassadresses who come to see you with little suggestions and things like that. She's a splendid, splendid human being, and as a rational, splendid human being she can use every emotion; she has to blackmail you to get to her point. Eventually we met – after cunningly contrived meetings with thousands of other people involved – in a little house which was chock-a-block from top to bottom with actors and actresses – all in separate rooms, I might add, but chock-a-block with them, all starving. After discussing it with her and knowing I was going on a very tough tour, I remember I had managed to save about £4. 10s. for a pair of snow boots, but we ate that in the first two days because all the actors were broke and I was the only one with money. I was God for two days; it was a splendid feeling. My first grasp of riches.

*What year was this?*

Oh, strike me. About 1950; I should think about 1950. That's something that always throws me – years; I can never remember the year I was born, I always get forms which say, 'State clearly the date of your birth.' I can't remember dates. I always live for today. I live in a marvellous dream world. Today is today.

*Anyway in 1950 you were living in a house with the members of Theatre Workshop. What kind of plays were you doing? What kind of audiences were you getting?*

Well, anything. If it walked and talked, and would sit still for ten minutes, we'd play to it. We were doing a tour of the North-east in the middle of February, playing to miners mainly, miners' welfare homes. We played *Henry IV, part 2*, *The Overcoat* by Gogol, and a mining documentary, of all things, to miners. This was a splendid thing to do, when we actually got there, because it was really testing to play a piece of what you thought was truth to people who experience it every day. Now we didn't go in for the dramas, the huge coal fall and the hero hacking his way through for hours. We simply took a normal everyday fall in which two men were trapped for no more than two hours. But it contained the essence of the possibility of being trapped for longer. Marvellous things came out of it, like the release of their everyday tensions. Men started to behave like the human beings they are, in spite of the slavery of the coal-mine. Everything came out, the things they should have done, and if they had a chance would do. It wasn't as dramatic a set-up as if they were going to die; but they felt that when once they got out never again would they get stuck in that situation.

*Did the miners react well?*

Yes. You see the marvellous thing about them was this: we were so broke we had to have hospitality. This meant that one of us, Margaret Bury or somebody like that, would go forward the week before – everybody took it in turns – and would con people into putting us up for the week. The people were waiting, loving to have us there on this kind of hospitality basis. We were actually living with the audience who had seen our play. It was extraordinary the amount of desire they themselves had to write, perform, and be part of this kind of drama. It shook me rigid at the time; of course, it was all the anger of the thirties coming out, I suppose.

They were marvellous experiences – marvellous people. And my God, honest isn't the word. You see, the only morality you can have, or I can have – and mind you, let's get this absolutely

Khlestakov, *The Government Inspector*, Theatre Workshop

35

straight, this discussion is highly personalised, I cannot generalise about other people in the profession, what they think and what they don't think – but the only morality I have finished up with, in this business, is the morality of keeping my word. I can rely on nothing else. I'm not interested in anybody's sexual deviations, anybody's religious deviations, anybody's whatever deviations. The only thing that binds me and a lot more people together is a handshake deal of giving my word. I found an immediate kinship up there. I mean, it's fairly normal, if there is an accident in the pit and there was one tragic accident, to cancel everything immediately – shows, everything; the place closes down for the day. It's a splendid thing that they feel this way. But they paid us our money, our guarantee. We always got £25 for playing, we were desperate, we needed it. And by God they forked it over with no nonsense whatsoever.

*£25 a night.*

Yes, we did one-night stands, we could only work in two a week at the most because we would travel huge distances in this terribly old lorry. We used to get orders from the police to take it into garages, and garages would sign on the bill, 'We are no longer responsible for the state of this vehicle'. We used a pantechnicon you see; we'd all travel in the back – the furniture, the set, the lighting; we provided the whole lot. In one village we stopped the tram. They had one tram coming up the hill – and somehow or other there was confusion at the time, and someone, who shall be nameless, plugged into the main power source through the window and the tram came to a grinding halt. So they had to make up their minds whether they had light in our show or a tram service going up and down the hill.

*This one-night stand touring lasted for what? Three or four years before Joan Littlewood finally found a home in London – Theatre Workshop, Stratford East?*

Yes, we did about two or three – then we decided to form a base in Glasgow; we had a lot of friends in Glasgow that helped. We played the Edinburgh Festival: remember we were pirates. We had to be. It was the only way we could exist. You see, they had the bricks and the mortar. We had nothing. So we had to con them, lie to them, seduce them into letting us have the bricks and mortar, even if it was only for a few precious hours. We'd go anywhere. Literally we'd go to ridiculous places, like in Yorkshire, or right up to Aberdeen to play, and con everybody. Yes, we were going to do a lovely play that everybody would enjoy. Yet, it was good family entertainment. . . . I remember once we took out a terribly serious piece of work, beautifully done by Joan, about the atom bomb. It was interesting because we researched it. Now there's two ways of doing this. Firstly there would be the normal, shall we say West End way, as it was then, the scientist living in a nice bungalow

Theatre Workshop 1954: A minor character in *Jupiter Night Out*, and Bob Cratchit in *A Christmas Carol*

with stained glass, a wife or daughter problem possibly, and he's trying to resolve all the way through the play, should he work on the atom bomb, or should he not work on the atom bomb. Our point was that science was there to be used; this was in the terribly early days, remember, it came as such a shock that science suddenly flung itself into the forefront of everybody's thinking, but it was not going to be resolved theatrically or dramatically in the way I've described. The way to get through was that science was our servant, so we decided to do, for want of a better term, a montage of the history of the atom right from the early days of the Greeks.

*It was a documentary play?*

That's right, yes. Which necessitated the play being split up into little sequences, using song, dance, any technique we could possibly lay our hands on. We opened at a miners' gala somewhere, and it was rather curious because we kept getting terrific rounds of applause and laughs at the end of every terrible scene, although they were beautifully quiet during the playing of it. I understood afterwards that for the first half they were under the impression that this was the latest sophisticated review, from the West End. It was actually billed as such: we had to use all this kind of con.

*This was the play by Ewan MacColl called* Uranium 235.

A brilliant man. What an absolutely brilliant writer. He really brought verse back again to me on this kind of level.

*In fact this play did come into the West End.*

We were adopted by a group. Again, you see, the profession feeds on itself. The support for this kind of thing unfortunately always seems to come from within ourselves, and we were adopted by Sam Wanamaker, who was one of a group of actors who backed and supported the play in the West End. We ran for about three weeks, I think.

*This was before finding your home at Stratford East.*

Yes, this was long before. That came – well, God sent it out of the blue; we were literally in the wilds of Scotland, broken down somewhere, and suddenly we got the telegram and somebody train-journeyed all the way up to say that the theatre was available. It was MacColl, again, who was influential in getting it. So we took it and we were grateful. Grateful is not the word; I mean, we played to twelve people in the middle of winter. I followed *The Lady Stripped by Bullets*, it said in my dressing-room; that was the show the week before; I played Aguecheek in *Twelfth Night*. You can imagine the fun we had; it was hysterical. Malvolio kept getting sweets thrown at him, which was a mark of favour from the audience who were used to going there. We had a splendid beginning, far better than walking into a sophisticated repertory-run theatre.

*Long Voyage Home*, Theatre Workshop

There are so many in London, they tuck themselves down the Haymarket and all over the place, and they build up a kind of repertory for a certain class of people, which I can't quite qualify, but they're people who go to see a certain type of play that's always on there, either cultural, or a variety type, or a farcical type of play. But rather than walk into that, we went into this free-wheeling atmosphere of the East End theatre, run down and disreputable.

It suited our sort of atmosphere perfectly, because we wanted to work in the run-down, the disrespectful, the cocking the snook. So it was absolutely splendid for us. The audience were really disrespectful themselves; they cocked the snook at the world. They didn't give a damn. It was far better than playing to a regulated set of penguins who were used to hearing a certain thing each week. That is why we had so much success. A splendid area to work in. Not only that; we had to work hard. I think we got £2. 10s. a week. Of course we all shared. The cigarettes by Abdullah were cut up every week; I remember we got five and a half each. There were even razor blades, wielded by Jerry who was manager, to give us our share. I remember George Cooper, brilliant actor, he didn't smoke, so he had the total run of everything: any chocolates left in boxes usually. I had the circle for cigarette ends, George Luscombe had the stalls, shared with somebody else.

*Did you live in the theatre?*

Yes. I lived in the dressing-room. Thrown out regularly by the Council, once a month, of course. I discovered a gas main. And since many years ago I had been forced into being a plumber's mate willy-nilly by a stark-raving-mad careers officer at an employment exchange, so I was able to put that knowledge to good use and I had a gas-fire cooker working: the only one in the building. It really was like a Marx Brothers film. It was all worked like this. I had a bed, the big label underneath it was 'Props. Don't Move', and this was on pulleys. And as soon as anybody offstage heard the cry, 'Walter Plinge is wanted on stage immediately, Walter Plinge on stage immediately,' they had to fly to my dressing-room and madly start shoving things in boxes and pulling this bed up, and shoving notices up: 'Don't disturb: Crockery for next performance; please don't eat the sausages.' It was hysterical.

*You mean this was the signal the law had arrived.*

That the Council had arrived; they were going to throw us out again. We had nowhere to live, we couldn't afford digs.

Believe me it wasn't an enjoyable experience. We were semi-starving half the time. And thank God again for Angel Lane. You see, this is the interesting point; I don't think it could be done nowadays; economically it wouldn't be possible. Where can you get bacon at 6d. a pound? These were the bacon ends, the bits they cut off; a plateful of ham ends for 3d. Now Angel Lane was full of this kind of thing, up and down; we lived like the old-age pensioners had to live – it was a practical, splendid experience.

I remember we sent somebody off to the Edinburgh Festival and told him to build a train. He had a bag of nails and a hammer; this is absolutely true; this was Harry Green. This boy had a splendid gift of the gab, what a word user. He wandered into a furniture factory, if you please, conned them somehow or other into giving him the bits and pieces, the tools and everything, and he made a whole seating for five carriages on a train set, out of nothing, absolutely nothing. That's the sort of way we had to work to exist.

*Can you tell us about some of the parts and some of the plays you did during this period at Theatre Workshop?*

I honestly doubt it. They passed in such a magnificent haze, one merging into the other. Well, we commenced a fantastic five-year run; that's the only way I can describe it. We did *Twelfth Night*, *Volpone*, *The Dutch Courtesan* and *Hobson's Choice*. We did what we considered were the classics, of different periods – we didn't care – we just threw them on, gave them a new slant. We even took what we thought were classics of the thirties, the American era. We took *Three Men on a Horse* and this was an absolutely magnificent thing because we put cartoons in the background, slid them in, gave the plays a new staging and a new life. *The Good Soldier Schweik*, oh, innumerable plays, Shaw – practically every Shaw we could lay hands on. We also did a magnificent *Enemy of the People*. New plays; we did musicals of the area; when there was a train strike, we did one about the train strike just down the road. You see we had this fantastic freedom, we weren't under great critical approbation, we could get away with murder then.

1955  Sir Politic Would-Be, *Volpone*, Theatre Workshop

*You were practically ignored.*

Yes, we were ignored. But this was splendid for us because that meant we could do anything we liked. When we played *The Enemy of the People*, well, the second act was set inside the huge big room in the house; so we said, to hell with that if it's supposed to be a meeting; we will put it in the theatre itself. So we had the entrances through the auditorium, the fumbling with the curtain and the whole meeting; we literally had half of Angel Lane working there, May who ran the café, and thousands of others all screaming and shouting. This was the first sort of living-incident-type theatre that we'd ever experimented with. Once it got us into trouble, I must admit, because of some Indian students. It was a fabulous week, and at one point the play was interrupted by somebody shouting 'Rubbish . . . I think this is a load of nonsense.' It's always a marvellous opportunity, you pray for this, because then you say, 'How do you mean rubbish?' and get your point over beautifully.

Unfortunately one of the Indian students who was the comedian of the camp had volunteered to do this. Well, he got as far as 'Rubbish' and he was set upon by twenty other people: 'How dare you say that?' Then a huge fight broke out. They were splendid days.

*Now I remember you as a brilliant Richard II at this time.*

Well, I don't know about brilliant; it was a splendid effort. It was not conceived as Richard II; we never did anything like that. We conceived a play in relation to its attitude to the time. The Old Vic was doing *Richard II*, so we thought what a splendid idea; we'll do *Richard II*, right? We'll have two *Richard II*s, then you can have a classical mean. People can visit the Old Vic's *Richard II*, discuss it, visit our *Richard II* and discuss it, and they can have a real go. Because every Sunday we used to throw the place open and have general criticism, people coming in and shouting and screaming what they felt and what they thought should be and should not be.

*Richard II* was one of the happiest plays I've ever been in – a silly thing to say, I don't mean it in that twee way, we were all lovely with each other. I mean purely and simply that the greatest joy for me and a lot of the other actors was working at rehearsals. Ah, that's when it's fantastic. It begins. You create. You create in rehearsal, then you spend ages and ages through the run of the play trying to recreate that first beautiful, savage getting of the idea. I'd envisaged it in silks and gowns and everybody looking lovely; it's all the verse, it's so beautifully done. Then you get down to the horrifying reality of the grey stone wall, that a man is saying, 'If only my fingernails could rip through the cages of these walls'; we tried to create the walls – it was a fantastic experience, the happiest.

*Now there's no doubt in my mind that Joan Littlewood, and you probably agree, is one of the greatest theatre directors in the twentieth century.*

Absolutely.

*Can you tell us something about the way she worked?*

Awfully difficult because Joan is Joan and was born Joan. Obviously marked out for this work from an early age. She came out of the slums and bad slums too. She ran away from home at some ridiculously early age because she knew that Komisarjevsky was working in Manchester, so she hitch-hiked down to Manchester. She bludgeoned her way through RADA; after winning star prizes there and goodness knows what, she ran away from it all to go and work as a stage manager; and so it begins for Joan. Later she went into radio, won silver microphone prizes: she brought this technique to the theatre, the technique of sound. Her work evolved out of herself and from the experiences she went through; it's just terribly difficult to describe. I can only say it is, in a cliché form, simplicity – the hardest thing in the world to get: this is genius surely, the simplicity of seeing the thing in its simplest context.

1955 Richard II, Theatre Workshop

Everybody's putting forward subtle reasons why the character is this, why the man should do this, why the world is like this; she can put forward the simple reason that counts. I mean, she would use tears, if it would get her point. She'd cry, weep bitter tears, and always when you didn't expect it. You were all primed to have a go at Joan, a real go, then would come the tears; or you were primed to be lovely and you'd get the screams. I mean, she would come on with that walk, off would go the hat on to the floor. 'Now listen, kids . . .' We knew what we were in for. It was splendid.

*Outside views of Theatre Workshop varied. Some people thought of it as a cross between a concentration camp and a trade union meeting. I think it's important to correct some of these views, because the profession never really liked Joan very much.*

Concentration camps! Certainly not concentration camps. You know the most precious thing we have is time, we have so little. There's no time for champagne. There's very little time for night-clubs, even when you're a so-called success. The kind of thing we

Joan Littlewood

were doing was a twenty-four-hour day. I would rehearse four hours in the morning on *Volpone*, and four hours in the afternoon on *Volpone*, and I'd go on and play three hours of *Richard II*: pretty tough. As soon as the curtain dropped at eleven o'clock, I would be starting the first fencing lesson.

Now this produced an atmosphere of its own. There was literally no time to do anything else but concentrate; people lived, breathed, and fed on it: you had hardly any time for food.

*This was always extraordinary to actors living in a commercial atmosphere who were paid so much money for doing so much work. It was very difficult for them to understand how Joan got this kind of loyalty, this kind of love.*

Well, one thing we must really get away from is the idea of a personality cult about Joan. Joan was nothing apart from the material she worked with, and if ever Joan had bad material, actors, etc., there was very little she could do with them. Joan was the beginner, the suggester, the bringer of ideas, but they all found an echo within the people she was working with, and they were loyal to her ideal. We had company meetings in which she was really ripped apart at times, believe you me; there certainly was no iron hand about it whatsoever. Consequently the actor found a freedom he'd never had before. If he said he couldn't do a thing, he was allowed to say why he couldn't do it. Some actors had cried out for freedom for ages, and Joan gave them that freedom. Then for the first time they were face to face with their deficiencies, their lack of knowledge; they were at the lowest point of creative endeavours in their lives. After they'd dressed themselves up in a world which relied on 75 per cent bull and 25 per cent knowledge – that was the commercial world – they used to scream and say the commercial theatre is terrible, it's this, that and the other. When they were given their chance to have a go, it hurt them to find out how much they had relied on tricks, on make-up, on lighting. At Stratford East we used little make-up, if any at all, it was completely *verboten*; we had three-dimensional side lighting, or the House lights up: anything that made the point. This was no help to the actors who came with their tricks.

*Joan wouldn't allow them.*

No. Not in the actors she was working with. I wouldn't allow it when I was on stage. And they could see that. They had to work; to fight. You see, what was most important was the fact that you had to fight for your character. It's not all beautifully drilled: your character now. No, after you, partner!

It was get straight in there. Believe in the man. If for instance you played Hitler, not that I'd ever want to play the man, but the first premise is that you must love the character. You've got to learn to love him or you can't play him, or any other character. You can't play him with tricks. You can, but it's terribly unsatisfactory.

You've got to get that audience transfixed with the ideas you're putting over. They had to find out what the character was and get on to that stage and fight for their character, because if they didn't they would get trampled under the rush of everybody else fighting for theirs, believe me.

*But how did she work? Presumably she didn't start off with all the actors sitting round in a semi-circle with a read-through, which is the way most plays in the commercial theatre begin. How did she begin to tackle a play?*

Well, she would – if she felt like it – have a read-through. But that was dependent on how far the actors themselves were advanced. The tragedy was that the actors were inevitably seduced away from us by the commercial managements when they were only half-way through Theatre Workshop's programme. This meant sometimes a complete recouping of cast for a new season. If we began a season in this way, nobody would let them read through and find out how bad they were, and point out how bad they were. We would start with the research, the general discussion from the character point of view: what you feel, what you are, what you were doing today coming to the theatre. A gradual feeding-in movement. For example, the start lay perhaps, with Joan, in the auditions for this kind of thing. She would sit out front and people would come along with beautifully prepared pieces and she would throw them: 'Right. Have you seen any of the Theatre Workshop's work?' and the man would say, 'Yes, I saw last night's piece of work.' 'What did you think of it?' 'Quite good.' 'Right. Well be a charlady, telling me about last night's production.' This would throw the actor completely. He would have to improvise, and this is where he got annoyed because he thought that this was going to be the usual stupid method nonsense that flooded the market. Joan did this to find out if he had any imagination. You see, an actor must be a good liar, a fantastic liar; give me the man who can stand up in the middle of a football crowd and start saying, 'Millwall was shocking last night, really shocking, and nobody's ever heard of Millwall.' But half the crowd is around listening, and that's an actor. He's got to lie, lie truthfully, he's got to have a fantastic imagination to supply what the author's left out. That would be the beginnings of Joan's work: get that imagination working, throw the tricks away, let's see *the* you; what are you capable of? Are you trained yet? What is the lapse between thinking the thought and the hand carrying it out?

*Let's talk just a little about the time before you went to Theatre Workshop. You were in a fairly ordinary commercial weekly repertory company.*

Yes. Ordinary in the sense that it had the usual inevitable pattern of theatres, but they all had an individuality of their own, these little repertory companies. This one was started by a man desperately interested in theatre, a scene-painter called Jimmy Lovell, one of the most splendid men I ever met. He'd been in the business for years.

It was started by him, financially under-capitalised, until 'the committee' was brought in and that is the fatal stage.

But I was started off by this extraordinary man; otherwise I wouldn't have been in the position I am now. I was taken to him by a friend, and he said, 'Righto, we're desperately short; get on there, play a detective inspector, a cockney.' This was terrifying, my cockney was foul. I walked on to the stage and I couldn't move and talk at the same time. I had to cross first, then speak: it was disaster. I said, 'That's it, I'm off, I don't want to do any more.'

Then he saw me in the street: 'You, I want you. Didn't you get my letters?' 'No, I didn't get your letters.' 'I want you!' 'What is it?' 'For the front legs of the cow in the pantomime.' Well, what had I got to lose? So I played the front legs of the cow in the pantomime.

*Successfully?*

Yes, because I had eyes that moved, and ears that went like that on strings. I really tore the kiddies' hearts, you know what I mean? Nicked the show in other words. Because I was playing an animal. Jimmy Lovell obviously saw in this, funnily enough, a characterisation. I sometimes say, even though it was bovine, it was one of my best! He handed me down a little note – while he was madly working the lights – would I like to start work with him at thirty bob a week in the repertory theatre. It's only because of splendid men like this, in the individual repertory theatres, that there was a source of intake for the profession which was varied; instead of everybody coming from a specific area or a specific class.

Well, I became everything. I was a stage manager, I painted the scenery, I lit the stage and I dressed the set. I also acted. Now it was a Conservative Club and we had the top floor. I had to carry huge flats, sofas and settees on my back up the fire escape, which gave me a constitution for life in the theatre. We would open with a new play every Monday, dress-rehearse it all day; then we'd do the show at night and so on every week. I would then start on Saturday night breaking the play up by eleven o'clock, work all through the night, putting the new set up for the next week's show; I then got about three hours' sleep. I turned in Sunday morning to light and dress the sets for the dress rehearsal, the following day carrying the things backward and forward. I ended up playing the lead, big huge fantastic leads, while doing all these things; it wasn't until some old actor stumbled over to me and said, 'Harry, you know you're a bit of a fool; when you are starring here you shouldn't be doing this, you know.' I hadn't thought about it. I just went to Jimmy and I said, 'Jimmy, he says I shouldn't be doing this.' He said, 'He's dead right.' Jimmy was another one of those marvellous dream men. So I stopped and just played lead parts from then on.

Towards the end of it I started to get nibbles from the West End. But this coincided with the beginnings of me saying: I'm sorry, I disagree with the load of rubbish I'm performing on this stage. You begin to get a bit of a – not a social conscience – a sense of power. Not that you influence people's lives or whatever – but you do to a certain extent make their thinking concrete. Our job is to get under the concrete, under the things that all people would like to agree on. Now when we've arrived at a stage in life where we can all say, 'That's it,' it's static. Right? Take the supposition that all coloured men are treated badly and we must be sympathetic to all coloured men. Right, thank God we've arrived at this situation; now let's leave it alone for ten years. But it's up to us to get inside that and say, no, no, no; you can't rest there because it's not really true. Coloured people in England are beginning to be accepted, so consequently they're not all good, they're not all bad, they're just like you inside; we must cut away at this gloss. You see what I mean? Whereas the kind of plays I was doing were just confirming, confirming and confirming.

*Confirming these prejudices?*

Yes, absolutely. All the time.

*Well, from the front legs of the cow to a string of marvellous parts at Theatre Workshop, you then left Theatre Workshop, or did you really ever leave it?*

No, I never really left Theatre Workshop. It became more and more apparent that money was needed. I became popular. We started to get Press notices towards the end, and television extended a sort of feeler in my direction, so I worked in television. This suited me perfectly because I was still able to work at Theatre Workshop; in other words, I could get the money to bring back to Theatre Workshop. The actors, as always, subsidise this kind of work. I then got fascinated by television, because remember one thing that did come out of Theatre Workshop work (and let's forget Stanislavsky for the moment, he's terribly important, but let's forget him absolutely because he needs a whole programme on a tenth of his work), what came out was truth, absolute searching truth. This truth was tailored to a medium known as the theatre, in which the huge gesture is used, so that it can be seen, where the nod and the wink wouldn't suffice. Sometimes one had to sacrifice truth for the presentation of the theatrical effect. Television really allowed me to use this truth. I simply walked from one group theatre to another. It's only now the sheer horror of the fact has suddenly hit me, that a lot of people may be watching us, because here we are; we're sitting together, we're in a good studio, the boys are around, I know them well, I know all the lads, you see; it's a group. I know the cameraman. When I work on a show, I get to know him, I know his speed of walking; if he's a quick man by nature; if he's slow – whichever way he may be, I get to know him, he gets to know me, in the short time we have together. So I'm walking into a group set-up. But I stayed with the Theatre Workshop while still enjoying the fruits of the truth in television – and the money – until about two years ago. Even when I was doing *Steptoe* I was going back there, doing shows, doing seasons, and building a building. Then finally the break came with Theatre Workshop. We had to break it up because of financial problems. The inevitable end of the *avant-garde* is when it becomes the classical, and another *avant-garde* should come into being to attack it. This has always been so in the past, I think, through economic reasons. By the time an *avant-garde* theatre gets to its maturity the money's fading. The period of any theatre of that kind is about fifteen years. It starts as an idea, it grows, it it gets a highlight period towards the tenth year; then gradually it tails off, and I do not know any group theatre, any foremost repertory theatre of the past, which has not done that. It's at the end of that fifteen-year period it should burgeon out, and Joan wanted to do this with what she called her 'happydrome'. This was to take the form of a hugh pleasure-park arena with a really fantastic theatre, theatrical conception. Theatre Workshop could no longer carry the weight of these ideas that were being propounded; that is why it finished, and I finished with it.

*You think it was inevitable.*

Absolutely inevitable – for many reasons. It was founded during the hangover of the thirties, it existed and drew its blood from the thirties, right up until 1955 I should say: now we're in the sixties. The theatres are not good enough. They've all got to be burnt. Get rid of them. I've been in terrible trouble at the Bristol Old Vic when they've been showing all the Americans around. I used to get up in the gallery and say, pull it down, burn it, because it's a postage stamp of a stage. You've got to build these kind of places that Joan envisages, fantastic sort of open areas, you've got to put 10,000 people into them. I agree it's like the Roman spectacle; but that's the ultimate end of the classical theatre. I don't mean the cruelty and the barbarity but from the extent of the spoken word. That is a theatre – to keep up with the sixties it must be like that.

*You mean the form, the way it is presented, not the idea of theatre itself, but the stage and the relationship between the stage and the audience, the whole house has got to be completely changed.*

Yes, it's got to be no longer a relationship between the stage and the audience because in a sense the whole thing is a stage. The audience has really got to participate. For example, when the Beatles take over a huge baseball stadium, you get real audience participation. I know that the screaming and all that kind of nonsense is not to be encouraged, but by God that is audience participation. The emotive thrills are really being felt; the audience are not just waiting for the interval to rush off to the bar in some cloistered, terrible, heavily centrally-heated or freezing sort of atmosphere.

*Well, to go back about two hundred years: you were playing Macbeth when the invitation came to play Steptoe. Can you tell us something about that?*

Well, not really. I'd had a sort of bad mental time. I wasn't going bonkers but I had rather a lot of strain, a lot of overwork, and I was sick of being under the critical eyes of London. The opportunity came up, and I was very grateful at the time because it helped me enormously to play at the Bristol Old Vic. Irrespective of what I think of the stage, the people who run the theatre and their actual policy work is fantastic. As usual the plays came first and the list of plays was splendid. There was *Mother Courage, Macbeth*, a modern play, *Period of Adjustment*, a Tennessee Williams play – in other words the really good repertory system type of plays. I took the job, went down there and played for a season.

Prior to this, I had met Galton and Simpson slightly and told them how much I really admired their work, I really did; and I said if ever they felt like writing anything – of course I never envisaged in a thousand years coming over into light entertainment –

*You'd seen their Hancock scripts?*

Yes I had. And another thing – I envied them like mad. I'd gone through a period when television was awful, about eight years back. It's changed now, thank goodness. Anyway, I looked at television, and all I saw that was making any kind of good – what's the word? – social comment was the Hancocks, the Eric Sykes, this kind of half-hour comedy programme. Oh, I did envy them. So Galton and Simpson remembered this conversation, obviously took me at my word, and this thing about the rag and bone man thumped through the door. I read it and immediately wired back: 'Delicious, delightful, cannot wait to work on it.' In between this, of course, I'd worked with the Langham Experimental Group. That's where I knew a lot of the people in the BBC, Galton, Simpson and a few more. You know – we went through the mutual admiration phase which lasts off and on for about two days: 'I just love your work, have another glass of wine, thank you very much.' And then we got down to cases.

That's really all there is to say about that episode. Except that the work done by people like Hancock, Sykes, Bentine, and a few more, is a great period, and in so many years' time it will be revived as a classic period of really fantastic social comment.

*What did you think about the part of Harold when you read the first* Steptoe *script? Did it look easy to play?*

Yes. Yes. With that ease that comes with, 'My God, this is brilliant.' You see, good work is always easy. You don't even have to learn the lines. They're there, they're right, and they're the lines you should say.

1963 Harold, *Steptoe and Son*, BBC TV

No, no. Well, not me, because they didn't know anything about me. They had written, as every good writer writes, they had written a character. And that was it, I fitted in. What they had actually written, I must say, was slightly wrong. I looked at it and we all learnt from each other in this relationship, Galton, Simpson and I, Brambell and Duncan Woods, the very brilliant director. For example, in the original, the old man was eighty-five and I was seventy. Now this is splendid but there would have been no involvement for the audience; because everybody would have sat back and would have said, 'Ah, look at those two splendid old men, what lovely old men.' Because when I had to say lines like 'I didn't get rickets through overeating, did I?' they'd have said, 'Ah, what a lovely old man saying that.' But when a thirty-eight-year-old man says that kind of thing, it's getting through to a majority population in a power position of thirty-eight. So it stops them just laughing at the images of old men, you see. So I said, 'No, we must shift the ages down.' And there were a few more touches like that, but they were only touches.

So then we began to build this relationship between us, of getting the points over. You see, the rag and bone trade didn't mean a thing; I wasn't interested in a documentary about rag and bone men. I don't give a damn whether their prices are right, wrong or otherwise; that's dismissed, that's thrown out of the window. But it gave a perfect format and a set-up to range and slash all over the place. I mean with Harold, the domestic work is over and done with in five or ten minutes. Then it's all politics, sex, general economics, the church: it's about a thousand and one things, but it's certainly not about the rag and bone business. That was of no interest to us.

*This kind of contemporary comment had up till then been very rare in comedy series.*

Oh, I wouldn't say that. It had been rare in my life; but no, no. Bentine and, as I say, a few more had been making this precise point in varying ways. They may have made it more in the comedic (that's a terrible word to make up but let's stick to it) – the comedic visual sense. We used words. Not one of our scenes, surprisingly enough, relies on double takes, joey-joey, grimaces or whatever you wish to call them. They rely on words and timing. Have you noticed the pace at which we play them? Very, very delightfully slow and true to the subject matter. Now in the hands of a couple of hack charlatans, bad managers or whatever, they'd have said, 'Come on now, speed, speed, speed, bang it over lads, let's get it over quick; chop chop, lads, get the laughs; kick high and smile at the gallery.' But we had the time to play it properly; that is the important thing that came out of *Steptoe*. There was no

need for comedy to be fast-fast-fast and joey-joey, or to be fast-fast-fast and compensate by a pause while comic business was done. It could all go along in its own truthful flow.

*And you played to a studio audience?*

Yes. When I first played to them I got quite a shock. But I didn't find them getting in the way.

*It didn't create a problem as to whether you were playing to the camera or the audience?*

No, not at all. Because I've had prior experience of playing to cameras. I neither want them there or do not want them there; I don't care either way. I can, to a certain extent, assume where the laugh-points – or the ones I want to be laugh-points – are going to be. Surely the lift of an eyebrow or the twist of a face can get a laugh on a fairly serious line if you wish it to. It's the control of this that is important. That's why I say, 'Look at the contact between Willie Brambell and me.' Willie is holding it, but the point has to go over without a laugh getting in the way, and I am holding back certain things. Remember, the dialogue isn't screamed out and you've got gales of laughter sometimes, so it takes playing. The thing must register but not look as if we're shouting over our laugh, to get it over.

*There's a terrific confidence there about what you're doing all the time. You seem to know exactly where the cameras are, for instance. Did you discuss the shots with the director? Did you always know where the cameras were at any one time?*

Yes, it's terrifyingly important. Oh yes. You could say this is being camera-conscious if you wish, but it's terrifyingly important to know. You see that camera is there all the time. Otherwise I won't get freedom, funnily enough; especially as the men will get to know me by my movements. So consequently, I'm not going to lose the most important point of the play by being off shot. For instance, reaction in comedy, at least this form of comedy, is a line. It is written in. I mean, if you say to me, 'The place is burning,' right, you cut to me; I've merely got to say in reaction, 'Is it?' Or I've got to say, 'My God!' – with a pause. But that is a line; the camera must cut to me; you must see the reaction. Or we mustn't see the reaction. So this must be planned, and the camera and the other actor must know this and must be ready to hold it up so that this reaction can go in.

*It seems to me, having just looked at an early episode of* Steptoe *and then a later one, that the two characters have stayed remarkably consistent over a very long period.*

Yes they do. But the character does change, you know, awfully

1963 *Steptoe*

subtly each time. Now this is the first time I've ever actually seen any recordings of *Steptoe*, and first I must get over the shock of seeing them.

*You don't often see your television work?*

No, no. Not at all, because Harold looks nothing like that to me. I can see me in there.

Let's begin at the beginning. You see, I envisaged a character, let's say (and I've had to play it before today) a romantic lead. Now I am conscious of the fact that I've had a broken nose. I wish this would have healed attractively like it did with Ian Fleming and a few others like that, but you see unfortunately it didn't. It's just grown big and flabby and it wobbles. I got a thorn stuck in my eye during the war which has scratched it, marking it indelibly. Now I can see all these fantastic imperfections. Shaving as a youth I accidentally took too much skin off here and the hair won't grow there. I'm aware of these imperfections. So I envisage in my mind's eye what the author intended this man to be. Now the author is stuck with me, and I play him for that. It is that that gives me the ability to be able to con you, with a bit of luck, into thinking that the nose is fairy aquiline, the double chin doesn't actually wobble, and yes, the teeth do sparkle and they are clear and white. If I were to watch any of these episodes, do a make-up test or anything, I'd be finished. I wouldn't be able to do it, I'd be so concentrating on trying to bend the character back again.

Now does the character change at all? He does. He changes in the sense that they wrote further facets of the same man. Take the girl I meet in the early episode. I am waiting for the idealised dream. This was still to do, remember, with getting away from the rag and bone trade, the going into some other business. So we're down to, 'It's time I got married and started off on my own.' And I see now something curious took over which I wasn't aware of, an almost bourgeois approach to marriage, the playing it quietly, the deference, the cosy table not set out like the table in the restaurant, but set out like a kind of little home we'll have in the suburbs with the little motor car to wash every weekend like everybody else – and it's all played out on a very gentle level like that.

And the meeting with the girl in the later episode is different again. She's a French *au pair* girl. Now with Harold, when you actually see him meet the girl and the things we did, you see his normal reaction to sex. First of all there was, 'Caw, I'm right in it here.' Next you get the character he's trying to evolve within himself, the excusing of this on the ground that no, this is love. First of all there's sex and after that there's the conscience thing that makes him change it; it's got to be love you see. First of all he meets a French maid, an *au pair*. Of course he's thrilled about this, who's been about with an *au pair*? That's a piece of one-upmanship, and he's got the night all worked out. They're going to go round the

1964 *Steptoe*, with Wilfrid Brambell

51

QUEEN MARGARET COLLEGE LIBRARY

town, he's going to become the suave man-about-town showing her around. But before that, he sits down with a French record, he's going to learn French, he's going to have a few words ready, he's going to do this marvellous thing. But, as ever the old man puts his oar in it, which makes Harold have to defend the reason why he's learning French. Because he is then beginning, and this is the only way you can show it, he's beginning the retranslation of the things of this world into the dream world after the sex. 'Oh yes, she'll have a château over in France of course; I'll work you in if I can. I'll stick you up in the old tower up there and I shall be running around looking after the vineyards and the estate.' But it's the old man that started this. This is Harold's reply to the fight with the old man. In that scene, there were a couple of these moments I was talking about, those reaction shots. When the old man says, 'You're going to get us into the Common Market,' and he says, 'You great fairy.' In there – the feeling I had I remember quite distinctly at the time – Harold's got a reply which he's going to say – a real swear-word, or you silly old nit. But he knows he daren't say it because that will start off a completely different tack of argument which the old man is after. So he swallows it back. But that all happens in a reaction shot, then the leaning over from the table saying, 'Now listen' – and Harold goes back on to the tack. However badly or well it is done, that reaction must be written in the pause, do you see?

Then the old man drags it out of him, what the girl is about, what it's not about, because the old man is jealous and envious of the fact that Harold again has come home with a goodie that he's picked up from somewhere, and the old man hasn't got one that day. Usually, Harold turns up with the gramophone records, you know, a bit of the old '1812', the old man is jealous of this, so he immediately has to discover an urgent desire to hear Oscar Rabin, or whatever, on the piano.

*In fact this is a common element in the conflict between you two, Harold's middle-class aspirations which are mocked by the father.*

This is what I mean about getting in there and fighting for your character, lad, when they're treading on it. You see, I can't think of it like that. That's why I can't discuss it really, if I was to play it properly. Harold doesn't think of it as middle class. He thinks of it as being – because *he* will discuss the middle class – bourgeois, how middle class can you be, while he's carrying out middle-class aspirations possibly. You see what I mean, but I could never admit to that as an actor, and as Harold myself. No, no, this is not middle class, I mean this is what I was made for; it was an accident you ever had me, let's face it. I mean I'm sure there was a mix-up in the hospital bed. I was really made to chump round the old vineyards there, sniff the grape and say, 'A little too far up the hillside,' that's what I was really made for. This is hardly middle class – in Harold's estimation.

*You have appeared in a number of movies, including* Rattle of a Simple Man. *You made this after you had done some Steptoes?*

Yes, that's true.

*So you must have been concerned about trying to make Percy in that film different from Harold Steptoe.*

The problem there wasn't so much to keep him away from Harold Steptoe but something I failed in miserably, now I see it, to keep Percy away from going too far into what I know about the North; what I know about the lads, you see. There are varying accents around Manchester, there isn't a Manchester accent. There's Rochdale, there's Failsworth, there's so many around, and I tried to get this certain accent which comes from a certain area, which is emasculated, back in the throat, almost a feminine type of accent, which would have suited Percy because the accent is a weapon for the particular part. I also wanted to get away from the demotic, the town language which has been derived at by screaming over machines and cutting off and glottal-stopping the ends of words. You can get from Blackburn and places around there a delightful, almost South Country burr. The ends of the words are sounded and all the r's are rolled; it's a beautiful language, very smooth and rich. Now I see from a dialect point of view I ought to have kept away from that one, but I failed miserably; I let it control me too much.

But this man's problems were essentially terribly different from Harold's. Harold is in no wise effeminate through the influence of a father; on the contrary, he couldn't wait to get hold of a girl and

Percy in the film *Rattle of a Simple Man*, with Diane Cilento (1964)

get upstairs. Percy had got the absolutely opposite point of view: he's been brought up by mother, tightly controlled all the time. Then he'd really pushed it all into a motor bike, and he was happy that way. As he says, I'm a very happy man; he was. Because he'd never been exposed to the thrills of a love situation in any way. Nothing disturbed that equanimity. It's only his bet that disturbs the equanimity. I possibly didn't bring the point out well enough in the film. You see, I'm trying to make it up to the poor author, to show you what really should have happened.

*Do you like working in films? I mean rehearsal time for example; how much rehearsal time do you get?*

Oh God, you've gone straight to the point. It's terrifying working in films. It's not a question of me hating the medium, but I hate the situation in which I have to work at present. I formed a way of life in acting that requires rehearsal, polishing. I can't give an instant characterisation, just like that, and that's what I'm required to do. I'm expected to walk into the studio at 8.30 in the morning and give an instant characterisation. With *Rattle of a Simple Man* I asked for rehearsal time and so did Diane Cilento – we both insisted, could we have at least a week's talking and rehearsal together, to start with. But we didn't get enough, in some cases we just had a little chat on the set of no more than ten minutes, for the whole sequence; a running-through of positions. Then all hell breaks loose with hammers and lighting men who have fully two hours to light the set – and they need it. Then they start shooting and you do a take; in effect you rehearse on print. This is definitely bad for me because I've either got it in the first take or it'll extend to about thirty-nine takes before I'll get near it again. It's the business of creating from inside, and spending the rest of the time trying to re-create that marvellous thing you had at the beginning. For me, films – no. Not unless I can make them under an entirely different system than I'm asked to make them at present.

*But how do you get it the first time and not the sixth time, which is more usual?*

Intuition. Intuition and inspiration which help you to skate over, gloss over the facts; and so you use tricks. Now they're not *rehearsal* tricks, but they are tricks – tricks of behaviourism, and they save the day. You can't quite get the word properly; you know you're going to fumble the word, the intonation, and so if you can come up with something that makes up for it, the intention has gone over. It's tricks that make you get away with it on the first take and I'm never really terribly interested in it afterwards. Because I either had a director who says, 'Splendid, don't need to do that again'; or else we'll keep going, because what he actually does want, and what the film requires, they've just got to rehearse with me, even if it takes thirty-nine takes: and we could have had that by having the rehearsal first. I could have done this if I'd have come straight out of rep. with my bag of tricks, because in repertory I used to be brilliant when I was rehearsing at home! I would get the script, I'd see the part, I'd learn it, learn all the movements, the matchbox would be crushed at the right moment like an eggshell – brilliant. I'd go in with it. And I'd be very hurt if other actors had done the same thing. But we got no point of contact like Willie Brambell and I have got, because I refused to listen to what they were saying. They were saying it with an entirely different intonation. That's not what I'd expected and it's just too bad, because my reply is going to be this way. When I became an actor I threw all this away. With *Steptoe* I'll go in knowing my play, not learning it, but knowing my play, knowing what it's about, know what I'm going to do – on the rehearsal floor I learn the play. I'm free. If Wilfrid throws me a line a certain way it'll shake me and I have to reply; this is known as contact. But, of course, there's not much time for this sort of thing in film. There might be for other actors but not for me. I've either got to go home and work on it all night and take not a blind bit of notice what anybody else is going to say to me on the set – consequently I'm going to be hard, factual, technically brilliant; or else I get into this terrible mess of trying to have the best of both worlds. I get into a terrible mess, waiting to discover what it's about. And by the time I've discovered what it's about, it's over; we've wrapped up. We've got to move on to the next set and, fellows, this is costing a fortune having this Rolls-Royce for three minutes, you know. We've had it.

*Last summer you did a very successful Comedy Playhouse called the* Seven Year Hitch. *Joan Sims played the part of your wife – you were both instructors at a local dancing school. That was pure situation comedy with very little social significance. How did that appeal to you?*

One of the main reasons there was to work with Joan Sims again. We were together in repertory many years ago. And we both wanted to work together again; get the contacts going, you know. The other thing which lifted it out of the ordinary was that it opened with a marvellous dream world in which I, as dancing instructor, am teaching the dance. Behind that you reveal the crack in the façade of the actual home life.

I don't want to be too subtle or intellectual about it but we were trying to represent the people of 1960. Not awfully well perhaps but it is a beginning. It was a beginning for me to get closer to the 1960s in a situation comedy.

*It's interesting that that part is very close to Harold Steptoe, the same sort of age, the same sort of social background, and yet you managed to make him a very different character in a way that isn't at all obvious.*

Well that is for you to decide. As an actor, there's at least 75 per cent of you in any part you play that cannot be eradicated or eliminated. Only in the theatre can this happen because the audience is far enough away not to spot the small shadow movements that are basic to every person.

You have chosen to show me as three cockneys or Londoners. Consequently I can assure you that I was never, at any time in my life, faced with the fact: God, I must make this different, I really must make this different at all costs. I wouldn't have cared if they had all come out like Harold Steptoe vocally or any other way, if it suited the character. I'll tell you what you can say was very close to Steptoe, which interested me for some period of time, though I'm not so interested in it now, I was terribly interested in failure: human beings as failures. Now don't get me wrong; I don't mean to say desiccated, finished-off failures, but the whole concept of a human being in the world is now finished; he's redundant, an extension of a machine. He's over. So consequently there's a failure there.

*You have a kind of gentleness, Harry, which takes the edge off some of the lines and some of the situations which would, perhaps, in another actor grate. I mean very often you're playing a situation where you are very irritated. In most of the Steptoes you're on a very irritable level the whole time; yet you manage to do this without grating. Are you aware of this?*

Only so far as the character is like that. Anyway, most of the characters have been on that line. This brings me to what I hope will be the seventies; I'm going to try to oppose that more and more. If I am faced with playing some of the other characters that I have played – murderers or violent people of this age. For example, the character in *The Torrents of Spring* has a breakdown where he gets raucous, vile, really hard. Now power – real power – is controlled. You see, weakness is a kind of hysteria. Harold has a kind of hysteria; it's a modulated hysteria. But it is hysteria. Power is controlled. The voice is only raised to the right level of power. You know what I mean? I'm just being faced with playing characters who have been in essence gentle people, really. This is the more interesting point, everybody's got the same facets you see; everybody's a liar, I mean there's no such thing as a shy man. Percy, the man in *The Rattle of a Simple Man*, he's not shy with a dog, he's in command of a dog, he's the master of a dog. You can't always tabulate people, because some people will use gentleness as a camouflage. Harold Steptoe does this an awful lot – he'll duck out from a nasty situation by using gentleness.

*But you haven't played many violent men.*

Oh yes I have, but more in the past than now. As I say, in *The Last Mile* I played the killer, Mears, a very, very violent man. In *The Petrified Forest*, I again played a very violent man. Hal, even though he's young, in *Henry IV, part 2*, what a violent man he is. That's why Hotspur comes out best; Hotspur is gentle, beautifully

1966 Ernie Conway, *Seven Year Hitch*, BBC TV, wi Joan Sims

gentle; there is no domesticity about Hal. Yes, I have played hard men, what I conceive to be hard men.

*In your years at Theatre Workshop, Harry, you evolved a certain set of social attitudes and attitudes about entertainment. Do you think you've changed these in any way over the last few years?*

Yes, of course I have. Well I must do, times have changed. Time has moved on. You're on to something fantastically interesting, really worth-while talking about. Let's take Theatre Workshop, founded in the thirties; now what were the standards of poverty in the thirties? It's what Albert Steptoe says, 'You got a full belly, you know; what more do you want out of life? You've got a suit of clothes, you've got somewhere to sleep.' Now, the thirties is based on this. That's the breadline level. But what's today's breadline level? We almost forget the new standards of poverty. We must realise what they are. Now forget India; this is where the confusion arises; forget starving India, just for one second though. And let us establish what ours are – forget American standards of poverty which are even higher than ours; what are ours? I don't know, but I suggest we've got to lift them up to something like: it is an essential to have a television set. It is possibly an essential to have a refrigerator, especially as the dairies are now only going to deliver milk every two days. It is essential possibly – possibly – to have some form of motorised transport. So this is the end for these turgid magistrates leaning forward and saying: 'You are on national assistance and you have a television set on hire purchase and you have a car! I haven't got a car, but you have a car,' and he's choked. We've got to realise this – so how can my attitude stay the same as it was in the theatre that reflected the tail-end of the thirties and the beginning of the forties?

*How does this change them?*

My attitudes? Well on this level, what are people being deprived of? The mass of the people, shall we say, are no longer being deprived of homes, they're being deprived of television sets. They're being deprived of privacy, that's the bed-sit life; that's a terrible thing. Now here's a terrible world to explore. The life that is doomed to live in a bed-sit. Let's take some boy, any boy. He leaves an orphanage, apprenticed to some trade, got no real basic relationships; goes into a bed-sit life, lives in it as a bachelor, has a marvellous time, gets married, into a bed-sit life again. Ends his days in the equivalent of a flatlet run by a landlady or some other. This breeds – I'm sorry, I seem to have gone off on to a political discussion, do stop me.

*This is important because one of the great sustaining things about Joan Littlewood was that the people were being deprived of culture by some kind of conspiracy or other. That was what she believed and that was what actors believed. Did you believe that then? Do you believe it now?*

No, I didn't believe it then. I don't believe it now. Remember, Joan was educated; she educated herself. It's not the people's fault, it is the government or society, call it what you like – 'they', it's 'their' fault that only 25 per cent of the nation are educated up to the level at which they can enjoy culture, understand it, and have the leisure time to understand it. I think that was more Joan's cry; the pap that is fed over in the advertising medium does not stress anything cultural. It just says to people, substitute culture or whatever with this particular thing. In all honesty I'm not saying we're a nation of illiterates; I am illiterate compared with what I would like to be, because I didn't have the time to spend or to take off and enjoy the marvellous four or five years' learning, soaking up the world's learning, to be able to appreciate culture. I remember I was taken out of the slums and stuck in a new school; we had a huge laboratory and bunsen burners, it was full of stuff, but all we did do was cut up onions all day and look at the insides of the onions because they couldn't afford to run the gear. I mean the schools now are fantastic. How lucky to be born now with these schools, you know, beautiful. They're given the gear and they can use the gear. Pottery kilns, anything, anything.

*But at Theatre Workshop there was a contempt, a very just contempt usually, for what was called show business. Is this contempt that you shared then and still share now?*

The Supermarket tycoon in *The Hothouse*, ABC TV

It was a contempt I shared then and I would share now if it was still in evidence, but it isn't. Television broke it up, finished it off. What is the cry of the old show business personality? He doesn't get a chance any more. Where have all the musicals gone? Where have all the opportunities gone? The people who have survived are the artists. Artistry has nothing to do with show business. Quite honestly, artistry is truth, and if you've got a good truth, you can do it on an ice-rink, on television, as a ballet, do it as anything you want. So I don't see enough show business in evidence to be contemptible about show business.

But an interesting point is this; because I no longer see the evidence, I can now accept the term show business. In the old days one had to resist the show-business-type people who came in and dominated, people who described Brecht as gleanings from an East German dungheap. We had to resist words like show-biz because they contained all the contempt and despair we felt for the people who ran it. But now a new generation has arisen and they use this word freely, and if it means now the good, marvellous comedy stuff that comes over on television, on occasions, then I'll be happy to call it show-biz.

*Do you miss the theatre at all, Harry?*

No. No, not one little bit. You see, we go through phases – we go through phases in life. You don't give up the theatre, the theatre gives you up. At the moment it has basically given me up because it's going through a phase which I admire an awful lot but am not terribly interested in playing in. I can't quite describe it, but the plays I have seen I have felt: splendid, but I don't wish to be in them. Not that I'm anti them on any moral grounds or from any other point of view; it's just that I love the epic. I still love the epic instead of the particular, you see. In the theatre sense that is. Maybe there is going to be a return to this type of play. There will be, obviously, if we get the breakthrough I was science-fictioning about just now, then there will be a necessity to bring back the epic; but not at the moment.

*Are there going to be any more Steptoes?*

No. As far as I can see, no. They served their time. I think their time has run out. But again this is only my thinking; if it's possible to write more, I'm sure the authors will write them;[1] they don't particularly wish to, themselves. Of course, they are the main inspiration of the Steptoes, so I can't really speak for them.

Everything serves its time. The Langham Group we talked about earlier served its time, guided by the men who made it, Tony Pelissier, Mervyn Pinfield, and the methods they worked on. I say it was experimental, well it was; we sat all day, we did the dialogue, we improvised the dialogue; the dialogue was then taped all through the day, it was typed overnight, rushed back to us. That experiment was splendid for the time, but it is not big enough for the times to come; so there will be no more Langham Group. There will be no more Steptoes because that belongs to the tail-end of the fifties and the thirties in both senses. No, we must try at least to go into 1962 if not 1967 next year, and I hope the seventies as soon as possible.

---

[1] In fact a new series of Steptoe was shown on BBC TV in the Spring of 1970.

# Albert Finney

E VEN now, I should think, the image of Albert Finney which leaps to most people's minds is that beautiful smile on the face of Arthur Seaton, in the film of *Saturday Night and Sunday Morning*, as his fist lashed out in the opening pub brawl. Finney has come a long way since then, but the special quality of his acting is still a sense of bottled electricity in search of joyous, violent release.

The story goes that his headmaster at Salford Grammar School spotted a caged energy in the shy, sturdy boy who kept failing exams, and suggested acting as a possible outlet for it. He was proved right – first at RADA, where Finney's performances provoked excited, premature talk of a new Olivier; then, at the Birmingham Rep., where his Henry V was hailed as a prodigy and his Macbeth, in 1958, astonishing for an actor of twenty-one. Charles Laughton saw it and brought him to London to play the bewildered garage-hand who took out his daughter in *The Party*. Next season they played together at Stratford: Finney as the gentle Edgar in Laughton's *Lear* and as Lysander in *A Midsummer Night's Dream* dominated by Laughton as Bottom. Clearly, Laughton was a major influence, suggesting the sort of career a round-faced, northern boy might carve in comedy and character-acting. A dangerous influence perhaps; it takes a great actor to handle the big, flamboyant strokes Laughton used – and did not always get away with.

However, Finney's success as Olivier's understudy in *Coriolanus* led to more rumours of a new, heroic star-actor. But his first West End hit, *Billy Liar*, was a comic-character part you could imagine the young Laughton playing: a shy northern boy, whose ambition explodes in dreams of wild megalomania. Laughton had given him tracks to develop along; the discipline of close, detailed character-observation containing explosions of broad, boisterous self-release.

John Osborne's *Luther* gave the first hint that he couldn't follow those tracks for ever. Perhaps the part came too close to Finney's own problems as an actor: he had to rely uneasily on emotion rather than character-playing. Only in Luther's diatribes did he appear completely sure of himself.

Evidently it wouldn't always be possible to hide behind a mask of character, freeing his inhibitions in disguise. Other ways of controlling and channelling his energies must be found. After the New York run of *Luther* in 1964, he disappeared for a year, travelling round the world, thinking and taking stock.

The result, when he returned, was his joining the National Theatre. At once, as Don Pedro in *Much Ado About Nothing*, he showed that many of his problems had been solved. In a small comic characterisation, a sort of Latin operetta general, he managed to appear both easy and formidable. In *Armstrong's Last Goodnight*, he made John Arden's feudal Border chieftain a tongue-tied, noble savage, whose language was violence; brilliantly, he used the speech impediment to evoke both thwarted power and its discharge. And in *Miss Julie* he almost capsized the play by the power of his acting as the valet – a power that expressed itself both as menace and control. Technically he had arrived at the height of his powers, and his virtuoso doubling in *A Flea in her Ear* seemed a triumphal little dance of celebration.

Finney's career in the cinema has run a parallel course to his work in the theatre. As Arthur Seaton in *Saturday Night and Sunday Morning* the details of the Nottingham accent were handled as meticulously as Arthur handled his lathe and fishing-rod. Secure in a character he could feel was not his own, he could release his sheer animal vitality, whereas in his latest film *Charlie Bubbles* (he played the leading part and also directed), he brought to life a much more private and personal character – in all its relentless detail.

*Ronald Bryden*

CLIVE GOODWIN: *When we saw you as Arthur Seaton in* Saturday Night and Sunday Morning *six years ago, it almost seemed that we were seeing, for the first time, a working-class hero convincingly played. When you were making the picture, did you feel that you were doing anything particularly new?*

ALBERT FINNEY: I was aware through foreign films. An obvious example is Brando in *Streetcar*, a working-class Polish immigrant to America, who was being explored in a depth not usually associated with that kind of character. One did feel that to a certain extent in *Saturday Night*, and one hoped one was doing it correctly for that reason. I didn't feel I was doing anything special; but I felt very strongly about the reality of the character. I sympathised with Arthur's situation; having spent a small amount of time in a factory myself as a student, I sympathised with his feeling of being trapped at that machine for the next forty years of his life. I was on his side, and I did feel a lack of exploration of that type of character in the British cinema. But as it was my first film, I had enough problems of my own to concentrate on, without being aware of its meaning in the British cinema; I was just worried about the acting and how I was getting on with it.

1960 Arthur Seaton in the film *Saturday Night and Sunday Morning*

*Did reading Alan Sillitoe's book help you much?*

Yes. A lot of people afterwards felt that I was very good at drinking pints of ale, and that I had obviously slept with my friends' wives; which isn't true. I'm really a wine man myself; beer gives me terrible indigestion: I find it very uncomfortable. A lot of people, after that, thought that was me, but I'm really lower middle class rather than working class. Obviously the character situation was very near to me in my upbringing, although I had a very different childhood from that character. I hate to be labelled, so I did tend to react against being considered that kind of person. From my milieu I could understand Arthur fairly clearly and sympathetically; and reading the book did help. Although one's acting the part as written for the screen, it's wrong to bring in elements which are not useful to the interpretation of the film. I think that it's good to do as much homework as you can, so long as it doesn't get in the way. Reading Alan's book, which is a strongly felt book, a very emotionally involved book, enabled me to understand the character's attitude sympathetically.

*You made that film with Karel Reisz, the director you've worked with since and have plans, I think, to work with again. Do you feel a particular kind of sympathy with this director?*

Yes. I think it happened fairly quickly in *Saturday Night*. We rehearsed it for about four weeks before we started shooting; and very soon I felt a trust in Karel, a similarity of outlook. I felt that he was going about it the right way. I was then only twenty-three,

you know; I'm not being presumptuous about that, but I felt sympathetic to the way he set out to do it. I like working with Karel; I think he's very good with actors. We did a film after that called *Night Must Fall* which wasn't very successful for various reasons, but I think the work which Karel did with the actors was, in some ways, extraordinary. I also think it's true of *Morgan*, the film he did with David Warner and Vanessa Redgrave; he's very interested in the actors creating a character and not just relying on their personality. He encourages actors to explore a characterisation, and that's the kind of acting I'm interested in.

*Can you give me an example of what he does with actors that makes him different and better to work with than other directors?*

One does feel his absolute concentration on the subject and his extraordinary patience with an actor. It's very difficult actually to think of a specific example.

*But he makes you feel important.*

Well it's not so much important; you feel that you've got the time to do it properly, that it's really explored, that you can turn it over in your hands and have a look at it from each side. I'm similar in a way. I often approach work by walking around the pool a few times before I dive in; I then put a toe in and I say, 'Well I'll think about it'. Then I walk round a bit more. When I commit myself, if you like, to an interpretation or a way of doing things, I like to be convinced that that's the way it should be done. Karel's also very hesitant at first, very 'Well I dunno, I'm not sure', and exploring it. I think we have similar temperaments in that respect; that's why I like working with him.

*Did you find it easy adapting yourself to acting in front of film cameras?*

Yes, I think the process within the body, the process of acting inside oneself, is the same; the manifestation of it is fairly different, obviously. What was marvellous to me at that stage, and very exciting, was to discover the reality of working a lathe. Some of the scenes were done in the Raleigh factory and I did have to learn how to work it. In fact there's somebody somewhere riding about today on a bicycle with one of the parts made by me – I hope it still works all right. As an actor who'd just worked in a theatre for four years and trained for the theatre two years before that, I found it very exciting when I was being photographed working at that lathe. I could concentrate absolutely on what the character was supposed to do; there was no cheating involved. On a stage it would have been made out of cardboard, and part of my job as an actor would have been convincing the audience that that cardboard lathe was an iron one; whereas in a film you don't have to because it *is* an iron one. The reality of that detail I found very intriguing and enthralling; I could just do the job at the lathe in the hope that the camera

1960 Arthur Seaton, *Saturday Night and Sunday Morning*

E

could pick up what Karel wanted it to pick up. That was terrific.

I was also disappointed at the bits of cheating you have to do. When one has discovered that the cinema can be that real and that rewarding, then there are times when you've got to move your elbow up a bit because of the angle of the camera and cross your leg back this way because the shot demands it. So you suddenly find you're playing a scene which you rehearsed and felt very relaxed in, in an absolutely impossible position. That kind of cheating annoyed me.

But because of the reality of the story and the reality with which Karel wanted me to do it, I responded to it well; you know, for one's first picture. Before that I'd done one night's work on *The Entertainer*, which was a sort of living screen test for *Saturday Night and Sunday Morning*; it was just one scene.

*Let's go back now to your beginnings as an actor which I think was at Salford Grammar School, where you played some fifteen parts, which seems an astonishing number to play at a grammar school.*

It was an extraordinary period in that school's history, when there was a headmaster who was very keen on the drama, and he happened to have on his staff four teachers who were similar *aficionados*. At the age of ten and eleven I had revealed a theatrical tendency at my primary school, where I used to do very good animal imitations of ducks and pigs in the farmyard. But in the first year at the grammar school, when they did *Merrie England*, I was rather shy and didn't volunteer. Then in the next five years I was involved in fifteen plays. Only three of them were full-length; most of them were one-acters. We used to have inter-house play competitions, and there were youth-club festivals in Salford, and we'd always put plays in. I think it was extraordinary that it was at that period in the school's history that I happened to be there.

Some of the other teachers were very, very sarcastic about the school's dramatic activities. There was one who was marvellously outraged by the thought that schoolboys should be let off their homework in order to rehearse a play. When he knew that I hadn't done the homework because I was working on the play, he used to create a great scene of collecting all the exercise books, and then counting every head in the classroom, then counting the books and saying, 'There's one missing'; counting the heads again and then counting the books again; then getting the register out and going through who – and he knew it was mine all along. Then finally, after five minutes of pantomime, he would say, 'There's no book here. Where's your exercise book?' I'd say, 'Well, I haven't done my homework.' And then he'd say, 'Come here, you haven't done your homework; why haven't you done your homework? Don't you know that that's why you're here, to learn. Homework is a very essential part of your education. Why haven't you done your homework?' 'I'm rehearsing the school play.' 'I beg your pardon,

Finney,' he would then profusely apologise and conduct me back to my seat and say, 'I'm sorry if we interrupted you'. He used to send me up rotten because I didn't do any homework. But they were nice about it, really.

At that time I wasn't aware of wanting to be an actor, although I suppose I must have always wanted to be. But it was a school activity which I found myself doing. When I was in a play and was being made up – the staff used to make us up – I used to think, It might be quite nice to be an actor, you know. But no more than I felt when I played rugby or cricket for the school, and I thought it might be nice to play rugby for England, you know, or cricket for England; it was the same kind of childhood fantasy, it seemed to me. Except that acting appeared to be further away than the possibilities of being a professional athlete, because it seemed to me that actors were a sort of special breed. Nobody I knew was an actor. I didn't know where they made them; I mean they made them somewhere else, you know. I didn't know where they came from. So the possibility of my being a professional actor, although I did fantasise about it, didn't ever seem to be a reality.

*Did you take it very seriously or was it just a joke to you? Did you work on the parts?*

I did it seriously; in fact it was the only thing I worked at. I refused to work at anything else, through laziness and a lack of interest. They always used to say on my reports: intelligent but doesn't make any effort.

*I have a note here that you played Emperor Jones.*

Yes. I played Emperor Jones. I remember going down to the docks in Salford – which are called Manchester Docks, but they're actually in Salford – and studying the negro seamen because of the way they walked. And I thought, that's because I wanted to be able to reproduce the kind of movement that they had in the performance: that was when I was about sixteen. So obviously I did take it seriously. But I wasn't aware of its implications, you know, the implications of taking it that seriously. When the headmaster finally suggested I entered RADA, I said, 'What's that?' And he said, 'It's the RADA, that's the Royal Academy of Dramatic Art.' And I said, 'Oh'. He said, 'Would you like to go there; it's in London, and you'd be there for two years and you'd train to be an actor.' I conjured up a marvellous student life in London, living away from home; I could stay up after eleven o'clock and all that. And you know, painting the statues in Trafalgar Square, doing all those things you thought students did in London. So I thought that sounds the thing. I went home and said, 'The headmaster suggests I go to RADA.' My mother had just read Equity's annual letter to the newspapers saying what percentage of their members were out of work and she said, 'It doesn't seem very substantial. Do you think –?' Father, who's a bookmaker and therefore a bit of a gambler, said, 'Well no, let him go and if he doesn't like it he can always come back into the business'; and Mum, preferring me to be an actor than a bookmaker, said, 'Oh, he can go.' There was no opposition of any kind at all from them. And so I went to RADA. It wasn't until I was actually there, I'd been there two terms, that I realised what I was really doing. I thought, well I'm going to be an actor I suppose, and I sort of started to settle down.

What's extraordinary is that if I hadn't gone to that grammar school I might never have been an actor, because if I hadn't passed the eleven-plus and had gone to the secondary modern school, I don't think they did many plays there. And unless I'd shown whatever promise I'd shown in acting at the grammar school and if the headmaster hadn't suggested RADA, I would have sat the ordinary level education two years running and failed it, then left and become a bookmaker. If I hadn't gone to drama school, I would never have done amateur dramatics, I would have accepted the fact that I was now a bookmaker. It seems extraordinary, both circumstances, you know.

*There may be other Albert Finneys in the north who aren't getting their opportunities.*

Well, yeah. I mean it's not that long ago, but for the headmaster of a grammar school to suggest the theatre as a career is kind of adventurous, you know, really. And rather remarkable.

*Did you begin to take RADA very seriously once you realised that you could actually become an actor?*

Yes. I was very self-conscious in the beginning because I felt very unattractive, kind of podgy and awkward. I'd had a crewcut that summer to play tennis, and I thought it was rather good at the time, you know, very short. It looked good for the tennis you see, but it didn't look good at drama school: I felt very out of place. I wanted it to grow as soon as possible, so that I could look like an art student, like everybody else. And with my thick North-Country speech, I did feel very awkward and shy and self-conscious. I mean, when you had the diction class, having to get up in front of eight other lads and recite a piece – I didn't like that, I felt very awkward. Becoming aware that acting involved things like movement and speech, breathing and diction and all that seemed to me, at first, so complicated; I didn't want to do that. It was like being at school again, having to learn something. Because at school I just got up and did it, and that was smashing. You're not aware that the shape your body makes can mean something, really, consciously; or that the way you sound is particularly important. At first it seemed to be a little disappointing that I'd actually have to work at it.

Then, at the beginning of the third term, I played Toby Belch in a production we did of *Twelfth Night* and the director was an actor called Wilfred Walter who'd lost a leg; he'd become a teacher because of his injury. At the first rehearsal, when we were blocking out the moves and it came to my first entrance, I picked up the script and I said to him, 'Where do you want me to come in?' And he said, 'Come in from where you like, if we get in trouble later we'll sort it out.' And I thought, that's an awful responsibility. But he gave me such freedom by doing that, by not imposing on me a way of acting, that this freedom was actually associated with him directing me in that role. And instead of thinking that they're all laughing at me in the class, I felt, no, they've got to enjoy me. I felt a very clear, conscious change of attitude from being negative about myself, on display as it were, to being positive. It was so definite that I felt that they were going to learn from it, rather than laugh at it; it was almost an arrogant kind of attitude. I needed to be that arrogant about it because I was very self-conscious. But it wasn't until then I realised that this was going to be a career and I was supposed to be an actor. If I was, I'd better work at it and I did like working at it; and obviously that's why I was there; I'd wound up there because I liked it and I was all right at it.

*Did you have a problem about what kind of an actor you wanted to become?*

No, not really. There was always a strong concentration on classical training. I remember, as a student, seeing Richard Burton at the Vic, playing Coriolanus and Hamlet, and thinking he did it very well and I'd like to play those parts. Because you think you're a great actor when you're seventeen and you obviously think you've got to play Hamlet and the classics. So you see yourself going that way. One has terrible debates about the professionals of the time not doing it properly; because you're a young actor, every production's kind of dusty and archaic. But I did see a kind of power for myself; I felt that I wanted a great career, like Garrick and Kean and Irving, in that tradition. One sort of thinks, that's what I'll do.

*Do you think, looking back on RADA, that it was a good training?*

For me, yes. Probably because of what I said before, I'd never been aware of anything to do with acting, apart from getting up and doing it. I'd never been aware of the fact that if you want this instrument to be useful to you as an actor you've got to work on it, look after it, polish it, train it and condition it. I would never have done that if I hadn't gone to a drama school and it hadn't been focused for me. There were lots of complaints about the methods employed. I remember there was a great deal of talk, when I was a student, about improvisation, that was the big thing just coming in, which we didn't do. A lot of the American students talked about improvisation and the Actors' Studio, which was very big at that time, because of Brando's success in *Streetcar* and *Waterfront*. But I felt that the training at RADA was of tremendous value to me because, as I said, it pointed out things one should work at and do which I would never otherwise have been aware of.

*Now from RADA you went to the Birmingham Repertory Company. Was this what you wanted to do?*

Birmingham or Bristol were the two one thought of at the time, and it so happened that there was a place at Birmingham. It was absolutely the thing I wanted to do, partly because they did a play for a month and we had three weeks' rehearsal for each play, which seemed to me smashing, you know – and it was.

*Did you learn a great deal at Birmingham?*

Well, yes. The thing is that when you go, you're so full of yourself. I remember the actual thing of appearing on a professional stage with actors, people who were getting paid for doing this, not just students any longer, or fellow students, people who have been at it for fifteen years or twenty years. I was tremendously excited by that initially. But also the terrible thing of 'Here I am, folks'. You go on stage and Birmingham is going to see what's arrived. O.K., of course for four months you don't do any acting; you just say, 'Look at me, I'm the new thing.' Then I settled down a bit and got on with the proper work of acting: and I did learn. I was able later almost to chart my development through those two years, from going in there and saying, 'Look what's hit town,' to starting to work in a more serious way and becoming much too inbred about it and too intense. Because you thought you knew that particular theatre so well that you could judge your performance perfectly and you could take the play right down, because you felt the audience knew you so well, having seen you in ten plays every year, they would be on your side and that you could bring them right in when you wanted to. I feel in a way that I left just as I was finding my real legs; I thought I was just about to be using that theatre absolutely correctly. But looking back on it, it was smashing.

*Do you think that this kind of beginning in a live theatre, in a repertory theatre, playing a fairly large number of parts every year, is essential for a young actor?*

It was for me, and I say yes it is, because it's from acting in front of the punters in the flesh, from that contact and that working on a performance, rehearsing a performance and then playing it, that you understand the demands made by the theatre. There's also the experience of playing parts which you're totally wrong for, but which you get away with.

*Which parts did you do at Birmingham that you were totally wrong for?*

We did an adaptation of *Jekyll and Hyde*, and I played an inspector. I was nineteen, twenty, totally wrong, you know; I was just eligible in age to be a police cadet and there I was playing an inspector on this big case: I wouldn't do that now, but that's what you can do in rep.; you can make glorious errors and get through a performance when you're playing a character part, by putting on a beard with enough hair in it for twenty. You go through all that, playing different parts and messing about with the make-up. You have a glorious time, experimenting, which you probably can't do later. But if the spotlight is on you at an early age, by making a film and being a hit, I think then those days have gone for you; because you're always very self-conscious about being a success. That's what's so marvellous about going into a rep., you can make glorious errors, and not really worry. Not that one ever should, you know; one should do what one wants to do, and that's it, whatever happens, whatever the audience think about it. But in rep. you can really indulge yourself in those young actors' excesses, playing everybody over the age of forty as if they're 300 years old, all that aged acting. Smashing to be able to do that and get away with it. So I think it is quite good to go into rep. for those reasons.

There are actors who probably don't need it. I think I did. I think it is a good thing, but I used to be more definite about it than I am now, because we all need different things and there are different ways of doing it for all of us.

*You were a very good Henry V at Birmingham.*

Not bad for a lad. Yes, it was a very good time for me to play it, but I've never wanted to play it since. That doesn't mean that I felt my performance then was definitive, but I no longer find the role really interesting for myself. I don't know what it is. But at that time I found it very interesting to play. Douggie Seale directed it. And from the time I started to work on it, it just felt good.

*Did you have trouble with the verse?*

I don't think so. What I did then was probably better than what I did later at Stratford. When I was at Stratford I was much more conscious of having to do something with the verse; whereas I didn't break it up in *Henry V*, I didn't try to deliver it naturalistically. But I didn't let it worry me; I think I did it much more simply than I did later.

*At Birmingham, you were also a very young Macbeth. Is this a part you'd like to play again?*

Yes. I mean I was miscast. But they did ask me if I wanted to play it, because I was twenty-one, which was a bit ludicrous. I have a favourite newspaper quote about that, 'Like a juvenile delinquent in a kilt.' But I felt why not, I'm wrong obviously, I'm much too young for it; but at least by playing it now you'll know more what not to do when you do it properly. It's an extraordinary part to play. The feeling of evil in the play is very powerful, and I found it

1957 Henry V, Birmingham Rep.

very exhausting to do, even at twenty-one when I was full of energy. At first I used to take two hours over the make-up, lines, you see, and I used to come out looking twenty-one. But I spent two hours doing it with moustaches and beard and things; because I was thinking, now you're Macbeth, and I created it all to myself in the mirror. By the time I walked on stage I was dead; I'd exhausted myself. Then one matinée I thought, don't spend two hours on it, you're killing yourself making up. Today just go in, throw the make-up on and run on stage and do it. And I did. Somehow, I just felt it was much better for me, doing it that way; because I didn't go on saying 'I am Macbeth,' you know: it felt much freer. From then on I didn't spend two hours doing the make-up. So that was one of the things I learnt, that you can exhaust yourself before you get on the stage, if you get too intense in the dressing-room making up.

Macbeth is something I want to do again. I've got a lot of theories about it too, which I expect will be proved wrong in a few years' time.

*What are they?*

For instance, when Lady Macbeth's talking to Macbeth and saying, 'Tonight when Duncan is asleep' – the actors are usually shouting it across – she's usually saying rather loudly or in a very loud whisper, 'You just go into his room and take the dagger and go in and do it.' I can't believe this. I think it should be on a very high domestic plane. It's a similar situation really to a woman putting on her husband's overcoat in the morning and saying, 'Go in today and ask the boss for a rise, that's all you've got to do, darling.' And he says, 'Well, I dunno if I can really, I don't know, I don't think I can pull it off.' She saying, 'Don't be silly, you just walk in, he likes you.' It's obviously much higher than that, but the woman's got to instil confidence in him. I think she should very quietly build his confidence instead of hurling it at him, which seems to me would frighten him more than ever. The other thing is the black magic, the witches; they're always kind of running round the pot and saying, 'I have newt and toad and frog,' and throwing things into a cauldron; then you think, well that's not going to do anything. Think of the Voodoo Rights. For instance, in Haiti when they're cooking summat and about to stick pins in it, they believe absolutely in what they're doing. If they're cooking up summat in a pot with all kinds of nasty ingredients in it, they don't kind of throw it in and say, 'That'll do the trick'; they're intoning it with a belief. In *Macbeth* I often don't believe what's going on around that pot; it's all crazy, it's just some poison they're making, there's such a sort of pantomime going on. So often the witches look to me like three Ben Gunns emerging from the hills. I mean there are witches in our society, aren't there? Apparently there are people who, on the face of it, live and walk about quite normally, that happen to be witches or happen to practise black arts. I just feel that the evil realities of the play could be done much more truthfully, rather than saying, evil is a bizarre thing and making it obviously theatrical. I think it should be done in a much stiller way, a more insidious way.

*It was in* Macbeth *that Charles Laughton saw you, which led to your next part.*

He came round and said, 'You were bloody awful.' He hated my Macbeth. He talked to me about it rather a lot but he did offer me a small part in his play in London.

*Did you admire Laughton as an actor?*

Yes I did; he was the first kind of legend I actually had contact with professionally, which was very, very exciting. I admired him in his movies; I'd never seen him on the stage. I thought he was terrific in some of his films, there's such a sort of vulnerability in the man, such openness in his portrayal, you know; the professionalism hadn't kind of shattered off the vulnerability of his soul. He was rather a difficult man, but we got on very well when we were in the play in London – and I did admire him. It was extraordinary seeing him work in the theatre because he seemed to be less theatrical than he was in the films, he seemed to make it very tiny. He talked to me an awful lot about acting, and I just liked to listen to him because he was very intelligent about the theatre. He talked a lot about Shakespeare, because he was going to play Lear, and Bottom in *Midsummer Night's Dream* at Stratford the following year, and he wanted me to play Edgar in *Lear*. I didn't really want to go to Stratford, partly because I didn't respond to the parts I was offered, but I went because Charles wanted me to play them; I was flattered that he said come. My work at Stratford was rather bad, and actually the relationship with Charles deteriorated during that time.

One of the things I remember very clearly, he said, when he was talking about insanity, acting madness, and also acting royalty, that if you're playing a madman or a king, you do less – what makes the audience believe you're mad is the reaction of others around you: which is absolutely true. I mean a madman does not go around saying, 'I'm potty, run away from me.' He comes up to you, starts talking to you, and you believe he's sane until you realise that what he's actually saying isn't logical, then you think he's mad and it's you who gets away from him. It's the same when the Queen drives down the Mall, there is nothing she's doing in that open carriage which makes the people wave and say, it's the Queen. It's the spectators' belief that that is the Queen that brings out their reaction. Charles just saying that to a young actor of twenty-two, you just felt, well that saves me ten years. It was a very valuable piece of observation to get from a master.

Stratford 1959. Lysander, *A Midsummer Night's Dream*, with Edward de Souza (Demetrius) and Priscilla Morgan (Hermia); and Edgar, *King Lear*, with Charles Laughton (Lear) and Zoe Caldwell (Cordelia)

But he could be very difficult, too. Charlie felt a bit insecure about working in the theatre again in England, which he'd not done for a long time, apart from a reading of *Don Juan in Hell* which he'd done on a tour with Cedric Hardwicke and Agnes Moorehead. So he was nervous about directing and acting in a play for the first time for twenty-two years. He was rather nervous of playing Lear, and it was something he'd worked on a great deal. But I don't think he'd practised enough to be able to do it the way he wanted to do it. I don't think you can be in the movies and then come back to play Lear; you've got to put a lot of practice in on the boards. You've got to do a lot of theatre work first, because of its physical demands on the actor.

*This is something, of course, which you do yourself; you make a movie and then you go back to the theatre. Is this something you find easy to do?*

When I went to the National two years ago, I hadn't worked in the theatre for a year – since playing Luther in New York. Before that I'd done a film and before that I'd done Luther in London. So in the previous two years before going to the National, I had played one role, I'd done a film, and I'd had a year off doing nothing. Now although the first part I played at the National was a relatively small one, I did feel that my equipment had rusted out. Don Pedro, which I played in *Much Ado*, only has two speeches of more than two lines. But I found that the breathing equipment wasn't functioning properly, I couldn't quite time when to take my breaths any more, which before I could have done easily. It took me about three months of being back in the theatre to feel match-fit again.

If one wants to do serious work in the theatre, and play the great parts, I don't think you can do the pictures and just go back to the theatre for a year, you need more than that. The instrument needs more work than it does in the movies; you've got to be able to share it with people a hundred yards away. You've got to be physically fit to get through two and a half hours. If you play Macbeth you cover an awful distance on stage; you cover miles, going up and down the boulders, on and off for exits, up to your dressing-room at the interval for a smoke and a cup of tea. The fitness needed to play those parts necessitates very special training and it can only be achieved by working in the theatre. No matter how much you play badminton, you've got to play tennis to be a great tennis player. It's the same with acting; if you want to be a great theatre actor and play those great parts in a great way, you've got to practise in the theatre to be able to do it. The instrument has to be as finely tuned as possible and you don't do that by doing movies. You could be a great screen actor. But if you want to be a theatre actor, it's better for your own sake as well as the instrument's sake to treat it more fairly than just popping in to the theatre for a year – which I learnt by going to the National.

*At Stratford you had the dream of every understudy come true. Laurence Olivier injured his leg and you took over the part of Coriolanus.*

Yes, that was smashing. I don't know what was wrong with my work at Stratford. I mean it was more wrong then than it's ever been before or since, and I was aware of it being wrong. It was one of those times when you feel that everything you do – you know that kind of tunnel – and there's nothing you can do to get out of it. The more you try to get out of it, the more you're in it. My work was awful, just vile. Every time I went on the stage I felt, get off, get off, what are you doing? But when I went on for Sir Laurence in *Coriolanus*, all the difficulties I seemed to be going through left me. Because, first of all, the audience kind of expect you to come on in flannels with a book. Sir Laurence isn't playing – big groan. His part will be played by Al – Albert Finney. And then I came on, and I had the costume on, and so they immediately think I'm talented because I've actually got into the clothes. I've put the body make-up on and then I start and they can't see the book. And I actually got through it without drying, so they think I'm very good. If you're an understudy and you go on, the card you've actually got in your hand is that they think you might not be able to get through at all, and if you can get through with any degree of professionalism, they think you're very good. And I kind of felt, get in there. But it's terrible to hear that announcement – you know, you're in your dressing-room putting on the make-up – Sir Laurence won't be playing tonight; terrible groan throughout the auditorium. That's nice.

But I felt a kind of freedom doing *Coriolanus* because I had no responsibility; I was his understudy, it didn't matter what happened. It didn't matter if I dried; they'd expect it. If I fainted, well it's a lot of pressure on the lad, you know. So I didn't worry. All the clouds which were around the rest of my performances, all the rubbish, the tunnel I felt in with my work, all the difficulties blew out of the window. I just went on and did it. I felt very free. I don't think it was a good Coriolanus. When you hear Sir Laurence's tones ringing in your ears for the number of times he'd done the performances, it's very difficult for you not to be similar, because you're working on his blueprint. What is interesting, I learnt from that, is how a great actor can take the peaks and the valleys of a performance, the ups and downs of a character as written, and push them even further apart. You know what I mean? He makes the climaxes higher and the depths of it lower than you feel is possible in the text. It was marvellous to go through it during a performance, kind of putting on his clothes and feeling well they don't touch me here at all, you know. Just feel your own way – how big you are on the graph, as it were. Then you see he went right up there. I don't just mean vocally, but emotionally and everything, and he went right down there. That was a very interesting realisa-

1959 First Citizen, *Coriolanus*, Stratford, with Roy Dotrice, Julian Glover and Laurence Olivier (Coriolanus)

tion. But I was glad when he was back actually. The theatre management gave me a steak between the matinée and evening show; I did it six times and it was always with a matinée and an evening show. So I quite enjoyed it.

*You were ill yourself just about this time and so you missed a very good part in a play,* The Long, the Short and the Tall *by Willis Hall, which Peter O'Toole played. I think it was through missing this part that you actually said to Willis Hall, 'Why don't you write a play for me?' Is this true?*

Yes, sort of, it came out like that. Willis was about to work on *Billy Liar* with Keith Waterhouse who wrote the novel. I felt it was only fair, partly because I knew Willis from when I was at Birmingham. He'd written plays for the BBC in Birmingham, and I'd done one or two of them on the radio when I was at the Rep. I'd also done a television play of his from Birmingham. So I felt that our effort should be joint, that we should achieve recognition together. I felt it unfair that his first play to be done at the Royal Court was a great success and, because of my illness, had been done without me. So I thought it was only right that he should give me another one.

*He wrote the play with you in mind, and you did it and it was a great success.*

It was, yes.

Billy Liar *wasn't only a great success; it was also a very long run, which is something you don't usually like to do.*

Actually the producer, Oscar Lowenstein, was very kind and let me go after nine months, which he needn't have done, although he did know that that was what I wanted to do.

*Did you find the long run difficult?*

Yes, very difficult. It was different with *Luther* which I did for nine months, but not in one theatre. We did it for, I think, six months when we played it in England, then we did it on the Continent. The two plays demanded different things. I found the demands of *Billy Liar* more difficult to sustain. With *Billy Liar* it was more a lack of demands. But I did *Luther* altogether an awful lot. We did it for four months in America as well. It was such a demanding part to play that you could never not do it. I only remember – and I'm not saying there were only five performances where I wasn't too good or was off form – but I only remember five performances which I did not feel like doing. Even on the days when I went in and didn't feel right for it, I had to get up into that pulpit somehow, it made you do it. Whereas *Billy Liar* was easier to do and therefore the part demanded less attention, less concentration, and less effort; so, after a while I felt very frustrated by it. It was also the character, Billy was a weak character, and so I tried to make myself physically a

1960 Billy, *Billy Liar*, Cambridge Theatre

little smaller, physically a bit more vulnerable than I actually feel myself. But before long I wanted to satisfy other sides of my nature, I wanted to come on to the stage feeling strong. I wanted to act out other things, that is why I do like working in a repertoire. One night you may be playing Billy Liar and the next evening you might be playing Luther; then you're satisfying different sides of your talent. But when playing one character for a long time, one isn't, and I do find this very frustrating: I don't enjoy it. I also think it's bad for actors; it is for me.

With *Billy Liar*, after a while, I didn't believe in the play a great deal. I thought the play was very funny, but I think it could have been more beautiful. The novel had explored adolescent fantasising in a much more engaging way. It not only made you laugh but it also made you feel. The novel was written in the first person, so it

Billy, *Billy Liar*, with Trevor Bannister (Arthur Crabtree)

77

was very easy to enter into the private world of Billy. But in the theatre most of the fantasies had to be discussed by the other characters. There were other elements in the book which I thought were not really developed in the stage piece, and I lost faith in it a bit. It was like being in a colander full of lettuce and after a while you get through all the lettuce and you see holes in it. That's what I felt – and the long run became harder to do. Because I had not only to act the part but I had to act a belief in it once I'd stopped believing in its quality.

*In the film of* Tom Jones, *you had a very good scene with Joyce Redman where you ate a delicious meal together; there was no dialogue in that scene. In* Billy Liar *there was also a very famous scene in which you mimed the playing of the Last Post. Mime does seem to be an important part of your work. Is this something you consciously aim for?*

I don't think consciously. I remember that scene in *Billy Liar* being written into the original script, but it was not quite as long as it turned out to be; Lindsay Anderson, who directed the play, and I did extend it a little more. I felt that the qualities that that scene showed were probably, as I was saying before, more closely associated with the style of the novel than the play, and I thought it would be nice to extend it. I remember one day at home just improvising for hours, playing with a piece of wood which I used, a kind of garden cane; then finally working out a sort of line on the scene, as to how I could use the stick. So obviously I did respond to that; but it's not something I look for. I don't say, 'I'll put in a bit of mime here.'

That scene you mentioned in *Tom Jones* was silent because there were so many other times when I had to be seduced by ladies, that John Osborne couldn't face the thought of writing yet more dialogue where I was chatted up by another lady. We were having a meeting about it when we were working on the script, and we thought, well let's do one without words, let's get the idea of seduction over by the way the food is eaten: that's how that scene evolved.

*Did you work very closely with John Osborne and Tony Richardson, who wrote the film script and directed* Tom Jones?

Well, we did *Luther* the year before, and while I was in the run of the play we used to have meetings to discuss the film, to talk about the style of the film.

*The particular style of* Tom Jones, *the style of free-wheeling comic post-card vulgarity, was that something which was decided before or during the shooting?*

No, it was decided before; we decided to make a film in which we'd try to break apparent cinematic rules, which other people break; that's not new in itself. In the novel the author often refers directly to the reader, directly to his audience. You're in the middle of a chapter and Fielding will suddenly break the belief if you like, the reality of the situation that you're following, and speak to you and say, 'I like this sort of thing,' or 'I don't like this sort of thing.' There's one particular case which comes at the beginning of a chapter. You're following the narrative and then suddenly the heading of the chapter reads, 'In which we will discuss the behaviour of and the talents or the merits of literary critics of our time.' And he starts his chapter by saying, 'This is nothing to do with the history of Tom Jones and it might be rather boring to a lot of people because it's going to be about the critics of today. So if you're not interested in that, skip this chapter, go to the next one and carry on reading the story.' Now we felt that that spirit was very important to put into the movie. In other words, that we could break at any given time the convention, if you like, of the reality of what was going on on the screen, and just refer directly to the audience. It was decided that this should be done in such a way that it would be part of the whole, part of the style, and wouldn't be something that's tacked on for effect. I remember this as being an important issue when we were discussing the script.

1962 Tom in *Tom Jones*, with Susannah York (Sophia)

79

Tom Jones

*Now just before* Tom Jones *you played what is probably the most difficult part in your career so far – the part of Luther. Again it was directed by Tony Richardson and written by John Osborne. Was this something which you had many consultations about before you actually went into rehearsal?*

Quite a few, but of course John Osborne is much more closely involved with his own play of *Luther* than a film script of *Tom Jones*, and obviously much more vulnerable about it; he doesn't like to discuss it very much: he's sort of shy about it. I don't think John likes being at rehearsals of his own plays very much because of his vulnerability. He does put a lot of his own flesh and blood into them and he does often lay himself rather bare through his writing; therefore discussions with John were not predominant. We discussed it quite a lot with Tony but that was about the kind of style in which we would do it. The play is very simple in terms of its staging because there are relatively few characters who talk to each other at any given time. There are a lot of solo scenes, the sermons, for instance, and most of the other scenes are between two people. The way I wanted to work on it was to read it a lot with the other actors, so that by the time we got up to plot the movements, which didn't seem to be a complicated job, we knew what we were after.

*Did you do much research of your own into Luther the man?*

Yes I did; but I do believe in doing the character as he's written in the play; it's fatal to come with a theory about Luther from doing research. But I did read a marvellous book about him by a man called Erik Erikson, which is a psychiatric study of his relationship with his father and his mother; the power of his father's image on Luther was extraordinary, the complex fears of letting his father down. That book gave me remarkable insight into the kind of knowledge which I didn't have before. So I did do quite a lot of research in that way.

*In the play you have three sermons to give. How did you avoid the possible monotony of this kind of device?*

Well, accepting the fact that I did avoid possible monotony, I didn't see it in that way. I didn't ever say, 'Well I've got three sermons, therefore I've got to make them different.' I felt that each time he gets up, the circumstances are very different, and therefore the audience would accept it. They were dramatically very well spaced in the play; there's one at the beginning of the second act, one right at the end of the second act, and one in the middle of the third act. Actually it is a marvellous situation, that's what I think is terrific about the play, about the writing of the play. But I always used to grumble because the third act was terrible to act. I felt that John had emotionally got it out of himself by the third act and found it very difficult to finish the play. He is an extremely emotional writer, and when it's out of him, when he's exorcised it, he finds it very difficult to go back, to fiddle or retouch. But the actual way in which he used the theatre was interesting. I mean, all right, there's a character who's got to go up into a pulpit and deliver a sermon; but it's marvellous to use the audience as a congregation. Some dramatists would have put a few benches on the stage and had a few medieval extras shuffling on, and Luther talking to them. But actually using the theatre audience as a congregation is a marvellously powerful situation for the actor, it was smashing to act. I loved getting up into that pulpit, three times wasn't enough. One suddenly thought the auditorium was the focus of what I was saying, legitimately I was speaking directly to the audience. Not only was it giving them a different angle on the subject; but suddenly from being at a play, they're in an assembly of people. The power of the writing was such that I hope in one of the sermons I induced a certain self-consciousness in some members of the audience,

1961 Martin Luther, *Luther*, Royal Court

F

81

Luther

because one was talking to them about things which in many respects still apply today. It wasn't about realism or the indulgences of the Catholic Church, but lack of faith, and not just in a religious sense. To use the audience in that way is a very bold, theatrical stroke, and one that my instinct reacted to.

*You mean it was something more than just acting; you were also telling the audience the truth about themselves, which is something the actor doesn't often get a chance to do.*

Yes. Not only the truth about themselves; but one felt the response to it was not a removed piece of dramaturgy, but something as direct as it was in Luther's day. The audience pay their money, they come in by car, tube or whatever, they're in the theatre, and suddenly they're being delivered a sermon. I think that's a marvellous thing for an actor to have a chance to do. It's very important – the audience feel that they're buying that ticket; and they're getting something from that evening they couldn't get from seeing the film or a television play; it has meant something more to them than just learning the facts of that story; and the assembly of people has meant something also, their presence is just as important as the actor's: in other words, it's full value. Yes, I think John used the audience very well.

*You said in an interview, about the time you were making* Tom Jones, *'I want to surprise people, surprise myself, I want to get away from taking myself – acting I mean – too seriously.' Did you take acting too seriously?*

I do feel sometimes that I get a bit pompous about it, a bit earnest; I can't help it, I suppose. I do take myself too seriously – and it was good to do *Tom Jones* where I had to perform straightaway before walking around the pool and considering what I was going to do. I just said, I'm gonna dive in here, now. I tried to do things much more –

*Spontaneously.*

That's right – and not mind that the public would see a spontaneous reaction rather than a created, artistically achieved reaction. I like to feel that they're seeing my work; I like to feel that they're seeing something I have worked at, that I've considered other possibilities but this is what I think they should see. One of the reasons why we all wanted to do *Tom Jones* in a free sort of way was because we were all associated, John Osborne, Tony Richardson and I, with different kinds of work, pieces that provoked other responses in people than just pure pleasure and laughter. So for all of us, more for them than for me, it was important to do something in which one felt freer. But I wanted to feel that I didn't mind the audience just seeing me messing about, rather than performing in a very carefully controlled messing about way, because that is the kind of acting I normally do. After shooting *Tom Jones* for about eight weeks I got very bored; it went on for sixteen altogether. I felt I was slightly cheating; it was just using one's personality rather than creating character. When I saw the film afterwards I didn't think that I'd achieved anything in terms of characterisation; I just saw me in certain situations, I either smile or I don't, or walk fast or slow; I couldn't see the character's development. Of course that's specifically Tom; I mean that's the kind of story it is. He's a creature that things happen to, and so it's only interesting to see his reaction to the things that have happened to him. The character doesn't really develop from beginning to end; you can't follow a development of him, and at the end of the story you don't feel that he's now equipped to do this or that. As opposed to Arthur Seaton in *Saturday Night* where there's a definite development in the story; and therefore for an actor it's a much more interesting part to do, because you're aware of what you want to bring out at any specific moment. Well, that didn't apply to *Tom*, but it was very good for me to do it. But the reason why I'm not really happy doing that particular kind of acting is because I think I have a facility for acting. My danger is that sometimes I do it too easily.

I was very lazy as an adolescent, I spent as much time in bed as I should have done for the rest of my life. I could have hibernated from the age of eleven to the age of seventeen. I think that basically I would like a lazy life, you know, to sort of doze a lot, be in the sun and drink wine. During the last four years I have made myself work more and work longer hours, and I enjoy that too; but it was an effort at first because basically my tempo is much slower. I think that I need the neurosis of making my work more complicated and more difficult than it need be sometimes in order to avoid this facility, and to escape the feeling that I'm just getting away with it.

*Could this have been part of your motivation for completely turning your back on glamour, success, money, and going back into the provinces into rep., to the Glasgow Citizens Theatre to direct three plays there?*

I wanted to see what directing was like. I wrote to four theatres, two didn't reply. I went to Glasgow partly because they'd have me. I played a part there, Pirandello's *Henry IV*, and then I directed *The Birthday Party* by Harold Pinter. And as the next play wasn't chosen the company manager and I decided to do *School for Scandal*; I wanted to do that because it was very different from *The Birthday Party*. The main reason for going to a fortnightly rep. was not that I wanted to see if I could get the truth of *The Birthday Party* or the truth of *School for Scandal* on stage, or give the definitive production. I just wanted to see if I could stage something, and also to see that the actors weren't too offended by me being on the other side of the footlights.

*And what did you find out?*

One or two of them weren't too offended by it. I liked the experience tremendously. I felt that I was good for the actors. I mean good in the sense that they responded to me being out there. I think that they worked very well for me; it's always a good sign if somebody works well. It made me feel that I should do more of it. I don't think I illuminated much for any of the actors or changed any of them; but I felt that I did have their confidence; the experience was terrific for me. I mean with *School for Scandal* I overdid it a bit, you know; I made it a bit too jokey actually; I didn't work badly. I think the actors enjoyed doing it. I know one or two of them definitely did.

*This is something you'd always wanted to do.*

Yes. It had become a more conscious inclination. Because one does have thoughts about one day wanting a company, directing, and making directorial decisions about the kind of theatre one wants to work in, and not being content just to be an actor. I think that's the

1963 The King, Pirandello's *Henry IV*, Glasgow Citizens Theatre

thing that led me to direct there. From that I realised that I wanted to do more of it, spend more time on production: two weeks is pretty rough.

*How did you work? Did you improvise or did you work on the play a good deal beforehand?*

Because of the pressure of two weeks there isn't a great deal you can do, you know, the cast are all doing another play at night. You can only work them for so long per day; some days if everybody had had it by three o'clock I used to stop. I don't think there's any point in going on with a rehearsal if everybody's going to end up on the floor; nothing's gained and you just get bluer and gloomier about the piece. I think Pinter puts in the script his own punctuation, the dots or asterisks after a speech almost denote the number of seconds the pause should be; as well as writing the text Harold writes the orchestration; I tried to be as faithful as I could to what I thought this orchestration was. I hadn't seen the original which Harold himself had been in on, but I tried to give it the measure, or the tempo, which I felt it should have. So we didn't improvise a great deal on that.

On *School for Scandal* I worked very differently. I think that how you work on something is always affected by what that something is; every subject demands a different way of working on it. Those two plays are very different examples of theatre, and the audience's reaction to the plays is therefore very different, although the seats they're sitting in are always the same distance from the stage. *The Birthday Party* is a very concentrated situation and you have to take the audience to the stage. They're watching something that unfolds before them, they're asked to have faith in it, they're asked what they think it means, or what they think it's about. It goes on before you as if a wall has been taken out of somewhere and you're seeing a section of life inside a room. This is what happened on this day; these people came to this house and as a result of that, this occurred. It happened like this. What do you think about it?

*School for Scandal* is entirely different. It's a piece that is meant to be put up on a platform in public, it makes no apology for being theatrical, or not pretending to be real life. Not that you make the characters totally unbelievable or crazy; of course they must be in some way associated with humanity. But it's a different convention. At the time it was written, the theatre was different from what it is today; it hadn't gone through that naturalistic alley. I tried to rehearse it in a way that I felt belonged to the spirit of the play. During rehearsals I behaved as a director much more outrageously. I tried to joke, I was running about and jumping up on the stage to keep the atmosphere that I thought would evoke the right mood, the right feeling for that play. Whereas on *The Birthday Party* I rehearsed it in a slightly more intense way because I felt that that way of working on the play belonged to it.

*Do you feel this as an actor too, that every part requires a completely different approach, a different way of working?*

For me, the way of working on a play or a part always springs from my initial reaction to it. I don't have any sort of process of acting at all. Maybe I should have, but it depends on what I think it demands. The biggest aid one can have in a performance, or in doing a production, is achieving the right way of working on that particular subject or that particular character. Once you've got the correct attitude to what you're doing, you're a long way there. If you are able to enter into the correct spirit of that particular job, which is always different from the last one, or from any others you have done, you've got a good chance. It always is different for me, always.

I can't describe it, because different things happen. Why did one respond to Luther when one did, why did one want to do that part, and why didn't one do something else which was offered – one doesn't know. There's another interesting thing, concerning how I initially respond to a play. It can be a scene, one scene, that starts me off: it's just a question of response. I can read a splendid script and not respond, not want to do it although I know it's splendid. I know the writer's marvellous, I know it's going to be a terrific project, but it's just not made me want to be there, want to be in it. It has nothing to do with its quality; it has to do with how I am at the time that script comes through the letterbox and into my hands.

*Having successfully directed a short season in provincial rep. you turned your back on film offers and went to the National Theatre and did a full season there, playing in six plays. Did you enjoy your time there? You certainly turned in six remarkable performances in six very varied plays.*

Doing that amount of work and that variety of work is something I've always been keen on. Actors can explore themselves at the National or the Aldwych quicker than by just performing in the commercial theatre, where you probably do ten plays in ten years, if you're lucky. But in the repertory theatre to play six parts in just over a year was marvellous. The experience of being at the National, once I'd settled down again to the theatre and got my stage legs back, was an environment that one could explore. It was not only the plays, but different directors with such varied styles and different ways of working that was so enormously valuable to any actor, whatever stage he happened to be at.

*We can't talk about all six directors, let's just talk about one, Jacques Charron, who came from the Comédie Française, the Feydeau director. Now you played in* A Flea in her Ear, *which is a double role and also French farce. This must put enormous demands on an actor. Did you cope with it easily?*

None of us in the cast had ever played a French farce before, but from the moment Charron came to the first rehearsal, he was such a sympathetic man, such a nice man, one immediately felt his knowledge of that style of play; you felt he knew what he wanted and how the play should be staged. The spirit with which he did the production was so engaging and so correct for the play, that after three days' rehearsal you just walked into the rehearsal room and everybody immediately started behaving like they did in the play; there was such an atmosphere created within the rehearsal room, it was terrific. There are times in the theatre when you learn something about yourself as an actor or about the theatre as a profession in retrospect, but occasionally you come in contact with a director or a play that makes you realise you're learning at the moment. I felt that very strongly with Charron, because the style in which he wanted the play to be done was absolutely right, but I'd no idea how it worked. I'd never even played English farce, let alone French.

He was extraordinary to work with because he could hardly speak English – sometimes he would get up to demonstrate, not to say do it like this, but to give you the pitch. He did say, and he was absolutely right, that the play should be played at a certain pitch vocally; it couldn't ever be pulled down because then it would mean something else: he wanted it on a certain level all the time. Sometimes if you lost the pitch or you wandered at rehearsals up another avenue, he'd get up and say, no it should be like – and he talked gibberish you see, because he couldn't speak the English text, and he'd sit down. Then you'd get up and you'd do it in English. You think, well, how does anybody know what to do? But he made it so clear by his indicating the tempo he wanted it to be done in. It was marvellous to have a director doing that play who you knew could do it better than any of the cast. He knew how to do the footwork, because a lot of the footwork is terribly important. It's like choreography; in order to be at the right place when you had an aside, you had a movement across stage and then you had to stop; then the next second say something to the audience. Which foot you arrived on was terribly important, so that you could do the next step to the audience and things like that. That's smashing, to work like that.

An actor's instinct on playing a double role, you know, is to show how clever he is. He says, 'I'll make them as different as possible, so that one's A and one's Z will show what versatility you've got.' Then Charron said, 'Don't do it.' He said, 'What's interesting is to make them as close, because they are different. . .' Which is a sort of theoretical idea which nobody seeing the play would actually read into it; but he was absolutely right. One of the characters was a bourgeois, middle-class head of an insurance business, and the other was an idiotic boozy porter at a hotel. Immediately you think, well, they're as different as chalk from cheese, lovely, I can have a ball doing the two, the only resemblance is that it's the same actor playing the two parts. But that's not the play. Of course they're different. They must be different. But the play really is the similarity between them, because you have to make the audience believe that the one character in the play can be mistaken for the other. That's the point.

The acting also had to be very precise; again it isn't the kind of acting I'm too familiar with, because today we are bound up a lot in a naturalistic idiom. When we opened at the Vic, we played it for five performances and then the following week we played it on the Tuesday. After that another play was played on the Wednesday and I think we played it again on the Thursday. And that was the first time we'd really been away from it, or played something else since we started performing it. One just felt that the timing had gone a little. The amount of practice needed to do it as well as we'd done it when we'd been rehearsing and performing it constantly meant that we really had to be on the ball the moment we went on to the stage. Once it was in the repertoire one was only playing it twice or sometimes three times a week. Now it often happens, even with emotional plays, that the matinée serves – I don't mean that you deliberately cheat the matinée public – but it serves as a loosener up, this is inevitable. But with the farce, one always felt that the evening performance was like a diamond compared with the matinée, because one had got back on the ball, the precision was really sharp. To work on something like that for me was smashing.

*Out of the other five parts that you played, is there one that you'll remember particularly?*

I remember them all for very different reasons. I remember *Armstrong's Last Goodnight* because of its complexity. I mean the language that John Arden part invented and part took from medieval writings, the Scottish idiom, was so difficult to speak. Not only was I speaking a Scottish medieval dialect, but the character also had a speech impediment. At first people didn't realise it was an impediment because of the dialect and vice versa. And that was always a tremendous problem. Basically the character was a rather primitive, noble creature, a man of instinct, a rather wild man. But the mental effort of trying to make the audience follow the complexity of the language required a sort of – animal acting on one side with a mental clarity on the other, which was very complicated. So I'll remember that for its difficulties. I'll remember Harold Gorringe, in Peter Shaffer's *Black Comedy*, because I thought I went too far: a rather camp antique collector. And *Miss Julie* I remember because I found that a very strange piece to do. As the dawn of naturalism it's terrific. But I don't think it quite works now because we've explored naturalism in much more rewarding ways. If you're going to do the play today, I think you've not got to be too scared

1966 Poche and Chandebise, *A Flea in her Ear*, Natio Theatre, with Geraldine McEwan (Raymonde) a John Stride (Tournel)

of treating Strindberg too sacredly; we should have changed it a
bit more, somehow. That's partly my fault; I never quite felt the
reality of the situation. When Strindberg wrote the play in 1888,
he wrote a foreword in which he said, 'I don't want painted pots
and pans on a painted backcloth. I want real shelves and real pots
and pans.' Which shows the kind of theatre he was trying to break
down. Well, we've gone through that phase now, but one cannot
just perform it as it is because the social order has also changed;
there isn't such a stigma attached to the rough trade valet sleeping
with the lord's daughter as there used to be. And so the dilemma
on which the play hinges no longer has the same power.

*What can be done about that, do you think?*

I don't know. I think one should experiment if one wants to do the
play, experiment to make the situation more alive for the audience.

Don Pedro in *Much Ado* I also enjoyed doing, because of Zeffirelli. A lot of people said, 'Oh the verse went for a burton, you
know, doing it like one of those Sicilian films; Shakespeare wasn't
round about Sicily.' But I disagree. I felt Zeffirelli did something
absolutely fascinating with the play. All right, Sir John and Dame
Peggy did a beautiful production, when they did it a few years ago,
a beautiful production and it had tremendous values in it. But to do
it with Zeffirelli and to try and do it the same way is pointless. What

1965 Armstrong, *Armstrong's Last Goodnight*, Natio
Theatre, with Caroline John and Graham Crowd

Zeffirelli could give it was a tremendous Italian flavour, and that's something one could never do with anybody else. What was interesting was to go the way he wanted to go; to work with him was marvellous. Because I feel that the emotions in Shakespeare are often very Latin when you translate them into modern English terms. I thought that certain things in Zeffirelli's production were more Shakespearean than they are in a more conventional kind of production of the play, because emotionally he tried to make us much more open. All that jealousy and the church scene where the wedding's called off and the girl faints; all that kind of violence and emotion in public; it's not a thing you sort of advertise. It does happen here, but it's hushed up, that tends to happen a bit. 'Now behave, Jack, don't let anybody see you're upset.' You know, keep quiet, say nothing to nobody. But many things he did in the play were very, very true to the situation, and very Elizabethan, the first Elizabethan age.

*How did you come to join the National Theatre? Did you know which parts you were going to play before you went?*

No. After I had played Luther in America I took a year off. I travelled and didn't work, because I hadn't really stopped for a long time, and I wanted to analyse and to think. That was terrific; it was marvellous to do that. Then I came back to England and I still didn't know what I wanted to do. There were one or two things floating about but I thought the best thing to do would be to join one of the companies, you know, and just play a few parts. I phoned Sir Laurence, or I may have written to him. And I said, 'Can I have a job?' And he said, 'Come and see me'. When I went he said, 'There's nothing really till Chichester unless you would like to play Don Pedro in *Much Ado*.' This was early December of 1964, and Chichester wasn't going to start rehearsing till April. I said, 'That's not very big, you know, there are not many lines.' But I wanted to work so I said, 'Smashing.' And I went to the National and did it. The reason I went there was because I wanted to have a chance to do a few plays in a relatively short period of time.

*What did you actually do during your year off? What kind of analysis, what kind of thought?*

I just travelled. I went round the world by myself. Did nothing. Just looked and sat. It's very dangerous after a while; I mean – when I was in New York on the stage doing Luther I'd be in the middle of a speech, you see, and I'd hear a jet plane go and I'd think, Where are you going? Wait for me. Oh I wish I was – oh sorry. And then I'd go back again into the part but I kind of wanted to get away. Then the play finished and I went to Mexico. I had to see Mexico in three weeks, then I went up the West Coast and I sailed from San Francisco to Hawaii; I was in Hawaii six weeks. I flew to

John Armstrong

National Theatre. 1965 Don Pedro, *Much Ado About Nothing*, with Maggie Smith (Beatrice)

1965 Ben, *Love for Love*, with Joyce Redm (Mrs Frail)

1966 Harold, *Black Comedy*, with Derek Jacobi (Brin) and Maggie Smith (Clea)

Tahiti; I was there six weeks. I was on Tahiti a week and then I went to another island in French Polynesia called Riatea, where there's nothing, nothing; and I lived for three weeks there. I'd been travelling by that time quite a bit and I was in a very relaxed state. I used to get up every morning and just look at the reef. That's all I did. I used to get up, and look at the reef and then I'd have breakfast, and look at the reef, I'd have a swim and then look at the reef, have lunch, look at the reef. It was beautiful. But it's very dangerous because you get into a kind of permanent semi-somnambulant state, you see; and you're aware of nothing because there is no debating going on. Of course I was the only person at the hotel. It was a kind of quiet spot; and you just sat looking out to sea. There was no conversation and I wasn't even reading; by this time I was so wound down I hadn't the energy to read. All you're aware of is your thoughts. And as that is the only thing you're really doing, thinking, any thought which you think is important sort of goes across your mind in neon lights; and you start to think you're a great philosopher. You understand, you sit there looking at the reef and thinking; and you start to feel that you understand mankind very, very deeply. But it's dangerous and I felt that if I'd stayed there any longer I would have just rotted in that deck-chair and never moved except for a bloody mary or a coconut. I went back to Tahiti just for two nights, intending to go back to Riatea and get back into the deck-chair. Then I heard a jet go off and I thought, wait for me. I wanted to get away now, after winding down, so I started to come back to civilisation and wind up again. I need my neurosis, you know, I need to be sick, after winding down and feeling absolutely relaxed, because I know that's not for me. I can fantasise about being a beachcomber but I couldn't be one for too long. It's a lovely fantasy to have, to live there, build a house out of straw and help to people the island; but I couldn't really do it.

*Now that you've taken a year off, done almost nothing for a year, do you think that's now right out of your system or is it a temptation that you feel all the time?*

I like to keep the future sort of unpredictable. But I feel there's a pattern of intense work followed by a stop rather than continual breaks. I'm going to have a short break now because I've just finished doing a film, but I'll be back on it, doing the editing and all that, within minutes. After leaving the National, I was there for fifteen months, I left on a Friday and on the Monday I was starting to shoot a film in France; when I'd finished that I came back here to start doing my own film. I like to work at that tempo. I think that the pattern might well be years of intense work, five, six or seven years, and then stop for a spell, because it's good to do that. It was terrific just to do nothing, for long enough to have had it.

1966 Jean, *Miss Julie*, with Maggie Smith (Miss Julie)

*You mean to get really insufferably bored by it?*

Really, really bored by doing nothing. That's very good to do that.

*You've just played the leading part in a film,* Charlie Bubbles, *from a script by Shelagh Delaney, which you directed yourself. This was your first film as a director.*

It wasn't that I'd been looking for a subject or anything to direct. When I first read the screenplay, it was really an outline, a document of about sixty pages. I responded very much to the character and situation; I felt I wanted to act it. But I also felt very strongly about the way the film should be treated and I thought it would be wrong for me to hire a director to direct it in the way I felt the actors should be directed; that seemed to me rather illegal. So I thought, well why not do both, if you feel so strongly about the way it should be directed. In order to get the money, act; and so I did both. Which has been interesting. I mean it is hard, especially for the first time, to do both. The directing side of it I absolutely adored – an extra-ordinary experience. But what my performance is like I've no idea, no idea. I hope that because of my feelings about the subject, and because of my knowledge of the subject, through having worked on the script for eighteen months and then shot it for three and a half, that the characterisation has things built into it because of that knowledge.

*How did you handle the technical problem of directing a film and playing the leading part?*

Well, I had an acting stand-in. In a very complex dialogue scene, an interior, I would do it first with the actors, with nobody else about, just the acting stand-in watching. I'd do it with them and sort of discuss it, and then when I thought we'd achieved something, the acting stand-in who had been watching would come in. He'd not do what I did, he'd try to reproduce my timing and my movements, but he'd do it as if he was playing the part.

*It sounds as if it's a very personal film, which is rare for films made in this country.*

Well, I hope it is. There's all kinds of things in it which people will say, 'Ah you see, that's him, that's his story, that's the kind of thing that will happen to him.' There are some things in it which could have happened to me, really; some things which have happened to me, really. But I hope that it's personal, not that that means it's –

*Autobiographical?*

Autobiographical – but just that it's something that I wanted to make a film about; and I hope I've done it in a kind of personal way. You see, I like going to the cinema, and I do like personal films very much.

*The experience of both acting in a film and directing one is again not very common. Is it something which you'd ever do again?*

Well, acting and directing a film I'd say no, now. Take for instance Chaplin's early films, when he was playing Charlie the Tramp; Chaplin had nothing to do in order to establish the character he was playing, because the character was famous. It was Charlie the Tramp in that situation. So that his preoccupation was not developing the character; he was developing the story line and the comic invention which was brilliant. But the kind of film, the kind of character development that should be in Charlie Bubbles is much more intense, it needs much more awareness of the actor with his director, what path they're on and what line of thought they want the audience to follow. Now I think that makes it very difficult to act and direct. At the moment, having literally just finished shooting and not having started to edit, I feel that I'll never do it again. I would like to direct another film and not act in it, because directing and acting are two attitudes, outside it and inside it. The director's attitude of having to see it all, be objective about it so that he can channel it and choose and photograph it from the right place; and the actor's attitude being in and apparently unaware that there's a camera about.

*Did you think about style at all when you made the film? I mean what directors have influenced you? Is it a very English film do you think?*

I don't – actually when you say English film, I'm rather worried. It might be.

*I hope it is.*

I have obviously been influenced; one's favourite film directors are a few people, they're not just one. But there's nobody I think I've modelled myself on. What I've tried to do is to be as simple as possible, as direct as possible. In other words, show the people in the film, show their faces and let the audience read the characters: it's fairly straightforward. I don't think there's anything adventurous or unusual as regards what the camera's doing; it's not moving around or anything contemporary like that. Because I did want to concentrate very much on reading what's going on, and staging it very simply.

*You did just say that you would direct other films. Did you find the experience of directing a very rewarding one, more rewarding, more satisfying than acting?*

Well if it's not it's pretty close. What's marvellous about it is its total involvement. The last two weeks of shooting a film is extraordinary. Although it wasn't particularly long, it was only twelve weeks, you've just got to grit your teeth and get through it, you know; you can see the finishing post but you can't believe you're

ever going to get there. Something you've lived with and thought about for so long, then comes the actual relief of finishing, which is what I'm feeling at the moment; it's marvellous. It's like floating in hot goat's milk. I don't know what that's like, actually, but it always sounds as if it should be nice: that feeling is very good.

*Albert, you're one of our finest young stage actors, you're an international movie star and now you've directed your first feature film. Now you could do almost anything, I suppose. Do you know what you are going to do?*

No. I've no immediate plans for the future because I want to see what the experience of doing this film means to me, and I'm too close to that as yet to analyse it. Some time in the future I still have a feeling and a desire, in part of my mind, to have a theatre, to have a group or an ensemble, or be part of one.

1967 Charlie, *Charlie Bubbles*, with Colin Blakely

*They're all very different things.*

Yes. I mean be part of one in an involved way, in a way that just doesn't mean one's a member of the company, but has a concern and an interest in the kind of things that are done and how they are done. If I want to do that I'll obviously have to spend time in the theatre, not just a year but some years. The great classic parts like Macbeth or Lear; I still have a hankering to do all those. But as I said that'll need practice. As a stage actor, if I want to do those things, I think that the prime will be between thirty-eight and forty-eight, those ten years. In order to fulfil those parts, if I want to do them, I've got to be in good nick theatrically by then.

But I wouldn't say that's what I'm going to do because I also have fantasies, like learning the guitar in Madrid, and retiring, you see; then when I'm forty, of giving recitals on the guitar at the Albert Hall. I like to feel that if one did want to change one's whole way of life, one could do it. Sometimes I think it might be awful to feel that I've got to be an actor all my life. Might be marvellous to be able to do something else. You know, suddenly at the age of fifty to emerge as a chess player or something. Of course I'd always want to be good at what I did, or feel that I'd be good at it. But there's no sort of line on the future that I can see clearly, and actually I don't want to. As I've talked about the theatre and those parts that I'd like to play, it makes it seem that that's probably what I'll do, and part of me hopes to do that. But I wouldn't be at all surprised if I never did, you know, because I don't know what I'm going to do; and I kind of want to protect that.

*That's the way you want to keep it?*

Mm.

# John Neville

J OHN NEVILLE's greatest asset and handicap as an actor has been his face. It is almost too theatrically handsome: a blond, high-cheek-boned, Scandinavian mask, proud, sensitive, yet strong enough to carry expression to the topmost gallery. It is the face of a romantic hero, a stage prince – and for a long time it let him play nothing else.

From the moment he arrived at the London Old Vic in 1953 as Valentine in *Two Gentlemen of Verona*, he was type-cast as the golden Shakespearean juvenile: Fortinbras in *Hamlet*, Ferdinand in *The Tempest*, Orlando, Troilus to Rosemary Harris's Cressida. No one knew that, at the Bristol Old Vic, his great successes had been in character parts: Charles Surface in *The School for Scandal*, the Duke in *Measure for Measure*, Gregers Werle in Ibsen's *Wild Duck*. He became the Old Vic's matinée idol. Schoolgirls screamed at his Hotspur, for his Chorus in *Henry V*, trying to shout down the rival *claque* for Richard Burton as the King. Their alternating Othello in 1956 – Neville playing the Moor one night to Burton's Iago, Burton taking over the next as Othello to Neville's tempter – caused riots in the galleries, a war of Mods and Rockers. The Rockers called Burton Olivier's heir, crown prince of blood and fire. The Mods saw in Neville the successor to John Gielgud, the classic master of vocal music and noble melancholy.

Critics made the same comparison, mostly to Neville's disadvantage. His Richard II was less consistent than Gielgud's, they said, his Hamlet too resolute. It bothered them that Gielgud's heir should be more striking as Ancient Pistol in *2 Henry IV* than as Hotspur in the first part and should choose to play Autolycus in *The Winter's Tale* as a sly Cockney barrow-boy. It puzzled them that his Iago, a wily, spike-haired NCO, should be so much better than his statuesque Othello. As a classical heroic actor, in spite of a fine voice and technique, he seemed somehow hollow at the centre. It occurred to no one that this might be caused by another kind of actor trying to get out.

1957 Hamlet, Old Vic

He got out in 1957, exchanging the lead in *Troilus and Cressida*, in the Old Vic's American tour, for that of Thersites, the foul-mouthed misanthrope. In *Twelfth Night* he was Sir Andrew Ague-cheek, gentle, ponderous, absurd – a Neville hero, almost, made comic by slow motion. Finally he got away from the Old Vic and Shakespeare altogether, playing the lead in an American comedy, *Once More with Feeling*, then taking over the role of Nestor le Fripe in the musical comedy, *Irma La Douce*.

A hint of the man behind the matinée-idol face came with the *Henry V* he staged at the Old Vic in 1960; with a modern-dress Chorus, full of pacifist feeling and contemporary relevance – the type of production which might bring Shakespeare home to the kind of boys he'd first acted with in a Willesden youth club, during the war. But it was as Alfie at the Mermaid Theatre that he finally revealed himself; Romeo and Iago rolled into one Cockney accent, a comic character of utter modernity, lent the stature and technical magnetism of Shakespearean acting.

As theatre director of the Nottingham Playhouse from 1963 to 1968, he created brilliantly the kind of young theatre and audience he believes in. He repeated there his Old Vic triumph as Richard II, but a very different Richard from the one critics compared with Gielgud's ten years before.

*Ronald Bryden*

This interview with John Neville took place in the Nottingham Playhouse.

CLIVE GOODWIN: *Richard II was one of the most successful parts that you played during your seasons at the Old Vic. Can you tell us something about how you set about creating the character?*

JOHN NEVILLE: I don't think I tackled it in a vastly different way from any other of the roles that I played at the Vic. I should say that I've never considered any of Shakespeare's plays to be old-fashioned or archaic museum pieces. And so whenever I've tackled a character, I hope I've always looked at it in a modern way. Neither have I ever found all the masses of stuff that one can read about the plays from scholars, and erudite people, of any great help, however interesting. I think they inevitably leave out one very vital part of an actor's equipment: his personality. It would be impossible for me to play Othello in the way that Mr Bradley, the great scholar, might have played it, because we're obviously two very different people. Michael Benthall and I worked on *Richard II* very closely at the time, we started out from the point of view that at the beginning of the play Richard is a playboy king. So a great deal of that part of the play was taken up with one's attitude to the court, one's relationship with what are known as 'the caterpillars of the Commonwealth', as they're called in the play. One had a very close relationship with these young men. They were young bloods, amusing and witty company. The difficulty for the actor playing the King is the fact that there are two different characters. As he appears in the first part of the play; then, he goes away to Ireland, there's a pause, and he's not on a great deal. Then he comes back to England and appears to be a very different kind of character. We quite blatantly made no attempt to link the two; he came back from Ireland a different man, that is what he was, and that's the way we played it. From the moment he comes back from Ireland, adversity piles on adversity and the play is then a study of a man who faces that adversity. There is a certain tradition in the playing of Richard, all through the latter part of the play – the abdication scenes, the farewell to the Queen – that he stands outside himself and watches himself perform for the assembled company. As I said, there is a theory that Richard does this, and I believe – although it's difficult for me to say – but I believe that we didn't do this. I tried to sink myself in the role and be that man and, in addition, to look at him in a contemporary way.

*He is, of course, very ambitious; how did you marry the playboy concept with his burning ambition?*

Just to elaborate a little further. At the opening part of the play, what the audience saw was an extremely decadent court, a bad ruler, a ruler who has let the kingdom go to rack and ruin; and we didn't really play up the ambition too much. Here was the King in charge of his kingdom, but only just in charge of it. When I came do the play ten years later here at Nottingham, I saw it in a more

1955 Richard II, Old Vic

1955 Richard II, Old Vic, w
Meredith Edwards as Gau
(top), and John Wood (Pier
of Exton)

political way. It was at the time of a change of government in this country, and the play seemed to have very definite links with a change of régime, from a decadent régime to one that one hoped might be more progressive.

*One critic said that in adversity you rose to a kind of frustrated nobility; does this mean anything to you?*

I think what the writer meant was that when the King returns from Ireland, he receives three pieces of bad news in quick succession, and the way Richard reacted and dealt with this situation made him a nobler figure than he had been in the early part of the play, when he was just a playboy. I think Shakespeare knew what he was writing about; we saw it happen in Britain during the war and with the Jews who were put in the gas chambers.

*Had you been impressed by other actors that you'd seen play Richard?*

Yes, I was extremely impressed by Alec Guinness.

*But his interpretation was very different from yours.*

Yes, it was. I was at the Royal Academy of Dramatic Art at the time, when the Old Vic was at the New Theatre in London; Alec Guinness was playing Richard II and I was a walk-on as a soldier. I used to watch from the wings, and I was absolutely bowled over by watching him every night, seeing how he developed the role and how it grew and grew.

*But nevertheless, when you came to play it yourself you used a very different concept of the part.*

Yes. It was just a very different set of circumstances, different director, different designer; and it was all quite different.

*You were in the company of the Old Vic for six years and during that time you played twenty-two Shakespearean parts, finishing with Hamlet. Was Hamlet a part that you had always wanted to play?*

No, I'd never wanted to play Hamlet. When Michael Benthall started off on the five-year plan at the Old Vic, Richard Burton played it. Unlike many actors, I'd never had any ambition to play the part. But when we came to the end of the five-year plan, Michael Benthall said, 'As you've gone right through the whole thing, I think your apotheosis ought to be Hamlet.' So he said, 'Go away and read the play.' I went away and read it, then he said, 'What do you think?' I said, 'Well, it's a marvellous play, I would rather like to play it.' So he said, 'How do you see it? How do you want to be dressed?' I said, 'I'd like to be in a pair of jeans and a white shirt.' I'd been through a lot of plays in those six years, and I'd been in- flicted with a number of designers who were trying to rule the theatre at that time; it was a sort of natural reaction. Anyway, that was how we did it.

1965 Richard II, Nottingham

*I don't remember jeans and shirt.*

I started off with a black hussar's jacket; that came off very soon, and I was in a white shirt and tight black trousers nearly all the rest of the play.

*Can you remind us about the five-year plan?*

I joined the Old Vic, from the Bristol Old Vic, at the time Michael Benthall took over the running of the Old Vic; in fact, he rescued it from running into bankruptcy. He instituted a plan – it needed a plan of some sort – and the plan was to do all the plays by Shakespeare in five years, which we did. I was in a great many of them. It was a tremendously exciting period because it put the Old Vic back on the map. We were severely knocked at times by the critics, but then, that's what the theatre's about. Still it rescued the Old Vic from what would have been oblivion. Michael Benthall did a fantastic job.

*To go back to* Hamlet, *did Michael Benthall have a very specific idea of how he wanted it done?*

Yes, he did. When he did it with me he was producing it for the fourth or fifth time; it had been a favourite play of his from boyhood; I think he'd played it himself. Then he did a notable production of it at Stratford with an alternating Hamlet, Robert Helpmann and Paul Scofield. So when he came to do it with me he knew a great deal about the play. The thing he achieved was absolute clarity of story line and swiftness of action. It got those sort of notices for its direction rather than perhaps its acting: it was a really marvellous production.

*Yes, I believe it was described at the time as the definitive* Hamlet; *it did have great speed. What about rehearsals?*

We never had enough rehearsal time at the Old Vic the whole time I was there. We rehearsed the plays, usually, for about three and a half to four weeks. We rehearsed only four days of the week because there were matinées on the other days. We were always acting in the plays that were going on in the evening; so that we had little enough time to think about the roles. The plays went on to a full barrage of West End criticism; we never felt that we had quite enough time.

*How do you feel about rehearsal time in general? At the Old Vic, which is now the National, they sometimes rehearse plays for up to three months.*

I think this is much better. I feel that one can over-rehearse. I wouldn't want to be rehearsing as long as they do in Russia. I'd want to get to the stage because I rather like the audience.

*Let's get back to* Hamlet. *What was your approach to the character?*

I had a very definite outlook. At the time I was considerably

5  Mark Antony, *Julius Caesar*, Old Vic, with
Paul Rogers as the dead Brutus

younger than I am now, and the way we tackled it was that Hamlet was a very young prince who was disillusioned. I think there is nothing more horrifying than the disillusionment of the very young. It's so utterly shattering. He was completely disillusioned by the actions and behaviour of the older people around him: that is what we tried to show.

*I seem to remember that the relationship with your mother was rather more poignant than I'd seen with other Hamlets – was this a conscious aim?*

Yes, it was. I think one always has to take into consideration the nature of the circumstances when one is involved in a play. We had a particular director, a remarkable actress, Coral Browne, playing Gertrude; and so we worked out a mother-son relationship which was quite interesting.

*Did you see the Oedipus complex theory in your interpretation of the part of Hamlet?*

No, not consciously. But Coral Browne was rather young and very attractive and we worked out a relationship which came to a rather sensational climax in the closet scene, resulting in a kiss. It was certainly remarked upon by the critics and people who saw it.

*So the kiss came more from the characters of the actor and actress involved rather than any deep-seated theory?*

Yes, I think so. We tried to do it as delicately as possible so that it just happened. In this way one got a very marked reaction from Hamlet himself; he was puzzled, horrified and overwhelmed.

*When you say this thing happened, do you mean that it just happened in rehearsal or Michael Benthall said, 'Go on, kiss him'?*

I think it just happened, yes, as one might kiss anyone good night, but it was different.

*But this does bring up a larger question of the relationship between character and performance. What do you think about that?*

One of the things that I remember being taught at drama school was that when you tackle a role you have a number of things at your command, one of the most important of which is your own particular personality, and you have to match that up with the character that you're going to play. You must not cloud the character, or overwhelm it with your own personality, but use as much of it as is valuable to that character. There are therefore certain things in your personality, certain very relevant things that relate to the character, and so you bring those to the forefront and you take the other things that don't match up with the character and push them into the background. In this way, those things that are really valuable are brought into sharp focus. This is something that I remembered and I think one tries to do it all the time.

1957 Hamlet, Old Vic, with Coral Browne (Gertrude)

*This does mean, of course, that the parts which you will probably be best at are the parts which are closest to you temperamentally?*

That may be so.

*Of course, there is a myth around that one is best at the parts which are completely different from oneself.*

Yes, but surely that leaves out personality, because there are certain things in one's personality that one may not be awfully proud of, that one can use for characters that are different from oneself.

*And enjoy using.*

Yes.

*Did your interpretation of Hamlet change much when you played it over a period of time?*

We played it over a year at the Old Vic, then we took it on a tour of America; we also went to the Continent – France and Yugoslavia. But I wouldn't think that it altered very much in interpretation. What happens is that one gets more sure of certain things, and able to play the role with less strain. As a role, it is a tremendous strain to play. I remember when I first joined the Old Vic, Richard Burton was playing Hamlet and I was playing Fortinbras, which is nothing, no strain at all. He used to say that on the days when you're playing Hamlet – this is in repertoire, of course – you wake up in the morning and you know that that night you're going to play Hamlet, it hangs over you the entire day. I didn't really believe this was quite true until I actually played it myself, and it is quite true. It's such an enormous work-out, you use everything. You use your own personality, and if you play the role properly, you must use everything of your being; you are completely and utterly drained. I played it emotionally, I don't know any other way to play it, because there's a great deal of emotion in the role. It's very taxing indeed and I think you need to be something of an athlete both mentally and physically. I remember quite vividly the very first night I played it in London, it was quite a big first night for us all, I was actually physically sick at the end of the performance, I came straight off from the curtain calls and was violently sick.

*J. C. Trewin said of your performance, 'I remember Hamlet not as an actor's Sierra of peaks and valleys but simply as Hamlet. That is much.' Is this a tribute which you would respect?*

Well, it's very complimentary. I think it had a lot to do with the production, quite honestly.

*With the pace of the production?*

Yes, indeed, I would certainly say that, yes. It was a remarkably fine production and beautifully designed. One was given every possible

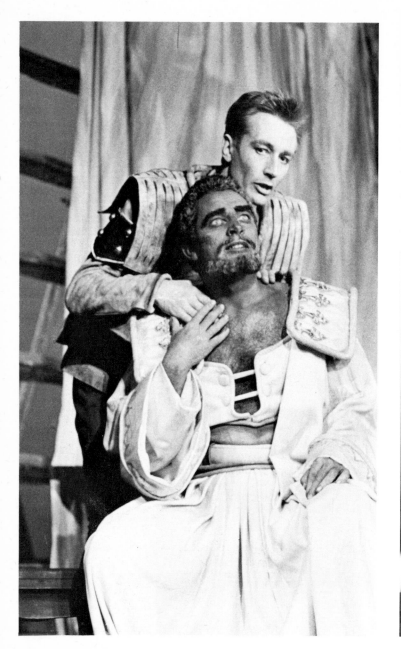

1956 Iago and Othello with Richard Burton, Old Vic

1955 Autolycus, *The Winter's Tale*, Old Vic

help to play the role, and one can't always say that of a director.

*Now in the 1956 season at the Old Vic, you and Richard Burton alternated the parts of Othello and Iago. This must have been a very difficult thing to do. I mean, how, for instance, did you avoid imitating each other, each other's inflections?*

We can both imitate each other, and did off-stage, but I don't think that came into it. It was such an enormous undertaking, and again one didn't have quite enough rehearsal time; we had a total of six weeks to rehearse it both ways round. What made it even more difficult is that we had one first night, and we did it the other way round the very next night. Initially, we rehearsed it quite separately, so that we both got our ways of doing each character quite clearly defined. I was particularly fortunate in that we rehearsed it with me playing Iago first, and I was for ever after very grateful, because it's a fiendishly difficult part to learn. It's difficult to learn because the major part of it is in prose, so you don't have the help of the poetry rhythm to help you. I got all that under my belt and poor Richard was left in the second period of rehearsal having to learn Iago, which was very, very hard. That was one of the difficulties, learning part of Iago; incidentally, it's one of the longest parts in Shakespeare. The whole thing was such a welter of excitement, it was, I think, probably more exciting than playing Hamlet, and extremely rewarding. Possibly one didn't achieve as much, but it was wildly exciting to do.

*Some of the roles that you took at the Old Vic were, of course, character parts – Autolycus, Aguecheek – did you enjoy these as much as the heroic parts?*

I always say that I enjoyed them more because I have always thought of myself as a character actor. At the Bristol Old Vic – I was there for three years – I played a great many parts and enjoyed the character roles most. Michael Benthall saw me play, I think, two of these, near the end of my time at Bristol. He saw me play Young Marlow in *She Stoops to Conquer*, which I played as a character role, and Gregers Werle in *The Wild Duck*, which was a complete character role; I had a slight stoop, a moustache and glasses. It may sound awful, but I was very good, it was one of the best things I've ever done. Michael said, 'I would like you to come to the Vic, but you've got to forget all this character stuff. You've got to play all the big heroic roles; that is what you've got to do, if we're going to make anything of you, and establish you.' This is, in fact, what he made me do, and he was right, of course.

*Well, I'd like to question how right Michael Benthall was, because Penelope Gilliatt once wrote that you weren't a born Shakespearean prince at all, and that you were not idyllical histrionical, but sardonical comical. What do you think about that?*

Othello

Yes, I think I would accept that; I enjoyed that piece of writing very much. It links up with my own attitude to most of the roles I played, even then. Nevertheless, I think it's very difficult to alter one's basic attitude. I've always looked on the heroic roles as characters; I'm still a character actor really, I tackle each part quite separately, and I find out what kind of man he is: to me it's always a character role.

*Penelope Gilliatt described your face as that of a handsome evacuee.*

(Laughs) Yes, I was a very handsome evacuee at one time actually during the war.

*I'd like to link that up, at this point, with the fact that you don't often use make-up as a means of disguise, you rely on your own face to play the part: you don't often cover it with bits of hair and stuff.*

I must confess, it's something that I hadn't given a great deal of thought to. I've always imagined that perhaps I used rather too much make-up. My kind of face is not what one could call a plastic face, it has very definite features which you can't alter very easily. Make-up in the theatre, if you're playing in big theatres, doesn't really mean very much to anyone sitting beyond the tenth row; all they probably see is an outline. But if you've got something of the character to give them in your body and your voice and so on, you can get that over though they can't actually see the lines that you've painted on your face.

*When you say character role, you mean you don't simply try to coast along on your own personality, your own physical attributes, you do try to change them?*

Again, this is what I was saying earlier, you find certain characteristics of your personality which link with the character and you use them like mad; and you hold in check those which don't relate to the character.

*Let's go right back now and ask you what it was that first attracted you to the theatre; do you remember?*

It was Shakespeare, funnily enough, although I hated Shakespeare at school, it was very badly taught. However, I did have one teacher who was enlightened and taught me a lot. My nightmare was being given twelve lines of a play to learn for the next day, and having to get up in front of everybody else and recite them by heart: I was so inhibited about this that I detested Shakespeare. But I was in the local church and the churchwarden took me under his wing. He used to take me out to various theatres, and for three years immediately prior to the war he took me with his nieces to Stratford-on-Avon where in the fortnight's holiday we saw all the plays there. I think this was when I first got the germ.

*Was there nothing in your immediate background to suggest the theatre?*

1954 Macduff, *Macbeth*, Old Vic

No, nothing at all. My parents had always taken me to our local variety theatres, which I simply adored and still do. I love the music-hall, perhaps this is where the sardonic whatever it was comes in.

*Where was this?*

This was in Willesden. I used to go to the Willesden Hippodrome and the Metropolitan, Edgware Road, and the Shepherd's Bush Empire; they were my three locals and I saw everyone there.

*You went to RADA, I believe, when you came out of the Navy in 1946.*

Yes.

*Now the records of your years at RADA are very sparse, and it is difficult to believe that you were quite as shy and nervous as it is said.*

I suppose it is, as I'd been in the Navy and I'd been right round the world and experienced the war. But I was very shy, inhibited, stiff, awkward, and I think RADA gave me just a tiny bit more self-confidence than I had before, but not a great deal. As I was such a bad pupil, it didn't really help all that much. I learned a great deal more after I left, and that wasn't their fault.

*Why were you such a bad pupil, do you think?*

Well, I had this great enthusiasm, this absolutely passionate desire to act, and I'd waited for three years while I was in the Navy, wanting to do nothing else. All I had to offer was this enthusiasm and a certain amount of talent, but not very much: there was nothing that they could do with me. I came into RADA with the first wave of ex-servicemen, which blew a breath of fresh air through the building; it badly needed it at that time. I was one of many, and I didn't shine.

*Your first job after RADA was with Robert Atkins in a season at Regent's Park.*

It made a great difference; this was a very good introduction for me. I hated it at the time, he bullied me a lot and was, I suppose, in a way rather cruel. But it was particularly good for me because I'm very obstinate and I couldn't believe that I was as bad as he thought I was. So, I really knuckled under and got down to it. I wanted to do it, you see, very badly, and he went on and on at me; he was great in that he was a tremendous teacher. People forget that, at one time just after the First World War, he ran the Old Vic for about nine years; he's also run Stratford; and he did these seasons in Regent's Park for many years. He taught me how to speak verse – I had a certain feeling for it, I must admit – but he taught me a great deal about the speaking of Shakespeare which I still consider very important. Obviously, one is in rebellion against the poetry voice and the old ham way of doing Shakespeare, but I still believe that, what-

1955 Pistol, *2 Henry IV*, Old Vic

Old Vic. 1956 Troilus and Romeo, w
Claire Bloom as Juliet; 1954 Berowne, *Lo*
*Labour's Lost*, and Ferdinand, *The Temp*
with Claire Bloom as Miranda

ever modern method you use – and I'm all for that – you've got to be clearly heard. If you've played in a masonic auditorium in Detroit, as I have, to five thousand people, that is where the teaching of people like Robert Atkins can be of immense value.

*Of course, there aren't people like him any more, teacher-directors. I think they're a great loss.*

I think so too.

*Do you agree that there aren't any?*

Just thinking about it, I suppose there aren't any of those elder statesmen of the theatre who can teach you how to speak Shakespeare, which is so important. There's a lot of inaudibility in the theatre still. I have to watch it, even in myself, in this theatre. I have to watch it and I go on about it until I'm quite boring about it to other people, but it pays off.

*Well, you played twenty-two major Shakespearean parts in six years at the Vic. Have you formed any conclusions about the speaking of Shakespearean verse?*

One has to bear in mind that the whole of theatre, and even the speaking of verse, goes through phases of fashion. Above all, the clarity of speech and the clarity of thought behind the speech is what I would stress myself, rather than the poetry voice, which I think is all too easy to do. This can be thoroughly boring for the audience, because it means that you don't get Shakespeare's thoughts over, you make a lot of beautiful sounds and it doesn't mean a damn thing. One more fact, which I think most young actors forget, is that Shakespeare requires masses of energy to play.

*When you left the Park your next job was a season of weekly repertory at Lowestoft. Now I think this was your first and only dose of weekly rep. Was it a good thing for you?*

Yes, I think so. It was one of the happiest times I've ever had in the theatre, possibly because one knew so little about it. It was extremely good for me playing a great number of parts very rapidly, with only a week to work on them. It's a horrifying thing to do, but it's a very good lesson in discipline and getting down to the job. But it's obviously something that one shouldn't do for long, one can get into bad ways of acting by taking short cuts and so on: I did enjoy it very much. I had the additional pleasure of working with a young director who was just new to the theatre himself, Stephen Joseph; we worked together on a number of mad projects at Lowestoft and had great fun.

*Is weekly rep. something that you would recommend for every young actor?*

I don't think there's anything wrong with doing it at the very beginning of your career and for a short time.

Old Vic. 1957 Angelo, *Measure for Measure*, with Barbara Jefford as Isabella

H

*You went from there to the Birmingham Repertory Company where you had three weeks' rehearsal for each play. Was this a profitable period for you?*

Yes, I got married in Birmingham. I was very much the boy about the place and my wife, who was much more talented than me, was playing quite hefty parts; I didn't have a great deal to do, but it was a marvellous company and it had a tremendous tradition. I was with a lot of extremely good people and I was the junior.

*It wasn't till you went to the Bristol Old Vic, which was your next job, that you really started to play big parts; you seemed, in some way, to turn the corner as an actor.*

I began to find myself, I suppose. I went to Bristol with Dennis Carey who was directing. We joined together. I went down just to play two roles, and then he asked me to stay for the rest of that season, and then the following season, and then the third, and I played all kinds of parts. In the final season I was the leading man of the company, and I really began to find myself as an actor and get a little confidence. The last role I played there was Henry V.

*Where did this confidence come from? Was it just the surmounting of technical obstacles?*

I think one gains confidence as a result of people above you giving you a little more to do and believing that you can do it. If they indicate that, it gives you an added confidence as an actor. Perhaps a lot of people even inside the theatre don't realise what incredibly vulnerable creatures actors are; the least thing, the least half-sentence, can completely destroy them, knock them off that equilibrium of confidence in what they feel they can do. I think a lot of directors don't realise it either, perhaps because they've not been actors.

*From Bristol you managed a fairly easy bridge into the London Old Vic because the two companies were connected at that time. In fact, you transferred with Dennis Carey's production of* The Two Gentlemen of Verona. *What do you remember about that production?*

It was the junior company coming to London at a time when the senior company was having a great deal of difficulty; they were going through a very bad patch. It was before Michael Benthall had taken over. We were all very young, and *The Two Gentlemen of Verona* is a young play with a great deal of freshness about it; Dennis Carey directed it, and we all contributed a great deal of energy and high spirits: it had an enormous success. It brought a great feeling of elation to us juniors, coming up from the country and taking the town by storm. But I wouldn't say – with deference to Dennis Carey – that it was the greatest production of all time.

*Apart from your stage work, you have, like most actors these days, appeared in a number of television plays. I remember seeing you in a production of*

1951 Charles Surface, *School for Scandal*, Bristol Old with Newton Blick (Sir Oliver)

*Anouilh's* Poor Bitos. *Now you've spent most of your life acting in front of large audiences in usually quite large theatres. Do you find it easy to adjust the scale of your performance to a television camera?*

No, I don't. I think this is because I probably do about one television play a year, if that, and consequently I always find it extremely difficult. If I was doing it all the time, I would become much better at it and learn the way of acting for the television camera rather than for a large audience in Nottingham: I can't say that I have learned that. I'm always acutely aware of other people around me, who are infinitely better at it than I am.

*I think you're being very modest, but still.*

No, it's quite true. A great many actors do a lot of television, but I don't. Obviously, the same acting problems are involved; but the scale of it, the way of acting to a camera or to three cameras in a confined space, is a slightly different hurdle one has to get over. I don't know too much about it yet.

*Do you think there's a difference in technique, or is it simply a question of adjustment of scale?*

As I said, I don't know a great deal about it. I think if you're acting the role right, that is from within, then you're on the way, as you are in the theatre; but the amount you project the role in the theatre is considerably more.

*When you left the Vic in 1959, after ten years as an actor in permanent companies leading a very secure life, you suddenly found yourself for the very first time on the open market. Was this a frightening experience?*

After playing non-stop Shakespeare for six years, night after night, I badly wanted the change and so I rather took it in my stride. With commitments of wife and family, perhaps I ought to have been a bit more frightened. But anyway, I had immediately a very good time doing an American play called *Once More with Feeling* with Robert Morley which, as it only ran eight weeks in the West End, could be accounted a failure. It was great fun to do and he was marvellous to work with. The next thing I did was a musical *Irma La Douce*, for six months; this was something that I was asked to take over when it had been on for a year. Taking over from someone else is something one has to think rather long about, but I thought it would teach me a great deal. It was something that I hadn't tackled before, on such a scale, and for a run; I thought that I would learn a great deal, and in fact I did. It was one of the most exhausting roles I've ever done.

*You sang and danced in it.*

Yes, a tremendous experience. I did it for exactly six months, because that is what I got the management to agree to, and I didn't

1964 Maxime, *Poor Bitos*, BBC TV, with Peter Woodthorpe (Bitos)

do it for a day longer. I had the marvellous feeling when I left of being both glad and sorry because I'd enjoyed it so much, yet I wanted to get on to something else.

*In 1958 you directed your first play, which was* The Summer of the Seventeenth Doll *at Bristol Old Vic. It seems strange that, with your classical background, the first play you chose to direct should be a very tough play about Australian cane cutters in the outback of Australia.*

Yes, I suppose it was. In effect, it was the play that I was offered. I'd seen it in London, loved and admired it very much. I knew a little bit about Australia because I'd been there during the war in the Navy, I knew a lot of Australians, something about their background; I felt I could give something to it and I enjoyed the experience of doing the play. But the next time I went back to Bristol was to direct a classic, *The Importance of Being Earnest.*

*Had you always wanted to produce?*

There are certain plays that I would be keen to direct, but I don't have the burning ambition that I must produce or direct everything. I suppose, secretly, what I'd always wanted to do was run a theatre rather than just direct plays.

Opposite: 1959 Nestor-le-Fripe, *Irma La Douce*, Lyric, with Elizabeth Seal (Irma)

1959 Victor Fabian, *Once More with feeling*, New Theatre

*Do you have any firm opinions about directors? You've worked with a great many, I mean. How do you think they should behave towards actors?*

I have firm opinions as to what they shouldn't do, which is perhaps a negative way of looking at it.

*What is that?*

I don't think they should get ideas above their station, which they often do; I don't hold with the mystique of the director: that it is so-and-so's *Romeo and Juliet*. Frankly, it's Shakespeare's *Romeo and Juliet*. It's so-and-so's whatever it is; I believe in the author, and I believe that his interpreter is the actor: that's the way it has always been. There are two people, the author and the actor, who are working with the audience, a live audience. I think the director can be very talented, but his job is to interpret the author to the audience and not interpret his own vanity or his own arrogance to the audience. If he tries to do that, he gets in the way of the actor playing the author to the audience, and I think a great deal of mystique goes on about it. Finally, a good director is someone who understands actors and their problems, understands what the play is about and is a good chairman.

*That puts it pretty succinctly. Are there directors whom you would cast in this role? Directors you've enjoyed working with?*

Yes. I worked a great deal of course with Michael Benthall, I did a lot of plays with him, and I would cast him in that role, quite definitely. Oh, there are a number, but perhaps I'd better not name them all because of those I leave out!

*Of course, Joan Littlewood agrees with you: she always said that the theatre won't flourish until the directors are all dead and buried.*

What you won't ever do away with is the actor getting up and telling a story that the author has given him. You can do without the director, you know.

*Now, you direct plays here in this theatre.*

Yes, a lot!

*Do you think you're a good chairman?*

I hope so, yes. That is what I believe in and hope it's what I do. You've got a team of actors, you've got the electrician and a scene designer; all these ingredients. They have to have a chairman, and the chairman has to say, 'Well this is the way we're going to serve this author' and it is your contribution to give the audience what the author wants. I believe that.

*This can work with a permanent company, of course. But you would agree it's much more difficult with a group of actors who are just brought together for one specific play?*

It may be, yes. But I believe in a company being together, very much; you get the best results. I remember when I was at the Old Vic, it was a new company each year, and the best work was nearly always done at the very end of the season. By that time, they'd been working together a long time and they knew each other well, they knew each other's foibles, problems and so on: the best work came out of this.

*Of course, there are chairmen and chairmen; what do you do in the case of a very difficult and obscure play? How far do you give the director his head? What do you do in a case where you have a definite clash of opinion over interpretation between a director and an actor? Did you ever have such a clash?*

Very rarely. I think this comes out in talk, doesn't it? If you're working with an actor and you believe that he can play the role – I'm talking now as a director, perhaps – if you believe that he can play the role, then there must be some point of agreement somewhere along the line. Usually, if you can explain to an actor, or he can explain to you, that what is important is what the author meant, if you can both reach an area of agreement on that, then there shouldn't be too much difficulty. The difficulty arises when people want to exploit their own arrogance and vanity rather than serve the play.

*Yes. Of course, very often one is having to produce a play that isn't really very good, and then one has a responsibility to the audience.*

Not at Nottingham!

*Never at Nottingham, I grant you, but in other theatres this can happen sometimes. Doesn't the director then have a responsibility, even as chairman, to make the company produce something which isn't perhaps there?*

Yes. Obviously there have been times when you know pretty well, as an actor, that the director doesn't think too much of the play and perhaps he's damn right. But nevertheless, I believe that if you're doing that play it is your job to make the company believe in it, wholeheartedly, because if they don't believe in it they won't make the paying customers believe in it, and that's what's important. Those people who sit on those seats and have paid money are very, very important. We believe that here: they're important, and if they're not there we're out of business. In theatres like the one we're in now – and perhaps I shouldn't say this – all the plays we do are different, but we hope that they've got some quality.

*In films, of course, the director's role is rather more important. How do you respond to that as an actor?*

There again, I make perhaps one film a year, and I'm quite ready to leave it to the director. I recognise fully that he has a much more comprehensive idea of what's going on than I have. He has many things to look after that I don't know anything about; I'm quite ready to leave it to the director. As a matter of fact, it's rather a relief to me to have no responsibility whatever, just occasionally.

*In 1960 you did a film called* Study in Terror, *in which you played Sherlock Holmes. It was a 'Jack the Ripper' story. Did you base your characterisation of Sherlock Holmes on things that you read in the Conan Doyle books?*

Yes. I read a great many of the stories. I'd always felt from having seen Sherlock Holmes in my childhood that he was perhaps rather more stiff-backed, stuffy, arrogant and conceited than he need be. I was a bit worried about his relationship with Dr Watson. I felt that he'd often been treated as an old duffer. I think there's a very warm relationship between them even though Holmes often teases Watson. This was something that Donald Houston and I worked on, so that this relationship had a sort of fun about it and warmth, rather than Holmes just being arrogant and condescending to Watson.

*You certainly succeeded in that. Do you enjoy filming?*

Yes. Very much indeed. I enjoy it rather more than doing television plays. What I enjoy about filming is the fact that you can go over a scene until you get it right, or nearly right. This is the great luxury, leaving aside the fact that you haven't got a live audience to play to.

*In 1960 you played Macbeth at the Old Playhouse, Nottingham. Was this your first appearance in Nottingham?*

Yes it was. I was asked by Frank Dunlop, who was running the Old Playhouse, to come up and play Macbeth, which I did; followed very quickly by Sir Thomas More in *A Man for All Seasons*. I also directed *The Caretaker*.

*And did your association with Nottingham grow from that first engagement?*

Yes, it did. I enjoyed myself here very much. I enjoyed the audience particularly, even in the Old Playhouse. What struck me most was the youth of the audience, this is what first attracted me. And so I came back again and did another little stretch and then a third, and then by that time this playhouse – the New Playhouse – was well on the way to being built.

*How did you come to be appointed Theatre Director here, at the Nottingham Playhouse?*

By that time I was well and truly associated with Nottingham. I had got thoroughly involved with the running of the Old Playhouse with Frank Dunlop, and we were both asked to come here as directors, together with Peter Ustinov: that's really how it happened.

1965 Sherlock Holmes, *Study in Terror* (film)

*Were you in on the design of the theatre?*

No, no. By the time I first visited Nottingham the designs were all set. I was only in on some of the slight modifications, but the fabric was well and truly settled by the time I was involved.

*I believe it was you who insisted, right from the beginning, on having a repertoire of plays – that is, running several plays at the same time. What are the advantages of this system?*

Yes, that was my contribution to the policy of the theatre; it was my plan that we should do a full-scale repertoire which wasn't being done anywhere outside London at that time. The advantages are that it's much more interesting for a company of actors to play: you're doing something different each night, you don't get stale, it's not like doing a long run of a play. But perhaps, more important, it's very good for the audience. If you're doing a number of plays, all of which are different in type, the plays can range from Victorian music-hall on one extreme, to Greek tragedy on the other; in fact, we have done that in this building. Then it is likely that you can begin to widen your audience. It is, of course, a little more costly to run this system, but it brings in great benefits; it increases the numbers of people that come to the theatre, without any doubt. We've widened our audience, since we've been here, to doing ninety per cent on a 750-seat house, compared with the Old Playhouse, where we were lucky if we did sixty per cent on a 460-seat house.

*What is it, do you think, that attracts people to this theatre in such large numbers? It is a very beautiful theatre, do you think that has a lot to do with it?*

Yes. I think the building has a great deal to do with it. If you give people the right surroundings, the right conditions, then it's likely that you will attract more people into the theatre. It is a beautiful building, but it is also a comfortable building, and you don't have to run down the street to get a drink, as you did at the Old Playhouse theatre. There are adequate bars, enormous foyer space for people to promenade and talk. People don't come to this theatre late; they come early, to meet; they have a meal at the restaurant, or a coffee at one of the bars; I think this has a lot to do with it.

*How often do you yourself produce the plays here?*

I don't produce every play by any means. I don't know what the proportion is; perhaps one in four. We have a team of people, there are two other directors on the staff, and we have our guest directors. Yes, I suppose I direct one in four.

*Do you find that satisfying?*

Enormously.

*More satisfying than acting?*

Yes, I find it enormously satisfying – if you do it well, of course; one doesn't always do it well. As I said before, I don't crave to direct every single play, and when I do direct, I always enjoy it, because it's something I want to do. There is a great satisfaction in creating and interpreting an author, and also in being able to help an actor to give a better performance than he might have done.

*How do you recruit your company?*

We recruit them less and less because we're becoming more and more of a permanent company. Lots of people want to act here, fortunately, and more and more of them want to stay. When we do have auditions we have them in London; but more often than not it's people that one has seen at other theatres, and if they're free, we ask them to join us.

*How often do you appear yourself?*

I've just recently gone through a phase of not appearing at all – that is, for the last four or five months. But before that I was appearing a great deal – in too many things, really; it's awfully difficult to keep a balance.

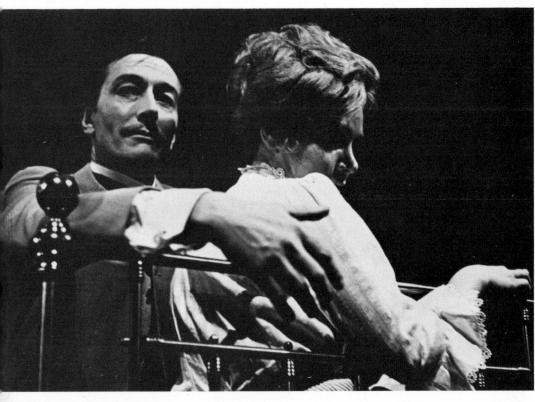

Nottingham Playhouse
Opposite:
1967 Iago, *Othello*
1965 Richard II
Left:
1967 He, *Beware of the dog*, with Ann
Bell
1966 Faustus

*You do about twelve plays a year, here at Nottingham. What guides you in your choice of these plays?*

Our policy is two-pronged; firstly, it involves doing classical revivals, because we reckon to be a classically based company; and secondly, in trying to find as many new English plays as we possibly can – that is to say, new work that perhaps no one else would do. The criticism is sometimes levelled at us that we're not doing any contemporary European plays; this is not because we have no desire to do them, or no regard for them; it's simply because there is no time available if we're carrying out our own policy.

*Sometimes the two prongs become one; you did a production of* Measure for Measure *in modern dress with six musical numbers specially written into it.*

Yes.

*This would seem to contradict what you said earlier about letting the playwright speak for himself and keeping the director out of it.*

Yes, I stand accused, and ashamed. But perhaps in my defence, I ought to say that I know the play very well. I was in a production at the Bristol Old Vic, playing the Duke, and then I played Angelo at the Old Vic; it's a play I have a great regard for, I don't despise it in any way. I'd always wanted to do it in a modern way, even when we were at the Vic. We had the idea we might do it in Vienna (the play is set in Vienna) at the time of *The Third Man*, just after the war, at the height of the black market. When one came to rethink it here, that was out of date, because it was ten years ago. So we plumped for doing it absolutely modern, sort of Carnaby Street, we felt that it had a lot of modern relevance. The morality of the play is relevant to the morality, or lack of it, in our modern society; but we never lost sight of what Shakespeare was trying to say. I believe we did it with integrity.

*It's quite a tough play. Did the musical numbers fit in easily?*

Yes. They were tough musical numbers, specially composed by a young musical director we had here. It was an enormous success; we had to revive it. I wasn't in it originally as I had directed it, but I took over the part of Angelo when we revived it.

*Few people will remember that you created the part of Alfie in the original London production. How did you come to play Alfie, when the play of that name was first produced at the Mermaid Theatre?*

I was asked to do it and I don't think anybody else wanted to very much. It's a pretty tough play, there were all sorts of reasons why people were rather frightened of it. Roman Catholic actors weren't keen on playing it, for instance, as it deals with abortion. It did cause a great deal of fuss when I played it here; there were letters in the local Press, of course, from the usual lunatic fringe. But the fact

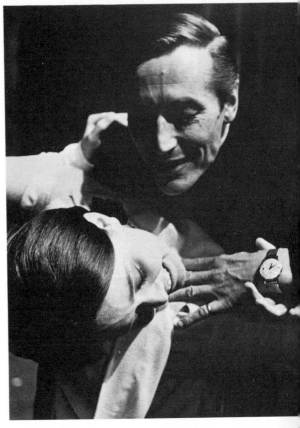

1965 Angelo, *Measure for Measure*, Nottingham, with Sarah Jane Gwillim (Isabella)

Alfie. Below, Mermaid 1963. Opposite, Nottingham 196

124

is, it's a highly moral play, written by a Roman Catholic who detests abortion. I had to do the play for that reason.

*Was it true to say that Alfie's background was not so very dissimilar from your own as a youth at Willesden?*

Yes, very similar.

*Is this the first time you've been allowed to play the part using that experience?*

Yes. The very first time. But it was a tough part to play and I think you needed, if I may say so, a certain amount of technical equipment to play it, which I would not have had if I'd played it much earlier in my career. I think the six years of Shakespeare helped me to play Alfie.

*It must have been quite a relief to settle back again into the old familiar cadences.*

Yes. It was marvellous. Quite early in the evening the audience were pretty shocked at what was going on, pretty bowled over; and one had to get on terms with them, because there were great stretches of the play where you had to talk to the audience and tell them a little story about your caperings or experiences, and tell it to them in a way that was palatable, or fairly palatable. This was a great challenge and something I enjoyed doing, being able to talk to the audience.

*It was something you'd done before in the classical theatre.*

Yes, a little bit, but you don't exactly talk to the audience when you say 'To be or not to be,' then you're talking much more to yourself. But Alfie is actually talking directly to the audience and working off their reactions.

*I believe you took a booth at the Nottingham Goose Fair recently. Can you tell us something about that experiment?*

Yes. I don't think it's been done before. We took a booth at the fair, it was a leap into the dark for us; we did a very fast-moving twenty-minute show with snippets of all sorts of things. I did a bit of *Alfie*, Christopher Hancock did a speech from *The Caretaker*, we did a couple of numbers from *Irma La Douce*, a Nottingham language sketch, all kinds of things, most of which had been seen in the theatre at some time. What we were trying to do was to get out and search for a new audience, an audience, perhaps, that wasn't coming to us yet. It was frightening and funny – a really great experience. I think one of the things that bowled us over was not only this great contact with a new audience, but the way we were accepted by the fairground people themselves, the people working on either side of us.

Nottingham Playhouse Goose Fair Tent 1964

*What did you have on either side of you?*

On one side we had one of those great big – I've forgotten what it's called – The Cyclone, I think, the great big wheel that goes round and round. On the other we had a children's railway and a toffee-apple stall.

*You didn't attract a special audience into your booth? It was just the crowd who were at the fair?*

Oh yes, the people at the fair; we had queues all the way down to the whelk stall.

*Do you think many of them came to the theatre as a result of it?*

It's difficult to say. We hope so. These are the sort of activities we do, in the hope that they'll see the kind of work we're doing and perhaps come back.

*I've never seen an audience anywhere in England such as I've seen in this theatre, quite so young, enthusiastic and so alive. Can you account for this?*

As I said before, at the Old Playhouse theatre I was struck by the audience, the number of young people; and we've increased that number enormously. We do a number of things to attract audiences. First of all, we try to give the greatest quality that we can in all the plays that we put on. We also play one schools' matinée every week that we're open, forty-four weeks of the year: that is building an audience for the future. This is the continuation of a tradition which was started at the Old Playhouse theatre. Then I started something called the Youth Workshop, which is a Saturday-morning youth club, not every Saturday morning, unfortunately, we can't fit it in with all our other activities, but it is something that we thought might attract the people who weren't coming to the schools' matinées. I always felt that the grammar school and the secondary modern school child might not necessarily find itself at those schools' matinées, or indeed in this theatre at all. So we started this club in order to get people into the building, show them what it was like, show them the sort of things we do, involve them in the activities, including improvisations on the stage. This has been a great success because it's resulted in people coming into the theatre who've never been here before, and they come back to see the plays.

We've also instituted a scheme, just recently, of actually going out to schools. We take a seven-man team from within the company with a one-hour version of *Julius Caesar*. We do one hour's teaching, instruction and rehearsal, that is rehearsing a great number of children in the three crowd scenes; then they actually do the finished performance in front of the rest of the school. We've been given a brand-new bus by a local firm to do this; we put the scheme up to the authorities and we've now embarked on it. Another thing we've done, from the time we opened this theatre, we moved the first night forward from Tuesday to Wednesday, and on the Tuesday night, that is the night before we open to the public, we have a student preview. This is open to anybody who has a student's card, and they can come into any part of the house for three shillings: the theatre is always absolutely packed. I think all these things help us to get a new audience, a young audience.

*There is in the foyer, for instance, a marvellous exhibition of American painting which I saw on my way in.*

Yes. We always have an exhibition of some sort in the foyer. This one was an exhibition we mounted in conjunction with the Midland Art Gallery across the road; these are all comtemporary American paintings.

*Do you think there are many other towns in England that could sustain and support a theatre like this one?*

Yes. Most, I would think, given the same kind of approach. But obviously one can't do this sort of operation without adequate money; the right amount of subsidy from both the national and the local authority is prerequisite.

*Do you get the right amount?*

No.

*This company has been on a great many tours all over the world. Can you tell us something about them?*

I'd done a lot of touring before I came to Nottingham, and we did do one very interesting tour from the Old Playhouse. We went to West Africa: Nigeria, Ghana and Sierra Leone; we took three plays, *Macbeth*, *Twelfth Night*, and *Arms and the Man* by Shaw. This was quite an achievement because it had never been done before. There are no theatres there, so we were playing in open-air cinemas, halls of different kinds, and on two occasions in a sports stadium. What was really staggering was the audience's reception of the plays; very vocal, very alive and animated. One was struck how very closely they followed the actual story line: Shakespeare's plot, which we don't follow any more, meant a great deal to them. For instance, the first time we did *Twelfth Night* in Lagos – as you know Sebastian and Viola are twins, and they never appear on the stage together until the end of the play – at the moment when they did appear together and recognised each other, the audience stopped the show for about a minute; they yelled, they screamed, they laughed, they cheered, and they cried; they threw their programmes and their hats in the air, and we couldn't go on. A great audience.

*Do you want this theatre to tour more?*

128 Yes. I think it's very valuable to tour foreign countries, for all the

obvious cliché-ridden reasons. But we find it very difficult because, if you're committed to a full-scale repertoire for the major part of the year, which we are, and absolutely committed to serving this region, then it makes it very difficult for us to tour. We would have to have a double company, and when we get money to do that we will do it.

*All your working life you seem to have preferred working within the framework of a company, an ensemble. Is this true, do you think?*

Absolutely true. I feel happiest doing just that. I was extremely unhappy in the period after I left the Old Vic, and went into what one might term the jungle. I didn't feel there was a place for me there. It may suit some people, but it didn't suit me very well. I'm very happy here, where – to put it pompously – one feels that one is serving a very clearly definable public; you know whom you're working for. But you want to have more of them, you want to chase after people who are not happy in the band, as it were.

*You began as an actor, then you began to direct, now you're an artistic director, which is something different. It means, of course, that a great part of your day must be wrapped up in pure administration.*

Yes. This is the thing I enjoy most of all. I suppose, really, that that has always been my ambition, to run a company, to run a theatre. It's difficult to describe why: it's very challenging, it's often very difficult; but intellectual problems of working out who should do what and where and why and how, I enjoy enormously. I don't always succeed, of course, but I do enjoy it very much.

*It's also gruelling and lonely. It doesn't have that immediate sense of enjoyment that one can get from standing on a stage and communicating with an audience. Nevertheless, you still enjoy it.*

I do, and to me it's part of it. I enjoy, on the one hand, doing an Alfie soliloquy to an audience – picking out one or two people and talking to them, I enjoy that. But to me the administration thing is absolutely bound up with this; one is working for and with a community that one knows something about. They're there, one knows them, and the administration part of it seems to me to be irrevocably entwined with the whole business, I can't separate it.

*Would you say that this urge to communicate was the basic reason why you want to act?*

It's the basic reason why one wants to act, and it's the basic reason why one wants to run a theatre: to attain the widest possible audience, and to attract those people who don't yet come.

1969 John Churchill, Duke of Marlborough, *The First Churchills*, BBC TV

I

# Eric Porter

AFTER *The Forsyte Saga* life will never be the same again for Eric Porter, either as man or actor. From a shadowy figure among the leading players of his generation, he rocketed to the front pages of the national Press; and his portrait of Soames is indelibly stamped across that rugged face, admired and cherished by most households in the United Kingdom.

Porter played the part throughout with his whole being; this actor of forty really was a septuagenarian, and when he lay on his death-bed, his eyes slightly glazed, the jaw fell open at exactly the right angle. But it is not a mask superimposed from the outside; every expression on that face is a reflection of the inner man, the complete man. His Soames was justifiably one of the finest acting performances of the sixties: it is significant that it was seen on television and not in the theatre.

Porter never went to drama school, but he was fortunate at the start of his career to work with Robert Atkins, Lewis Casson and Donald Wolfit, three actors who were not only fine directors but also first-rate teachers of stage craft. They realised Porter's potential and he was quick to learn. When he left Wolfit's company he shouldered his way into the Birmingham Repertory Theatre, where he remained for three years, playing a long succession of elderly character roles.

He reached London in 1951, a fully-fledged actor, and played Solyony in a star-studded cast of Chekhov's *Three Sisters*. The merits of his performance were immediately recognised; he could characterise and he had the authority that comes from stillness. These qualities were even more apparent in his playing of Bolingbroke to Scofield's Richard II. Then in 1952 he appeared in his one and only 'boy meets girl' part in *Under the Sycamore Tree*. He gave the youth a burning earnestness and sincerity which created a strong impression. But a criticism of his acting at this time was that the characters he created were unnecessarily peevish and dour – they lacked grace.

1965  Shylock, *The Merchant of Venice*, Stratford

This serious-minded actor is a perfectionist. During the next six years, spent playing seasons of classical parts at Bristol and the Old Vic or appearing with the Lunts in Montherlant's *The Visit*, he found his sense of direction and gained that knowledge and experience which enabled him to project his performance across the footlights with enormous confidence. In 1959 his Rosmer, in Ibsen's *Rosmersholm*, to Peggy Ashcroft's Rebecca West, won the *Evening Standard* award for the best actor of the year: he satisfied his severest critics with a rare piece of creative acting. Porter maintained a continuous interplay between the inner life of this one-time clergyman and the outward events of the plot. He endowed the broken idealist with a benign grace and made it appear logical that Rosmer could only expiate his sins by taking his own life.

At the end of the run he went to Stratford and became a member of the Royal Shakespeare Company. Porter thrives within the protective walls of permanent companies, and their way of rehearsing suits his meticulous method of working. Over the years he has played leading parts in twenty-six of Shakespeare's plays with many outstanding performances to his credit.

One landmark was the 1965 Stratford season when he played Barabas in Marlowe's *Jew of Malta* and Shakespeare's Shylock in *The Merchant* with equal distinction. The final test was his King Lear in the 1968 Stratford season. Perhaps a little lightweight, it was certainly not a pale shadow of Wolfit's performance – it was Porter's own individual reading of the part: keen, sensitive and intelligent; a careful interpretation of the text. The character of the old king was drawn with fine economy and the spoken word was never obscured by a parade of feeling (this is all part of Porter's credo). In any medium, his search for the essential truth in the part is always dominant, but his acting is not without warmth; this was evident in the playing of Soames, and even more so in his television performance of Cyrano when he fashioned a full-scale romantic hero.

*Hal Burton*

DEREK HART: *Twenty-six episodes of* The Forsyte Saga *represented what – a year of your life?*

ERIC PORTER: A little more than a year. We started with a month's pre-filming, down at Brighton and various other places, before we actually started rehearsals.

*Had you recognised the possibilities of portraying a character like Soames Forsyte before you undertook to do the serial? Had you read it?*

No, I hadn't read it, but I had listened to the original radio broadcast which was some twenty-five years ago. No, I never look forward to playing any parts, really – I'm much more inclined to sit back and wait until a script is put in front of me; then, if it excites me, if I know I can do it, and want to do it, then that's it.

*But have you never read the original Galsworthy book?*

Only when I came to do this.

*Then the whole impact of Soames struck you with a new force?*

Oh yes, indeed. One realised that this was probably one of the best parts to play on television in the twentieth century.

*As the serial didn't exist, initially, in dramatic form, this must have meant considerable problems of characterisation, as you went along?*

Yes and no. In a stage production of two and a half hours you generally have to get the whole character in, in that time; you have to meet the character (or, rather, you have to let the audience meet the character), you have to show whatever aspect the dramatist wants shown of that character. But with twenty-six episodes you have this marvellous, luxurious spread, this feeling of time and leisure. Each episode can show one particular facet of that character, with, shall we say, all the other facets waiting in the wings to be brought forward in their particular episode. We didn't know right at the beginning how some of the episodes were going to be dramatised, but we always had the book to refer to.

*But did you never find yourself being inconsistent with the image of yourself that you'd created at an earlier stage?*

No, because, as I said, we always had the book in front of us, therefore we could see the direction in which we had to go. Right at the beginning one knew what the end was. And without revealing what the end was going to be, one knew that the character had to be pushed to certain extremes. Take, for instance, the rape. Now it wouldn't have done for me to have created a character, right at the beginning, that couldn't have encompassed within his animal personality the possibility of rape, of being physically violent. Therefore, he's got to have something of the animal in him. But of course with Soames it's so kept down, so tutored, so instructed by his upbringing and his class and the whole background of his being.

*This means an intensity of concentration right from the very start, doesn't it? Because, if you know the overall pattern, in order to follow it through you have to have the character entirely under control at episode one.*

Yes, particularly with a serial as long as this; you've got somehow to have it so defined that it will remain absolutely clear and fresh – in episodes 26, 19, 15, 13, 8.

*How far did you find yourself taking on a physical stance which you felt was particularly Soames?*

This has almost resulted in physical deformity for me! At least, it did for the year I was playing Soames. When one is studying age (and I wouldn't say that I was an experienced geriatrician!), one thinks in terms of muscles, bones, tautness, tension, laxity, the whole thing. Now, obviously, the more upright the carriage, the younger, the more vigorous you are. Then one begins to observe that in middle age – and, let's face it, I've always played middle-aged parts, I was born middle-aged! – you begin to see the slow sag in the spine. Then it begins to go at the neck, the head goes forward, but there's still pride, so the head has to come up. Then the whole pelvic area is slightly shoved forward because of the tension in the back of the knees, trying to pull the knees back straight, so there's the slight sagging in the knees. You find, of course, that this is why people get shorter when they get older, because of this slight sag. Then you find, as you walk around, you can't help but behave in this particular way. Having once set oneself like that, that's fine. But at the end of a year it took me a hell of a long time to straighten myself out again!

It's one of those things that an actor does, almost like a computer, because he feeds a message into it, and then leaves it. An actor has many parts of his brain which he uses – one to keep remembering the words, one to watch the audience to see if they're laughing or not, another one to watch out if the scenery's falling down, etc. If you were playing Richard III, to take a very obvious example, the actor sends a little message to one part of his brain: take the deformity – then the shoulder goes up, the stroke, or whatever it was, or the paralysis that he was born with, comes into the arm, so the foot, the leg, is twisted permanently, so that one does that for the whole evening, and it doesn't matter whatever else you do, that deformity is there. This is a minute part of the performance, but it has to be gone into.

*Did you find any of the characteristics of Soames within your own personality? Or were they all entirely alien to you?*

No, I found a great many of them really: this inability to communicate completely; this inability to relax completely in personal relationships.

1966 Soames, *The Forsyte Saga*, BBC TV, with Ny Dawn Porter (Irene)

*This is you?*

This is what my friends accuse me of, so I suppose it must be me, yes!

*Anything else?*

I think I have a reasonably well-developed sense of property. But on the other hand I've something that Soames hasn't got, and that is a sort of puritanical idea that somehow property, money and all that, is wrong. I know it's silly, without money the world wouldn't go round. This happens to be our particular symbol of exchange; therefore one must accept it.

*Did you feel, then, that this gave you a kind of objectivity which helped you to get to grips with Soames?*

Any part that one's asked to play is partly objective, partly subjective. I don't think any part can be wholly objective; you have to use something of yourself. There are two kinds of actors. There are the actors who try to get completely away from themselves, put a great deal of make-up on – beards, moustaches, wigs, etc. – and virtually hide behind the *maquillage*. There are other actors who can only present themselves as if they were the part. I used to be wholly the first kind of actor. In fact, when I was at the Birmingham Rep. there was hardly a play went by, when the nose putty didn't come out, or the crêpe hair didn't go on. But latterly I have been presenting more of myself, possibly because I am, as I say, born middle-aged, and gradually growing towards it!

*Did you at any point during the recording of the early episodes have any indication of the likely impact that* The Forsyte Saga *was going to make?*

No.

*It was fantastic, wasn't it?*

Yes, not only in this country but all over the world. One never realised that people would be so interested in the Victorian and Edwardian era. One knew it was a good part, a part that one wanted to play; it was obviously going to be treated in a highly professional and first-class manner, so one wanted to be associated with it; but one didn't expect the avalanche reaction that there has been.

*During the thirteen months that you were doing it, and the twenty-six separate recordings, you must have had to keep in mind, at each stage, the development of what you were going to look like.*

The whole thing was mapped out very carefully both with the make-up people and with the wardrobe. Obviously, as I explained earlier about the stance, this was aided by the wardrobe; we made certain fittings which would assist the posture. But facially I started off with a front piece, a rather full front piece. Then we took that

Soames, with Kenneth More (Jo) and Susan Hampshire (Fleur)

off and I used my own hair. Then we added a dark moustache. After that I started to grey my own hair; then we had a half-wig, with a slightly grey moustache; and then, of course, for the final episodes I had a full wig.

Soames

*The gradual development of Soames from being extremely unsympathetic in the earlier episodes to a character of great sympathy in the later ones – was this something which you worked out, or did this grow as you got closer to the character?*

I never think in terms of sympathy, you know. People sometimes accuse actors of playing for sympathy, or not playing for sympathy as the case may be: I never think in terms of that. I try to find the character, what the character is intended to represent in the play, and then leave it to the audience. If they feel sympathy, then obviously the character is sympathetic. All I tried to do with Soames was to show him as a fully rounded character. Nobody, especially if you get to know them well over a long period of time, is wholly black, unsympathetic, or evil; even the worst types have some recommendation. Certainly I tried to show what was behind the frozen exterior of this man. Behind every person who is stiff and severe there is a soft person, or at least a gentle or a sensitive person, trying to get out.

*Did you watch the episodes yourself as they were transmitted?*

Every one, on both occasions; at least, as many as I could. The first time was to see the thing, one just hadn't seen it. With this present showing, I'm watching them in order to examine what one does in each episode, with an eye to seeing whether what one tried to do has actually come through.

*Has it?*

In some cases, yes, one is agreeably surprised; in some cases, of course, one is horrified, and you want to go and do it all over again!

*But do you remember very clearly what it was you were trying to do when you look at it? How long is it now? It's a couple of years ago.*

Yes, it's two years. There is nothing more evocative or nostalgic than watching an episode of *The Forsyte Saga*. As one watches each episode, so one is immediately transported back to the rehearsal room, what one did in the rehearsal room, the problems that one overcame in the rehearsal room. Then what we did in the studio. It's almost like – well, I suppose the nearest thing is going back to school, and you smell the desks, the blackboard and the chalk, and all that. Watching an episode of *The Forsyte Saga* can almost give you back the exact feeling of what happened during the particular fortnight that you were doing that episode.

*As a general rule, what do you look for when you watch a recording of your own performance?*

The general effect plus a very quick eye for what is minutely wrong, but wrong nevertheless. I'm not bothered by the odd wig join showing occasionally and things like that. I leave that to the wardrobe department or the wig department to bother about. No, it's missing, shall we say, something that should have been done, trying to fill in the gaps.

*How aware are you of the cameras at the time? I mean, do you pretend they're not there, do you ignore them, apart from walking to your marks, or do you play to them?*

No, you can never ignore the cameras in a television studio, they are too omnipresent. In fact, I don't think one should ignore the cameras, ever: that is your audience. They are the medium through which one is eventually going to communicate and therefore one should know about cameras: I'm very conscious of them. It's much easier to modulate one's performance to the cameras if you do know something about them. It's no good suddenly going into a great hysterical, emotional scene when, although the camera may be right across the other side of the studio, there is a telephoto lens on you and you're in close-up on the screen: it's not necessary.

*Well, how do you adapt?*

It's like having a sort of rheostat; you scale down or you scale up, just as one does in the theatre. But, of course, everything in the theatre is that much bigger.

*Do you miss the audience when you are doing television?*

No, not if one has had sufficient experience in the theatre to carry the audience in your own mind. One doesn't bother all that much about an audience's reaction in tragedy, or serious dramatic plays with not much comedy in them. The concentration is a kind of substitute; if one's got that, then it's fine. But in comedy, if one is playing Coward or Shaw, then there is a certain element of timing which you've got to present to the camera in order that the audience can receive it the other end. They may be laughing in their sitting-rooms or their lounges; you've got to allow for that or they will miss the next laugh.

*You're speaking now as somebody who's very much mastered television and films.*

I wouldn't say I'd mastered them; I'm still learning. I find it fascinating, learning, because I've got this sort of technical bent; and any television director will tell you that I interfere as soon as I get into a studio! I'll make suggestions for shots and things like that. They're all very co-operative – I haven't been hit yet!

*For many years you were very much against television. Did you feel that it needed a different kind of acting?*

I am still convinced – I mean it's an absolute truth, really – that the art of the actor remains in the theatre, because he has complete control over his performance from the time he steps on to that stage to the time he comes off it. Admittedly, it is in co-operation with a director who has staged the piece; it is also in co-operation with the other actors. But if the actor suddenly decides that he wants to take a particular experience a bit further, one particular evening, then he has the control to do that. Now in television and films, more so in films, we need the craft of the actor but not the art. Films, as you know and probably everybody else knows, are all shot in little penny numbers and then stuck together at the end of the shooting. In fact you can shoot the end of a film before you shoot the beginning. Television is somewhere in between. Now an actor has a certain amount of control within a scene which may be quite a long scene; he can still bring out the extra guns. He can still make slight changes so long as he knows that he's not throwing the whole camera schedule out. But he is, nevertheless, still at the mercy of Charlie-boy, up in the control room with his little finger on the button, and what the actor thought was a close-up is actually a two-shot favouring the other fellow!

*How did you come to be an actor in the first place? Accident? Long-term planning?*

Oh, accident, I suppose. I'd always acted, either the giddy goat or various other things at school! We were given a free period on Friday afternoons to do whatever we liked. This applied not only to the junior but also to the senior school. I hasten to add that, historically speaking, this was before secondary moderns and all that, so we had infants, juniors, seniors. In those periods one just amused oneself and, one hopes, the rest of the pupils by getting together, dressing up, doing all those sorts of things. I'm sure it still goes on somewhere. From that, it was a natural thing to go on to the old boys' club and youth club activities. It was during one of these that the youth organiser for the county came round and asked if I ever thought of doing this professionally. At which, of course, a blinding light filled my mind, and I said, 'Oh, isn't it marvellous, I can do what I like doing and be paid for it!' I'd been an avid attender at the Wimbledon Theatre which was our local theatre, and paying my 1s 6d in the amphi.

*You started with Robert Atkins, didn't you?*

Yes. That was in 1945. He was then running his second season at Stratford. And a terrifying experience that was, being interviewed by him, because after waiting around for an hour and a half they finished rehearsing and broke for lunch; I was shown in and introduced to Mr Atkins. As you know, he terrified people with those great bristling eyebrows. Poor, innocent, sixteen-year-old ignoramus came in, and the first thing Robert said was, 'What are your legs like?' which threw me completely. I realised later, of course, that he wanted to know what they looked like in tights, but it's a bit fazing for that to be thrown at you at your first interview.

*After your season with Atkins you worked with Sir Lewis Casson, and subsequently with Donald Wolfit. Now these three distinguished figures of the theatre were all very much of the same generation, and in some ways had similar styles of acting. Can you indicate the kind of things you learned from them?*

Well, let me say, first of all, that to those three people I owe an enormous debt of gratitude, because to have them as your masters, in your early days, I don't think there is anything to compare with it. They are each of them consummate men of the theatre, which is what I wanted to be – a man of the theatre. And, of course, their knowledge of Shakespeare was second to none. Now I had no particular love for Shakespeare at that time. In fact, having just left school a couple of years before, there was still that redolent feeling of 'Oh God, I've twenty lines to learn before tomorrow morning. What's this stuff all about?' I believe that still goes on, which I find rather sad-making.

*But do you feel that they directly influenced your style as an actor?*

I think they showed one that to be courageous in both size of thought and gesture is not to be ham – the big gesture, the big thought, the big feeling, truly felt. Wolfit's Lear influenced me enormously; all his performances did because he was a superb actor. As a craftsman, as a technician, there was nothing he could not do. His comedy-timing was absolutely spot on.

*Many people who worked in his company, at one time or another, felt that he was very intimidating and that he tended to suppress the talent of those around him. Now would you consider this a travesty of the truth or do you think there's something in it?*

It is in part true. Because, you see, he always encouraged me, until we had a slight disagreement over something, then he wasn't quite so encouraging! But no, I found him tremendously helpful and not – not squashing at all. There was one unfortunate incident at a school matinée of *Macbeth*. It's that sort of a play that young people do find faintly amusing, all the witches bits and all that. Donald used to make a speech saying that there was no subject whatsoever for laughter in any scene of this play, and would the younger members of the audience kindly remember that – etc., etc. Unfortunately I was playing the Porter, which, let's face it, is the only scene in *Macbeth* that has any humour in it, so I had to stand on my head, practically, before I could raise a giggle!

Birmingham Rep. 1949 Chubukov, *The Proposal*; 1950 John Henly, *The New Gossoon*, with Paul Daneman

139

*Then you went to the Birmingham Repertory Company. Now was this a considerable advance in your career?*

Yes, and it was consciously arrived at, because I came back from the Canadian tour with Donald Wolfit and thought to myself, the next thing I need is a good spell in repertory. Which is the best Repertory Company? The Birmingham Rep. had the best reputation at the time. So I sat on the doorstep, and in fact literally bombarded them with letters, telephone calls. Got at the producer and his assistant through various friends that knew them to put in a good word. I did everything to get into that place, eventually managed it, and stayed there for two and a half years.

*Do you feel that you missed something by not going into a drama school?*

At the time I probably felt I did, because soon after the war there was this sudden upsurge of people either coming straight from school or coming back from the forces, going to RADA and coming out into the theatre, apparently fully set up for a career. I didn't realise at the time, of course, that this is not necessarily a lasting feeling, because very soon after they came out they realised that they had got to start all over again, begin at the beginning, and learn their job. I may have felt I missed it, just as I feel that I probably missed a university education; but when I think about it, it doesn't really bother me all that much. I must say, I did go in for the examination for RADA, and they said, 'No, you're not good enough.' Actually that was before I went to Robert Atkins. RADA at that time was being used as a finishing school (it was towards the end of the war), débutantes and young men were sent to RADA merely because there was no opportunity of sending them to Switzerland, Strasbourg, Heidelberg, or wherever the place is they used to get sent to.

*After you left the Birmingham Repertory Company I think your next move was to London, the Aldwych Theatre, where you played in an all-star cast of* The Three Sisters.

I was discovered for the first time. I'm discovered – no, rather excavated – every few years! Yes, I was discovered by Tennants. First of all I had an unhappy encounter in *Penny for a Song*, with Peter Brook: I didn't eventually open in the part. Then I took over from Sidney James at the Lyric Hammersmith and played opposite Kathleen Harrison, as her husband (I was twenty-two at the time!): I used to terrify her every night, the way I broke a chair over the end of the bed. After that, in 1951, I went into the festival production of *The Three Sisters*.

*Then followed one of your few ventures into the commercial theatre, which was with Alec Guinness in* Under the Sycamore Tree.

Yes. That again was under the H. M. Tennant banner; I was ac-

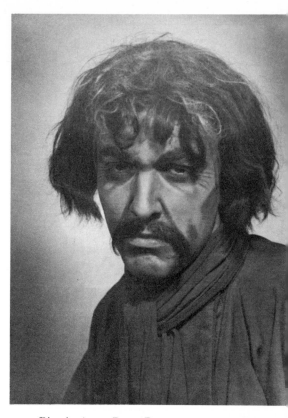

1949 Birmingham Rep. Peasant servant, *Diary of Scoundrel*

1951 Solyony, *Three Sisters*, Aldwych, with Re Asherson (Irina) and Harcourt Williams (Chebu kin)

tually put under contract to Tennants for two and a half years.

*You always seem to have played in plays which, for the most part, have been of some distinction. Was this an accident, luck, or was it a very carefully planned scheme?*

No – I can't say that it was planned, because one can never plan anything in the theatre. All I've had is an overall policy. I would always try to work with the best companies that do the best plays. If I've had a choice of play, it might have been playing something in the West End; or it might have been, as it was for instance in 1960, joining Peter Hall to help him create the Royal Shakespeare Company. I would go to the Royal Shakespeare, because a one-off play in the West End wasn't satisfying enough; but the idea of being a part of this new company, which Peter Hall literally inspired, was.

*Do you feel now that you have total control over your performance in a theatre? This usually happens to an actor, if he's lucky, at some stage of his career; he feels in total control of what he is doing, and hence in control of his audience. Now is this something which you invariably feel, or sometimes feel?*

I think 'sometimes feel' is probably the right answer. You see, one doesn't necessarily have control over a performance. One has, as one gets older, more experience and therefore more and more control over one's craft, which is applied at each performance. Depending on the difficulties of the performance, you find it more or less difficult to control it. Now for instance *King Lear*, I would say, is just about the biggest play that's ever been written, and therefore presents the most problems. You cannot control Lear, it's something that's got to happen: the rehearsals and all the performances are merely leading up to trying to make this enormous thing happen. It's an experience, it isn't a play.

*But do you feel in control of the craft?*

I am more in control of the craft now, yes.

*Is it a recent thing?*

Fairly recent, I would say. If you'd call the last eight or ten years recent.

*Am I right in thinking that at least twice in your career you threatened to leave the theatre altogether?*

Oh yes, I do that every week! I think most people, most actors, most artists who are seriously engaged in their work find the problems occasionally too much for them. If you go too hard at the work, then there are too many problems; you want to say, 'No, stop the world, I want to get off.' On two occasions this has happened to me. I had to say, at the time, 'I'm giving it up' because I didn't have enough money to have a long holiday: which was prob-

1952 Boy, *Under the Sycamore Tree*, Aldwych, with Daphne Anderson (Girl) and Alec Guinness (The Scientist)

ably all that was needed. I think that's really all it was. It wasn't a fantastic malaise or anything like that, but there were problems that I couldn't get over, and one needed to get away from the trees to look at the wood.

*You have a reputation as an actor for being very faithful to your author. You try to interpret very exactly what you feel the author meant and don't try to impose your own character on the character that the author has created. Now, you've played in quite a lot of Shaw plays. Do you feel that there are special requirements with regard to Shaw's dialogue?*

I think it's applicable to all dramatists, if the dramatist is serious in his intention and lays down a clear indication of the way it should be done. The indication may appear vague, as some of Shakespeare's plays appear vague and loose. But if you examine the text carefully, you will see that very clear indications are given as to what is required for that play. Now Shaw, of course, is even clearer. He's crystal clear in his indications. Not only do his prefaces set out the whole mood, background, reasons, anti-reasons and all that for the play, but during the play the stage directions are extremely clear. And, of course, the prose itself is so beautifully constructed and so well worth speaking.

*I remember Lewis Casson saying how the whole of Shaw's speeches are orchestrated in a way which is very rare among contemporary dramatists. Did Casson help you a great deal with Shaw?*

He didn't have time to help me personally, because we were doing *St Joan* and I was only the fourth monk from the left at that time and he was playing Cauchon! But to watch him! And the proof of the pudding is in the eating: he says it was orchestrated – he was quite right, because if Sir Lewis, as occasionally happens to all actors, used to dry, forget his words, he would go on singing the tune until he got back on to the words again. And do you know, I'll lay you ten to one that ninety per cent of that audience wouldn't have noticed.

*You recently played Jack Tanner in the BBC Television production of Shaw's* Man and Superman. *How do you think Shaw adapts to television?*

Some speeches have to be cut down for television, and some speeches are in effect spoilt by television. For the simple reason that in the theatre you have one focus, one position. It's like an aria, as it were: you have a set speech and you go through that speech. But in television a camera will break it up and, as soon as you break the visual image, you've somehow lost the oral concentration: there isn't the continuity.

*Did you feel that* Man and Superman *was dated?*

No! Certainly not the ideas, it's the same old male-female battle, the

1955 Horace Van der Gelder, *The Matchmaker*, Br Old Vic, with Jessie Evans (Mrs Levi)

1954 Frank Elgin, *Winter Journey*, Bristol Old Vic,
with Norman Rossington

1968 Jack Tanner, *Man and Superman*, BBC TV,
with Maggie Smith (Ann Whitefield)

battle of the sexes; the ideas in the play are still very clear. I think one tends to think of Shaw as dating; really his ideas have been so absorbed into the general currency of our ideas that we tend to underestimate his original impact.

*As an actor don't you feel that Shaw's characters are sometimes rather lacking in heart?*

I think this is probably true not because Shaw himself was lacking in heart, or anything like that, but merely because his main interest was to get his *ideas* over.

*And he trusted in his actors.*

Well, certainly he was very wise because if you get the best actors then they will be able to fill in the gaps that the dramatist will leave open; a good actor can even make something out of a bad play.

*You played, didn't you, in the Dürrenmatt play,* The Visit, *with the Lunts, Alfred Lunt and Lynn Fontanne?*

It was an extremely stimulating experience, a tripartite experience, because firstly it was by Dürrenmatt, who was a new influence in the theatre, introducing black comedy. It was directed by Peter Brook; and, of course, it had the Lunts. So the stimulus was three-fold. I learnt an enormous amount from Alfred Lunt.

1958 Burgomaster, *The Visit*, Theatre Royal, Brigh and New York

*Can you indicate what kind of things?*

I would say, primarily, simplicity and economy. You know, the half-raised eyebrow is better than the fully raised eyebrow, etc., even on the stage. Alfred is the kind of man who acts with his whole body, which is why he has got this tremendous reputation for back acting. He could turn his back on the audience and still express exactly what he meant, because he was acting with the whole of his back; not consciously, but the whole thing went right through him to such an extent – it's like Blackpool rock, you know, cut it any-where it still says Blackpool!

*But surely this is rather in conflict with what you were saying earlier about your masters, Wolfit and Casson and Atkins, who were teaching you not to be afraid of the big gestures, the big thought and so on. Now you're talking in terms of the man who teaches you that economy is the thing rather than the large-scale performance.*

No, this isn't a contradiction. This is the two ends of the scale, which you must have. I think it was André Gide who said you must go too far before you know how far to go. Therefore, you must be able to go in both directions, you must be able to scale it right down or expand right out. But somebody who sits happily in the middle never does anything. It's like covering a whole syllabus, it's no good specialising.

*Peter Brook, as you said, directed that production. Is he the kind of director that you like working with?*

He is partly the kind of director I like working with. I will work with any director with whom I can maintain a rapport theatrically – and he has this. He has his problems, which used to be the inability to create a personal relationship with the actor. He could create the theatrical relationship, because all the actors respect and admire him; but somehow, there was always a personal thing which wasn't there. I believe it is now.

*Do you yourself have a great inclination to be a director?*

I would like to extend myself in that direction, both in the theatre and in a film or television studio. But this is a terrible habit that people get into these days, you know; they do a couple of films or a couple of plays and they say, 'Well, of course really what I want to do is to be a director.' And lo and behold six months later out comes their first film. But I don't know whether I haven't got the push or whatever it is, or whether I would be a little too painstakingly careful about what I did and how I did it, which would probably absorb all the budget before we even got on to the floor! I don't know. It may happen, it may happen.

*Coming back to your past career, you went as you said in 1960 to the Royal Shakespeare Company, Stratford. This was shortly after you'd won the* Evening Standard *award for the best actor of the year for your perform- ance of Rosmer in Ibsen's* Rosmersholm. *Now you indicated earlier that you liked to go where you were part of a company. Did the Stratford idea work out as you had expected?*

Oh yes, for the first few years at any rate. But events seemed to over- take it. First let me say that, way back in 1956, Peter Hall had originally proposed having a company of actors at the Arts Theatre, a house which could hold some 200 people, and pays 4½d as salary, you know – nothing. The company were then going to subsidise themselves outside the Arts Theatre in other productions, or in films or television. At the Arts the actors would do whatever plays or parts they had always longed to do. So when it came to 1960, Peter Hall virtually said to the same group of people, 'What about coming up to Stratford?' – and again I said yes.

We sailed through the first year on the great cloud of inspiration that Peter had given us. He has a remarkable ability to inspire people; the gift of the gab, I believe it's called! I think he could talk the Queen into abdicating if he wanted to! But, as I said, this was overtaken by events. First of all, the need to get a subsidy from the government – any subsidy; we used not to have one, you see, in 1960. Then finding that the subsidy we were given was too small and that the company couldn't operate, in the way in which it was conceived, on that pittance. Then there was the fight to get it

1959 Rosmer, *Rosmersholm*, Royal Court, with Peggy Ashcroft as Rebecca West

K

increased. Now, the more energy you take up in fighting for money, the less energy you've got to give to work in the theatre. I think probably that is why, in the end, Peter felt that he was worn out or burnt out, to a certain extent.

*It has been said that Peter Hall developed a Stratford style of acting which is a very precise one. Do you feel this as a member of the company still?*

No – sorry to say it quite so abruptly as that. I think we have a Stratford policy, a broad policy, which is to examine the plays of Shakespeare with as careful and as loving an eye as possible. Not to be fooled by what's been done before and accept that it must be habitually done in that particular way. Nor necessarily to go altogether for something new, just because it is new. The idea is to expand ourselves within the play so that we enrich the plays for the audience, and enrich ourselves at the same time. But as regards a Stratford style, this may be apparent in the design or in the approach to design, but I don't think we have yet managed to create a style of acting. Because there are an innumerable number of different styles which come together at the begining of any season; there are always new additions to the company, even though some of the old hands go on. To my mind, there should be – then again it is a question of money – but there should be a form of studio work going on continually. We sometimes manage to cram a tiny little bit in at the end of the season, but it should be going on all the time in order to create a homogeneity in the company.

*Do you feel that Stratford has lost some of the spirit it had in the first couple of years, in 1960–2?*

The pioneering spirit always has to die, does it not, and be taken over by the administrative spirit, shall we say? Once you've set a thing up you've then got to run it. Well, Peter did the inspiring. He did the setting up, he gave us a vision of what could be, and worked at it for eight years. Now he's handed over to Trevor Nunn, who I think is a remarkably brilliant young man. We've only been going nine years, you know; Rome wasn't built in a day.

*What is the normal procedure with the Stratford rehearsals?*

You mean for just putting on a production?

*Yes. For instance, you are not only involved in the occasional studio work, but the physical side of acting is also very much stressed.*

Owing to lack of money, there is not sufficient time devoted to this. But we do try to give to each play its needs. Now, for instance, any play involving a battle scene, the *Histories* for instance, that was a very busy physical year, the sword-fighting went on pretty well continually. It had to; you must keep this going all the time, keep fit, etc., for the simple reason that sometimes fatal injuries can result. I myself had half my thumb nearly chopped off in *Cymbeline*

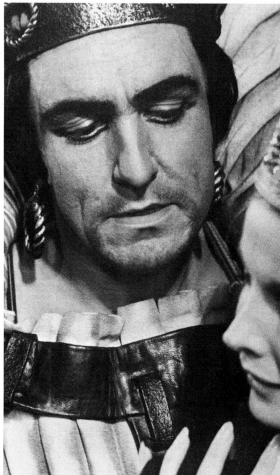

Stratford 1960.

Top, The Duke of Milan, *Two Gentlemen of Verona*, with Denholm Elliot (Valentine)

Bottom left, Leontes, *The Winter's Tale*, with Elizabeth Sellars (Hermione)

Bottom right, Malvolio, *Twelfth Night*

1961 Thomas Becket, *Becket*, Aldwych

Below and opposite:
1962 Macbeth, Stratford, with Irene Worth
as Lady Macbeth

in 1962. There is certainly a concentration on the physical side. Now this year, with *King Lear* for instance, we started a very simple thing, limbering up before we started each day's rehearsal. This, of course, has an immediate effect mentally, because if you are awake physically the blood is going around, being fed to the brain, and the brain is more awake: it's as logical as that. Then, of course, improvisation and things like that are sometimes very physical.

*You said just now that the History cycle made a very busy physical year. Do you not feel that you adapted your performance of Richmond when the plays were recorded for television at the end of the season?*

I'm not sure that one can do Shakespeare successfully on the television screen. Of course one adapted; in fact the whole of the production was adapted for television. We weren't given enough time, of course, and it was an adaptation which took place in the theatre.

*But how far did these productions illustrate Peter Hall's general attitude towards the plays as a whole?*

That season expressed it very clearly. The examination of the plays brought out an enormous number of new illuminations.

*During the production of the History cycle you had as many as three directors on the same play at the same time. This surely led to confusion, didn't it?*

1964 Bolingbroke, *Richard II*, Stratford

No, because in that particular cycle of plays there are very clearly defined areas of activity. With *Richard II*, there is for instance the Bolingbroke–Northumberland faction; then you have the Richard faction – you see, Bolingbroke and Richard II only come together just before the end of the play when they meet at the castle for the abdication scene, so their paths are quite separate. Clifford Williams took over the Bolingbroke political faction and Peter Hall was directing the Richard faction and their coming together. Obviously this was done with a great deal of consultation between all parties. In *Henry IV*, on the other hand, there were three factions: there was Henry IV having established himself as King, this was still Clifford Williams continuing; there were the low-life scenes with Falstaff, Prince Hal; and there were, of course, the other political factions coming in, the bishops and others. Oh yes, it worked quite successfully.

*The Stratford Company is very much a company in its fullest sense, isn't it? I mean the days of rolling up to the theatre, rehearsing, doing the performance, getting home, are over really. It's much more than that now.*

Ideally speaking, shall we say, yes it is. Sometimes, you see, an actor is playing both at the Aldwych and at Stratford. Then all he can do is roll up at the stage door, get the make-up on, give his performance; then go back afterwards to the Aldwych for another performance of another play.

*Do you like this emphasis on physical teamwork as well as the theatrical teamwork?*

Yes indeed, when one has got the energy and the time to do it. Now, for instance, this last season has been a sort of pathologic experience doing *Lear* and *Faustus*, it certainly took me by surprise. I didn't expect it to be like that at all.

*In terms of physical strain?*

In terms almost of mental strain. There is an oppressiveness about *King Lear* which is almost insurmountable. Paul Scofield felt it too, according to Peter Brook; he said Paul felt this enormous oppression about the play. I doubt very much whether one can really give it one's all more than twice a week, and preferably at widely spaced performances. It's something that rolls towards one like a great thunder cloud, the sky gets darker and darker and everything that one does is coloured by the thought – I've got to play *Lear* later on this week. It's been a very depressing season!

*You said that maybe you can reach something of the ideal performance twice a week.*

I don't say the ideal performance – just to be able to *do* it. The ideal performance you might reach – maybe twice a season.

*Do you have any awareness of when that is likely to happen? I mean, do you feel it coming on you or do you suddenly realise, half way through the performance, that this is happening?*

You feel it almost as soon as you walk on the stage; certainly not before then. This has nothing to do with you, it's something that happens. It's something from the audience, something from the rest of the actors: it suddenly goes click. As soon as you walk on the stage you know that it has happened. Half the company will say something about it as soon as they walk off because they've all felt it. It's the only reason why one is an actor really; and there are only very rare occasions when one gets this feeling.

*You first played Lear at the Bristol Old Vic in 1955, thirteen years ago. How much of your current performance did you base on the earlier one?*

One tries not to base a performance on anything that has gone before; one tries to look at it entirely differently. But, of course, one is still the same person, the same actor, and reads the same play with the same sensitivity and imagination.

*But you're thirteen years older now.*

Yes, but I don't think it makes all that much difference. We're talking about basic approaches now. Obviously, details are entirely different, and even the appearance. The Bristol make-up was quite consciously based on the self-portrait of Leonardo da Vinci. This year's

1963 Pope Pius XII, *The Representative*, Aldwych

Stratford production, contrary to a number of critics, is not based on Tolstoy or any of the Russians – this was a criticism that was levelled at it. I don't think we mentioned Tolstoy once during the whole of the rehearsals. The Stratford make-up grew out of a conception based on the play, what it needed and what our production needed to express it. As you say, I'm thirteen years older; and there are areas of the play which we now probe which were never apparent in the Bristol production.

*Which ones, for instance?*

Well you see, Trevor Nunn is one of those directors who does his homework to the *n*th degree, so he came fully charged with all the analytical side and the psychological, spiritual this and that very much at his fingertips. This was a tremendous help at the rehearsals, because he was able to answer almost any query that one would put up. At least, he would be able to give us a satisfactory reason or an indication of where we could find the answer. There aren't any particular areas that I can think of now – you know, it's just that the whole play, for me anyway, this time has gone deeper.

*You were speaking earlier of some of the physical and mental strains involved in playing Lear. What about the strain of the make-up? Is this a problem?*

At times certainly. I have to be in the theatre at least two hours before the curtain goes up in order to do the whole thing – literally from top to toe. I have to whiten my whole body in order to try and make it look old, because in this particular production I do what one didn't do at Bristol and I don't think many productions do – that is, when he says, 'Unbutton here,' meaning take off all our clothes, I actually do go down as far as one possibly can. The make-up is a problem, shall we say, but not so much a strain. What is a strain, during the summer, is the wearing of the costumes, which I've not actually weighed but I've got three separate cloaks and tunics, each of which must weigh something like 50 lb.

*Have you changed your performance a lot during the course of the season?*

No, not a lot. Because it was quite firmly directed at the beginning and therefore we have retained the basic structure. Obviously there's still flexibility within the structure in order to expand or contract.

*When you embark upon the playing of one of the great classical roles like Lear, do you make a point of studying all the scholarly commentaries?*

I never read anybody else's comments on characters or performance. I might occasionally investigate or consult a book about a particular aspect of meaning in the text. For instance, one likes to work from the Arden Shakespeare which is a very good text.

King Lear. 1956 Bristol Old Vic; 1968 Stratford

*You indicated earlier that you have been influenced to some degree in the playing of Lear by the performance of Donald Wolfit.*

Ah well, that is different because –

*Yes, I was going to ask you whether in fact you take in what you remember from other performances rather than what you read about them.*

You can't take from a performance what you read about it because a performance is a living visual experience, it is the one thing that the theatre still has over television and films. No, you can only take from a living performance. Since I was in Wolfit's *Lear* for so long, there are obviously certain things, certain tunes, certain lines, that I cannot eradicate. He got the meaning out of the line, the line meant that to me; therefore if I say that line, somehow I have to, or can't escape giving it, that inflection. But as regards academic studies, I'm not very good at that, I'm afraid.

*During your years at Stratford you played in two of Marlowe's plays,* The Jew of Malta *and* Doctor Faustus. *Now from an actor's point of view do you find Marlowe a difficult playwright to interpret?*

Yes and no. The difficulty arises from the fact that one has to fill in a great deal of what Marlowe left out: this is certainly the case with *Faustus*. It is one of his earlier plays, and is, to my mind, a lesser play than *The Jew of Malta*; in fact, it's hardly a play at all. The fragments that we've got are almost non-existent really; there are so many different versions written by playwrights, managers, other actors, that you can virtually take a choice of what you wish to play. In fact, during the rehearsals we would frequently come across a line which didn't quite sound as if it fitted in with the rest of the main concept; so we'd go to another version and find the similar line, slightly different, which would fit in. He's a much lesser playwright than Shakespeare, but he did lead the way. He showed Shakespeare what could be done, and Shakespeare did it.

*You also played Shakespeare's Shylock as a companion piece to* The Jew of Malta, *didn't you?*

Yes. This was the most extraordinary contrast. The two approaches to the actual subject of Jewishness, shall we say, are totally different. Shylock is bitter, introverted, driven inside himself by the antagonism of society; Marlowe's Barabas is the complete extrovert, and as soon as society antagonises him, he hits back with everything he's got, which is not inconsiderable! These two entirely different characters present a sensitive approach to a problem. Barabas shows us a man's determination to win through and prove himself in the face of everything, but with no bitterness – well, if there is bitterness, it is humorous and sardonic. But it is not the biting, acid bitterness that there is in Shylock.

1965 Barabas, *The Jew of Malta*, Stratford, with T[ Church (Governor of Malta)

1968 Faustus, *Dr Faustus*, Strat

1967 Cyrano, *Cyrano de Bergera*
BBC TV, with Georgin
Simpson (Orange girl) an
Jerome Willis (Le Bret)

*You've seldom played in comedy, have you?*

Oh yes, I think I've had a fair share of comedy. Not so much in the last ten years, because I suppose it just happens that I've got that sort of face or personality or whatever it is, that seems to say, oh yes, well he's a big butch type, he can play the big butch parts, the Bolingbrokes, the Henry IVs, and things like that. I would like to play more comedy; in fact I would like to play more modern comedy. Jack Tanner, for instance, is high comedy. There is a necessity there to be conscious of the comedic element in an audience even though one was playing in a television studio. It's a question of opportunity, yes. I certainly don't try to avoid it.

*After* The Forsyte Saga, *you did* Cyrano de Bergerac *for television. Was this your choice?*

Yes, it was. The BBC was very kind and asked what I would like to do. I did name one or two plays which unfortunately, because of film rights and various other things, weren't available for television. For instance, answering your previous question about comedy, I would like to have had a shot at *Alfie*. Which may set you back by the heels somewhat –

*But* Cyrano *it was.*

*Cyrano* it was. That came as an inspiration at one point, because although I've always liked the play, for some reason or other I had for the moment forgotten it, and then suddenly it came back with a rush and I said, of course, and we did it.

*Do you see a pattern for your career from now on? Or are you entirely at the mercy of every wind that blows, theatrically speaking?*

I don't see a pattern. I just see a continuation, one hopes, of the policy I explained earlier, of doing good plays with splendid companies. In this respect I shall obviously go on working for the Royal Shakespeare Company on and off, as I have been working for them for the last nine years. I also don't wish to do only Shakespeare for the rest of my life. In fact the pattern is one of jumping from medium to medium, in order to keep oneself fresh in all three – theatre, films and television.

1965 Shylock, *The Merchant of Venice*, Stratford, with Janet Suzman (Portia)

# Vanessa Redgrave

VANESSA REDGRAVE established her potential as an actress in 1961, playing Rosalind in the Royal Shakespeare's *As You Like It*. 'This Rosalind is a creature of fire and light', wrote Bernard Levin, 'her voice a golden gate opening on lapis lazuli hinges, her body a supple reed rippling in the breeze of her love. This is not acting at all, but living, breathing, loving.' It was a performance transparent with emotion, a lovely unselfconscious abandon. Here was an actress, you felt, miraculously endowed with the gift of being and giving herself on stage.

It wasn't a miracle, of course. Vanessa Redgrave comes from a theatrical home, three generations of players. But this did not make her a natural actress; her early photographs show a reticent, thoughtful child, awkwardly tall for the stage. She trained for three years at the Central School of Speech and Drama, in repertory at Frinton-on-Sea, then in minor West End parts. Stella, in Robert Bolt's *The Tiger and the Horse*, sums them up pretty well. 'Intellectually and morally advanced, but untried emotionally, she has the candour and generosity of an even younger person, but can also be awkwardly didactic, unseasonably serious.' In those days, she suffered from stiffness, worry about her height, a tendency to withhold movement for fear of gawkiness.

But in *A Touch of the Sun* and *The Tiger and the Horse* she played opposite perhaps our finest emotional actor, the best British exponent of Stanislavsky's doctrine of playing from the bowels. Michael Redgrave's Orlando, in 1936, was the father to his daughter's Rosalind. It was a gale of feeling – significantly her playing of the part coincided with her passionate engagement in the cause of nuclear disarmament and her arrest during a sit-down demonstration in Trafalgar Square.

But after Rosalind, what? How to jump the gap – which all English actresses come up against, for lack of women's parts in our classical repertory – from romantic heroines to the mature, complex women of Shakespeare, Ibsen, Chekhov. In 1964, she appeared as Nina in her husband's, Tony Richardson's, production of Chekhov's *The Seagull*. It was a different *Seagull*, a different Nina. Instead of the usual feast of Russian emotionalism, we were given an icy, objective study of bored middle-class *rentiers*, playing with their feelings. Nina, their victim, became the one character strong enough to break away and work seriously at her profession. In the last scene she returns and recites once more the vision of a dying planet written for her by Konstantin. Usually the actress fills it with tragic feeling – Nina understands desolation now. Vanessa Redgrave brought the words out dryly, almost contemptuously. This Nina felt no regret for innocence lost. She'd had enough of poetry, passion, despair. 'I'm a seagull – no, that's not it.' Ruthlessly before your eyes, she cut free the part of her mind which hankered still after symbols, youth, romance.

To some extent it seems a mutilation. Of all our actresses (as her Catherine showed in the television serial of Hemingway's *Farewell to Arms*) she has the gift of surrender to emotion, like a gull in the wind. But clearly, like Nina, she's come to distrust this facility; and in the long run it is not enough. The great roles call for more than romantic acting, identification of oneself with the character. They need observation, detachment, placing of the character in his context and society – the kind of acting known technically as comic. Vanessa Redgrave has always had a saving comic intelligence. As the rich, spoiled Leonie in the film *Morgan*, we saw her sharpen it.

In *The Prime of Miss Jean Brodie*, she wielded it like a spear. The stage has known tall English roses before, who could incarnate the beauty of Shakespeare and Tennyson. None of them could make it funny. That's the weapon which may see Vanessa Redgrave through the trough English actresses face in mid-career.

*Ronald Bryden*

CLIVE GOODWIN: *The critics stood and cheered you on the first night, when you played Rosalind in* As You Like It *at Stratford in 1961. It seems as if you were born to play that part. Did you feel that when you first knew that you were going to play it?*

VANESSA REDGRAVE: What was great about it was that when I read it for the first time it was a script, it wasn't an old play or book.

*You'd never seen the play before.*

I had, and I hadn't ever liked it particularly, except that you go wild if someone says do you want to play Rosalind, because you know that it's a smashing and a strange part. But I'd never seen any production that made me love the play as I did when I actually read it. I don't know why it was, maybe I had read a lot of Elizabethan literature and poems, at a time which was very vivid sensually and physically for me. I feel as if I've lived in it to a certain extent, through Elizabethan prose and some of those Elizabethan short stories, for instance. I guess I had read so much that, since most of *As You Like It* is written in prose, it didn't seem removed from me. Any strange antique turns of expression seemed like a fun way of talking, like the way we talk now, mixing in all sorts of things which will sound like very antique, weird ways of speaking to people a hundred years from now; it's just our free and easy way of talking.

*There are some phrases that come to mind, there was one in that speech 'Come to my cote'.*

Yes, one can think of 'cote' as being like come to my 'pad'. I don't know that I did it like that, but 'Come to my cote and woo me', I felt was like 'Come to my pad'. I think that was partly because of the kind of work that Peter Hall had already been doing. I had already got something of his feeling for words although this wasn't Peter Hall's production.

*Peter Hall, the director of the Royal Shakespeare Company.*

Yes, in his work on *A Midsummer Night's Dream*, which was the first time I ever worked at Stratford, one of its interests, apart from some of the performances in it, was that he helped actors rediscover the language. So that instead of talking in an old, antique, Shakespearean way the actors found ways of taking a sentence and making it sound like a modern sentence. For instance – the girl playing the Fairy, instead of dancing around in a fairylike way and saying, 'I will now go and hang a pearl in every cowslip's ear,' was terribly tired and said, 'I'll go and hang a pearl in every cowslip's ear.' That's an example of Peter's direction. I think he was the initiator of a new outlook. In the same way Peter O'Toole brought out 'Thou flea, thou nit' in *The Taming of the Shrew*. Shakespeare's packed with these sort of things, isn't he?

1961 Rosalind, *As You Like It*, Stratford

161

L

1961 Rosalind, *As You Like It*, with
Bannen (Orlando) and Rosalind Kn
(Celia)

*Jan Kott, the Polish Shakespeare expert, said recently that* As You Like It *is really like Christine Keeler around the swimming pool. Did you have this kind of modern attitude towards the play?*

I think that's a particularly odd sort of comparison. I haven't read Kott on *As You Like It*. I read him on some of the Histories and I really don't go for it much.

I never looked for a modern parallel, nor did Michael Elliott, the director. All I was trying to explain was that Shakespeare's speech was totally familiar to me, although it's a special speech, a very meticulous prose, with very difficult phrasing, lengthy strings of words which you have to treat as you would a phrase of music – begin, follow through and not let it drop. I don't think the actual situation in *As You Like It* has a modern parallel and I wouldn't particularly try to find one, because I was taught to think about it by Michael. This was the way he saw it. The journey to the Forest of Arden was almost like *Pilgrim's Progress*, it was the progress to the place where you may find yourself and also find another person, and make a union with that other person. This was for him the whole central theme of *As You Like It*, everybody who goes to Arden was looking for themselves, and most of them find themselves and the one they love. Jaques doesn't, of course. Now I don't think this very mystical approach has a modern parallel because today there is a general kind of fear of abandonment of self that will lead to knowledge of self and knowledge of somebody else. It's easy to think of *As You Like It* in terms of a romance because it is a delicious romance, and it's a comic romance. But it's a very ambiguous romance because you have the girl as a boy; you have this strange Elizabethan ambiguity of a man wondering if he is in love with a man or a boy or who he is in love with. For us today there's just no parallel because for a start there's no ambiguity. Either you're a man and you love another man, or you're a woman and you love another woman, or you're a woman and you love a man. I mean it's fairly clear. But it was troubling in Shakespeare's time, I guess, and very fascinating and enriching.

*You don't think Shakespeare wrote that simply to get over the problem of having boys play the girls' parts?*

That's what they all say, but it doesn't interest me thinking about it; that's for the scholars to think about. The marriage ceremony, at the very end of *As You Like It*, in all the productions I've done, which were goodish productions, I guess, was treated as a rather jolly, happy, romantic dance, a wedding feast. But for Michael the middle of that forest was almost like a church, but much bigger and, at the same time, more intimate than a church.

> 'Then there is mirth in Heaven
> When earthly things made even
> Atone together.'

Rosalind

163

We've lost interest in this marvellous paradox of a quest, and joy and mirth, atonement, guilt, remorse, exquisite pleasure, all touching each other like this, and producing a kind of a harmony; I don't know if we're after these kind of things at the moment, are we?

*I don't think we are; though a lot of people are telling us that we are. Let's get back to the question of the speaking of verse. I think you once said that there is a speech of Imogen's in* Cymbeline *which is one of the most difficult in all of Shakespeare.*

That came up because Imogen is a part I want to play again, since I wasn't ready for it when I played it in 1962. As you know it's written, from Imogen's point of view, in roughly two halves: the first half when she is a woman, and the second half when she is disguised as a boy. It's written very differently when she's a boy, she speaks very little except for one passionate speech which is almost reportage. It's the speech when she discovers the body without a head, the only long speech there is in the second half of the play. It's almost like that reporter who is describing the R101, the airship that crashed in flames. Do you remember? There's a sound recording of the reporter who is reporting its flight and then suddenly saw it burst into flames. He is describing it on the spot as it happens, he's going wild, and words, strange words, are coming out jerkily; not ordinary words, but words that, if you see them in cold print, seem like melodrama. People have always thought that *Cymbeline* was rather melodramatic; I've never thought it was – not when it works. In the 'Oh for a horse with wings' speech, you have a situation in which she has just read a letter saying 'come to me', it is from the man she loves, Posthumus, saying, 'come to me, meet me at Milford Haven'. I've always found emotional situations very easy to sense and to be involved in immediately; to be flooded with longing, excitement, happiness. To visualise Posthumus is something that is very easy, particularly if you've been playing all the scenes beforehand in which you have doubted whether you are going to see the person you love *ever* again, waiting for news from him, and have almost given up hope. However, for the first time, I discovered that just emotion will not do.

*When you say emotion will not do, what exactly do you mean?*

Now let me try and find what I mean. Emotion is like a flow of energy which is there inside you whichever way it's being directed; whatever thoughts are stirring this energy, it comes out in a thousand different ways. It is an energy which is contained within you and is then channelled out. With a naturalistic play you can let it almost come out anyhow. But Shakespeare has used certain words which convey with such exquisite differentials his changing thoughts, so that if they are overlaid, if they are stuffed full of all this emotion, overstressed – although something quite

164

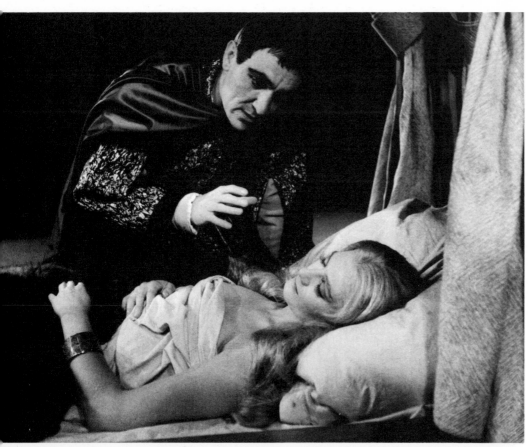

good may be happening with you – it's not good for Shakespeare; you might as well be improvising or doing any old play. Shakespeare has found some very particular, marvellous words to convey things that are far more precise than a great splurge of general emotion can convey. When I watched the recording of *As You Like It* just now there were a few good moments in it, but what was killing me was that I wouldn't let the words just speak for themselves. I wouldn't speak anything simply; I was overlaying, overlaying, overlaying; it's so heavy and overdone. I wasn't like that all the way through the telly production, I remember – but I think I was influenced a lot by what I'd done in the theatre at Stratford. I don't think one should do it on stage either. But the stage is asking for things to be overlaid because you're trying to reach up to that 'remember the boy at the back of the gallery, face out front and give it to 'em', you know. And it is true that in giving it to the people way back up there, you start to overlay. I have often sat and watched a production from the front row of the stalls which I have previously watched at the back of the dress circle, and felt appalled by something which I had been extremely interested and excited by from the back. I try to remember that when I act – you can't remember it enough. But unfortunately, watching *As You Like It* just now, there was one point when I was quivering: everything's there; I remember I was certainly feeling it and I think you can see that I'm feeling it; but the emotion is just too much because those words will do everything for you. A good example is Lear's speech, 'Blow wind and crack your cheeks'. Every time you use the word 'thunder' for instance, the word 'thunder' has the sound in it, an immediate connotation; you don't need to say 'THUNDER'; 'thunder' does it. In the same way, 'Will you come to my cote and we'll meet?' can be said very simply.

*Let's go back now, Vanessa, to the day you were born – in fact I'd like to ask you if this story is true. The evening of the day you were born, your birth was announced from the stage of the Old Vic by Sir Laurence Olivier where your father was playing Laertes and Sir Laurence Olivier was playing Hamlet. Sir Laurence said: 'Today a lovely young actress was born.' Now that seems that it was a foregone conclusion you were going to be an actress.*

Well, I don't know; I mean, it makes a gorgeous story to tell people; but are you after why I did in fact end up being an actress?

*I'm interested to know if you always did think you were going to be an actress or if you ever wanted to be anything else.*

I wanted to dance; I trained to be a dancer for a long time – that's what I wanted to do – goodness knows why. Something about the combination of music and movement fills me with something. I think I would have been quite a good dancer, probably very good; anyway, I'm far too big as you can see. And so acting was the near-

1962  Katharina, *The Taming of the Shrew*, Stratford, with
Derek Godfrey (Petruchio)

est thing. The thing about acting – and I try to remember it sometimes, when I'm bogging myself down making far too many difficulties for myself – is that it is simply a question of make-believe:
for me it is anyway. When I was a child there weren't many things to
do because of the war, and being in the country you could get lots of
outside fun: we used to improvise, day long, weeks on end, for years
and years. It was like the Pearl White series. My brother and I
improvised situations with characters; so from that, and knowing
that there was a profession close at hand, a profession in which you
could go on doing this, I just carried on.

*You mean that you found it was a game you could actually make a living at?*

Yes. Sometimes I think it's very much part of Dame Syb.'s acting,
particularly when she and Sir Lewis get together on their evening's
entertainment, when it's just the two of them in their chairs and
they have nothing else at all. You'll see them doing a scene from
*The Trojan Women* perhaps, Sir Lewis will be playing the Messenger
and Dame Syb. will be doing Andromache's speech about the death
of her son. Suddenly Sir Lewis will turn his back to the audience
and lift an imaginary trumpet and go bo-bo-bo-bō, bo-bo-bo-bō,
making Dame Syb.'s sound effect for her. I've always remembered
that, because it's so simple, it's nothing and yet it's everything. I
thought of it a lot because, with a play like *Cymbeline*, many people
find it hard to take, hard to believe in. I don't find it particularly
hard; but at moments when I did I thought of Sir Lewis lifting that
trumpet to his lips. I think of the hundred and one times in the production of *Cymbeline* when I lifted a piece of material, and I was then
in the middle of a storm because I put it round my shoulders –
something stupidly simple like that. It makes 'if' a reality, something becomes alive and immediately you have thunder whether
there's thunder in the production or not – it may be much better
for the production if there isn't any thunder, but it is there in your
imagination.

*So you began your career conventionally enough by going to a drama school,
the Central School. Is that what you wanted to do?*

Yes, it was absolutely what I wanted to do. There was a brief
moment, because of the singing and dancing, when I thought I'd
start musical comedy, right from the bottom, and carry on training
as a dancer and singer; you know, audition to get into choruses and
so on. But then I thought I really do want to be in plays and it's
going to be much more difficult getting into plays if I've never
worked on the processes of acting. So I went to Central. It was a
very important time for me because I was a very, very slow grower,
very, very slow.

*Mentally?*

No, I don't think so slow mentally, but with a hundred different blocks. I had tremendous voice problems all the way through Central, which I couldn't seem to get rid of, and didn't until afterwards, when I guess all the work that had been done at Central took effect. In fact I'm still benefiting from sensations that I learnt to recognise in the placing of my voice; where I'm trying to place it in my head and my nose; getting it away from straining at my throat, the loose jaw. When I first learnt these things they weren't any use to me, because I couldn't make them work, but I can now.

*Did you enjoy your time at Central? Did you learn a great deal?*

I read a great deal, because I hadn't really read anything of drama, literature or poetry, ever before. I don't know, it's always hard working out what you learnt and when you learnt it, and even why you learnt it. I think I first discovered at Central what a play is about, why am I in this scene, what has been my background, what do I want as a character, what am I after. In fact a lot of these things happened through discussing them with the other students, and by reading Stanislavsky. When I was a student, I didn't realise that the *doing* is three-quarters of it; through an infinite variety of *doing* something, you discover what it *is* afterwards. Whereas at Central one tended to be too careful, too fearful, too cautious, too inhibited.

*Would you say more or less attention might be paid to Stanislavsky in the training of young actors and actresses?*

I think a lot more attention could be paid to Stanislavsky in so far as there is, still, a great deal of very messy acting. By which I mean that one generalises situations, generalises actions, physical actions, tries for effect instead of just aiming for what you want as a character and then letting what happens happen – because somebody else doesn't want you to have it, or is in conflict with you. Stanislavsky writes of particular ways of finding concentration, of true concentration; this I found very helpful but then there are a hundred ways of finding concentration. I find it difficult talking about it now because that is a stage I went through then. A great deal of what I read of Stanislavsky I still find to be true in certain circumstances, but not in others.

*There must be things that you have found out in the last five years about acting, things which possibly you would have liked to have been told about when you were at drama school. Are there?*

No. I can only find one specific thing, and that's from where I am now. I would like to have worked five hundred times more, increasingly rather than decreasingly, through the years of training on my voice and movement. So that it became such a habit that I couldn't deviate from that kind of work. A great deal of ground was covered which is still in my mind, but I had so much work to do, I think one could have worked far harder on these things as a group, because I now think it is of the utmost importance for one's body, that means one's speech and movement – if you can separate them, which you can't really – to be so obedient to the impulses that come, that they obey you.

*Do you still work on your voice and movement?*

Yes I do, a lot. This may be because for so many years I had such difficulty, and still do; and because I studied ballet and am insatiable to do 'forty more' – when I'm already tired out with doing the first forty. I don't know. Every night before the performance I do certain physical exercises which I have done with Litz,* either in her open classes or alone with her in the course of productions. I do them every single night because I know that when I'm strong and my back is the source of strength, I feel the earth beneath my feet, I feel something going right up through me, I feel something very strong and yet clean and washed all the way through. I could be very fast or very slow, my mind's very alert; whatever the mind arrives at, my body is ready to do because I'm not stiff. As Jean Brodie I couldn't do it if I didn't work on my voice and movement every single day; because the lengths of sentences dictate absolutely – that I must be able to speak at certain speeds, and without taking breaths here and there. Then I can develop a speech following absolutely the impulse of the thought, so that the words come out quickly and I'm not bothering about whether I can be heard or not. I know I can because my voice is placed bang there and in my nose a little bit, my jaw is relaxed, my back is supple, so that the air flows quite easily without fixing my ribs to hold my breath – the breath is streaming up; and let's hope my mind's working too.

It's very hard to be specific because as soon as I want to say anything about what I think, it changes; I then think of a contradiction and it is the contradiction in work, and in everything, that fascinates me. What besets me about acting myself, or watching other people, is that there isn't a pattern and we shouldn't look for a pattern at all; it's an effect which I don't think has any relation to holding a mirror up to life. If one's trying to hold a mirror up to life, which I guess one is, then don't let us think, as so many playwrights would, that we're dying to make a pattern, either as actors or producers, – trying to make a pattern out of it. What's interesting is that there isn't a pattern and we shouldn't look for a pattern; try and seize the odd moments and let them make up what they will.

*You made your reputation as a classical actress. Yet, in one of the few television plays that you've done,* Maggie, *you were seen standing literally at a kitchen sink. Did you enjoy that experience?*

I did because I had done a whole stint of Shakespeare and I wanted very much to do a modern play. As I told you, in *As You Like It* I

* Litz Pisk was director of movement at the Central School of Speech and Drama and has choreographed dances and movement for stage and film productions.

overlaid everything, stressed every single word. But by the time I did *Maggie* it had all quietened down a lot. It has nothing to do with the fact that it's modern or Shakespeare. There shouldn't be any difference. But I'd cut down layers of sheer movement, facial movement, stressing all the words and so on. I was still popping my eyes though. So the lesson from *Maggie* – you know it sounds terribly silly, but the lesson from *Maggie* is, never pop your eyes.

*Do you think there is a definite technique required for acting in front of a camera, or is it just a reduction?*

No, it isn't a reduction at all. At least, I don't think of it as a reduction, unless you think in terms of the sheer volume necessary for reaching that boy at the back of the gallery.

What's different is that you learn to trust on thought and impulse much more. That's to say, you learn that if you are really thinking something, it can be seen. On top of that you don't have to indicate facially, physically, vocally, as the theatre encourages you to do; the thought in one's mind will come through. You learn to catch the rhythms and temperatures of the way we all go about in our normal everyday lives.

*So you did in fact learn something from television which you could take back to the theatre, because Ralph Richardson once said that what you learn in the theatre you then sell to the cinema.*

That might be a way of putting it but I feel that what I'm learning through working in the cinema may help to make my work in the theatre better.

*I'd like to change the subject, Vanessa. You've always been very politically involved. You've been arrested three times on various CND demonstrations and you've canvassed for the Labour Party. Has this political interest had any influence on your career as an actress?*

I don't think it has had any influence on my career. It has seemed to me to have an influence on all my parts.

I can pick out three things, if one thinks of it totally in terms of acting. At the time I was playing *As You Like It*, the very first season at Stratford, I became involved with the Committee of 100. There was the Berlin Crisis, and one of the first big sitdown demonstrations. Everybody who went to that demonstration didn't know quite what would happen, but thought that it was going to be the clink for about a month or something like that. In playing the performance that night before I went off to that demonstration, I found that my whole body, my eyes and my ears, were more awake than perhaps they had been for years and years. It sounds rubbishy to talk about it; you know how old Wordsworth goes on and on about, oh if I could recapture the vision of a child, because everything was so keen, so acute, it makes you so aware of other people, of yourself, of the wonder of just what we are physically, mentally – the horror, the particular and the general. Well, during that performance I felt as if I must be acting better because I was more aware of the people I was playing with than I had ever been before. It is something of that feeling of 'you may be seeing them for the last time'; this is dramatising it a lot because I knew I'd see them again.

It brings us back to the Elizabethans and what drives me as an actress. It drives Nina in *The Seagull*, it drives any kind of acting, really, since what we are after is people trying to communicate with each other; interacting with each other, doing things to each other, asking for things from each other, looking for an awareness of other people in ourselves. I have found that awareness, as a result of experiencing things much bigger than anything I had ever known; of events, of situations that had a reality such as I had never known. Because after all one lives, mostly, a very calm, safe, quiet life; socially speaking we may go through emotional drama but that's something else: this increased my awareness.

Another example is when the English Stage Company were working on *Joan of the Stockyards*, which actually I never got to doing because I was ill. I had read up reams of material about the years of the Depression; I'd read the biographies of Aneurin Bevan, I'd read about political action, the strikes, the background, the social circumstances of people, the attitudes and words of conflicting sides, conflicting opinions. I had myself been through a three-stage political development in that I had started from somebody who believed that all was right with the world and how wonderful everything was, to thinking something's a bit wrong, I ought to be giving a bit of the happiness I've got to somebody else, i.e. you start giving to charity and so on; and then to thinking that there are certain things that we as groups of people can do to help each other as individuals. I'd gone in fact from being a very religious young girl of the Church of England to being a Liberal, to being a Socialist, myself. I'd been through all these trains of thought; I had also started as a Conservative.

*Joan of the Stockyards* also goes through being a Salvation Army worker, sincerely wanting to do something for the poor, then becoming a Liberal, and finally realising that all this was still not enough. And so my own development, whether you call it political, social or just as a human being, plus all the reading that I've done because I'm interested in politics, meant that I had an understanding of the play that I would not have had otherwise; even though it may not have made me act it any better – that's another thing.

When people talk of the Brechtian approach to acting, they fix not on important things but the externals. They think of bare stages, of lights that can be seen, fairly ordinary costumes and a few certain well-chosen physical props: what's called the epic approach

1964 Nina, *The Seagull*, Queen's, with George Dev (Sorin)

172

to scenes. But I think the Brechtian approach is this, to remember always that when you are hungry, a whole lot of values do not exist for you and cannot exist for you. When you're not hungry values can start coming in and all sorts of particular discriminations: there is a world of difference. It's as basic as that. If I'm hungry I may murder. I may. Me. I might murder. Because I'm hungry. If I'm not hungry I will not murder.

*You said there was a third example.*

In *Joan of the Stockyards* there's a great deal of action which concerns groups of the unemployed hanging around the factory gates practically at starvation level, agitating for work. This continues right throughout the play; these people manœuvred by the owners of the factories, the Salvation Army people and the middlemen in the play. Well, I was thinking how fantastically difficult most of the actors found it to portray convincingly what it was like to have been cold for six months, to have eaten rubbish – or less than rubbish – for six months, to have been angry for six months, and then the way you act when you get a bowl of soup. The actors were saying, what's this awful noodle soup; need I drink it? I'm not getting it down on them; this just happened; it's natural in our social circumstances – we are comfortable, we have lost the perception of the fact that there were things floating in the liquid. If you have a historical awareness of what it was like, it doesn't matter whether it's the 1920s or the 1600s or the 1300s, actually to have bits floating, then put yourself into that state of mind, and you, as an actor, could never say to the director, must I drink this soup? It would be so vividly aware to you how you would need that soup. That's what I was thinking of.

*Have you ever turned down a part because you disagreed with the sentiments expressed in the play?*

Oh no. I mean I'd probably be even more fascinated by disagreeing with it. But when you say disagree with the sentiments of a play, do you mean that the play might arrive at or present a conclusion that I don't agree with?

*Yes.*

Present a philosophy that I don't agree with. No, I don't think I could do that.

*You've just made a very successful film,* Morgan, A Suitable Case for Treatment, *and in it David Warner played Morgan and you played his wife, Leonie. This was really a new departure for you as an actress. How did you come to be cast for it?*

I don't know, Karel Reisz just wanted me. I think he'd seen me at a party and I was looking lovely that night.

1964 Nina, *The Seagull*, with Peter McEnery (Konsta

174

*Were you nervous when you saw the script?*

Oh no, it was a marvellous script, because the director Karel Reisz and David had worked so closely together and spent a lot of time on it.

*Had you seen the television play?*

No, and I hadn't done a film for nine years. So I had a kind of Pavlov dog reaction; because I had been very nervous when I'd done the film nine years before; at that time I had never done a film before and I was shaking with nerves. But when I started in *Morgan* I realised that time had moved on and things were different.

*Had you turned down film parts in those nine years?*

No. Nobody wanted me. It's as simple as that. But the lovely thing about Leonie was, it was the first time I had had a part in which I, as a character, hadn't got a whole load of principles, a whole load of motives, a whole load of wants, fixed wants; I just responded totally to the situations I found myself in and reacted without any kind of pattern at all. Maybe because of Leonie, because of working with Karel, or working with Tony [Richardson] and then working with Michelangelo Antonioni, it has totally changed how I feel about working on acting.

*Michelangelo Antonioni who was directing the film* Blow Up, *which you've just finished shooting?*

1965 Leonie, *Morgan, A Suitable Case for Treatment*

Yes. So that what one is after in acting is this: knowing that I, myself, in my own real life will do things in a situation that as an actress I would find inconceivable, noticing more and more that contradiction is the essence of any kind of human activity, that is what I'm after. When I was working with Karel Reisz on *Morgan* I would start to say, 'Well now, how do I think of it, what is the character about?' He said, 'We'll discover each bit as it comes, and finally it will all add up to something or it won't.' And that is now how I conceive of things; I conceive of our lives as being like that. Maybe it adds up to something or maybe it doesn't, but the particular event of each moment is sufficient unto itself.

*Technically, of course, there's a big difference for the actor between working in the cinema and in theatre. For instance, the amount of physical freedom you have is much more limited in the cinema, especially working with a director like Michelangelo Antonioni, who I understand is very particular, very deliberate about your physical line and shape in a part.*

Yes. I'll try to be very precise because if it's a good director, it all ends up much the same. It's his vision, his perception and how he looks at things that counts; it's totally one man's pair of eyes and ears and mind. Take Michelangelo for instance, if there is a scene in which two people are talking to each other, he will have worked

1965 Leonie, *Morgan*, with David Wa
(Morgan) and Robert Stephens (Na

out – how I don't know of course – but he will have worked out already, before you come along, that he would like you to sit down at this moment and to sit down perhaps like that; and then suddenly to stand up like that and walk over to a very precise point against a wall so that one is nearly, but not quite, juxtaposed against another physical object, whatever it is, a cupboard, a pillar, a beam, a chair. Well that's really neither here nor there; it's just that he works that way. But within that framework there is a freedom of communication; I'm trying to understand what he wants me to do and, at the same time, feel that I do.

Then for instance with Tony [Richardson], we'll all get together and we'll say, well now we've got these chairs and this bit of room; let's just see what happens. Then we, the actors, will talk and maybe we'll slump in the chairs any old way, or maybe we won't even sit in the chairs at all. Then he'll begin to create something out of what one's doing, and eventually – or probably very quickly, if it's Tony – he'll catch at something we've all arrived at together, which of course he is actually seeing visually.

*Antonioni is completely different.*

Well Antonioni is different in that he has already decided before he starts shooting the actors that what he does will communicate something not only visually, but of situation and character. But it's only two directors' different ways of seeing the same thing, the visual image. For the actor it is something wildly different. The interesting thing is that I feel as free doing all the physical movements that Michelangelo gives me as I do when I am doing them myself in improvisation or in a group. There is no question of there being less or more freedom, it's just different, that's all. That's why I'm crazy about acting for movies at the moment – it may be something to do with being a woman, I don't know, but I want to be part of somebody's conception of some funny mess-up that we all get into. Some man's vision of that is more interesting to be part of than the kind of combined, co-operative, compromised hotch-potch that actors and the director in the theatre may feel about a play. We know that, exciting and marvellous as it is, again and again too many compromises have to be made in the theatre. Well, one man may not make a good movie, but what is interesting is that you are part of a particular idea if he's a gifted man.

*You mean theatre is a mess if you like, with a lot of people involved, whereas cinema can be an intense personal experience, with certain directors like Michelangelo Antonioni or Tony Richardson, who have a single-minded vision?*

At the moment I'm more excited by working for that. I'm more excited for somebody to ask me to do something and for me to do it, because I now think I shall discover more by unquestioningly

1966 Jane, *Blow Up*

M

and trustingly doing immediately what they ask of me to do. In that way I shall discover more than working it all out and raising doubts and raising questions into which come all my inhibitions, all my doubts as an actress and as a person. We all know that in the theatre, interminable times, we've all bogged ourselves down with query, with doubt, with speculation, which may well be thoroughly fruitful; but immediately doing that one thing that one is told to do may open more windows than one can dream of.

*Let's go back to the theatre. You have had a great success with* The Prime of Miss Jean Brodie. *What attracted you to this part, had you read the original novel by Muriel Spark?*

No, I hadn't, no. I read the scripts first; then, obviously, I read up on the book immediately afterwards. I don't know, Brodie's such a muddle for me. I mean it's like being on the moon and I can't remember how difficult it was to get there, but I do know it was very difficult to get to the moon.

*The director, Peter Wood, has said that there were a number of Miss Brodies and that eventually they all came together to make one. Is this true?*

The thing that first got me about wanting to play the part was that I was fascinated by the stuff that fascists are made of or fascist admirers are made of. And the fact that she's a romantic woman with dreams of heroism, self-sacrifice, with tales of the ancient heroes of bygone days, all the Victorian literature, all the dredged romances of the years, imprisoned in a physical frame which was not romantic nor heroic, with a job which allowed nothing except encouraging the pupils and looking forward to their future, and for living through them, living by proxy. All this fascinated me. It was therefore on this serious level that I thought about it. Then I realised that in fact she was full of every kind of contradiction and that a great deal of the play was extremely funny; and I thought, oh it's not serious then, I see. So I took out a lot of chiffon scarves, I practically had one on both wrists at one point and I was waving my scarves about, and every other word was in Italian because Brodie likes speaking Italian.

*This was during the rehearsals.*

Yes. In other words I camped every second, in order to try and find the character: some of this still remains. But how I eventually found her was by thinking out what she wanted to be like, how she wished she could be like Anna Pavlova; there's something special about Anna Pavlova's look, and the whole embodiment of the ballet-omania of the twenties and thirties; of the fire and emotion of Sybil Thorndike as St Joan; Florence Nightingale of course was one of her heroines. I thought of all the Burns Jones paintings, the Rossetti paintings and all the poetry of the aesthetes. However, we still didn't get there because we thought, well she longs to be,

1966 Jean Brodie, *The Prime of Miss Jean Brodie*, Wyndham's

like Garbo, Pavlova, Thorndike, and so one made her dress in
colours and in materials and designs that were, to a certain extent,
a successful realisation for her dreams. We got all the way to the
dress parades, you know, four days from going out on tour.
And it wasn't until I was in those damn clothes on the stage
that I suddenly knew that what was vital was that Brodie in fact
is, and looks like, a dried-up spinster, and that that is what makes
her ironic and pathetic; that she is *not*, during any single minute
of her breathing life, she is *not* what she wants to be. That is
the contradiction. So then we found the plainest, simplest, neatest
clothes and just added an Eastern bangle, or an Eastern belt from
one of her voyages.

*And did the physical line of the part go through the same kind of pro-
cesses?*

Yes, it was the Scots you see. Because you have to decide as an actress, when you know you've got to do an accent, either to start off
doing the accent right away, or let it come later; it's a decision you
always have to make. Well, I didn't really mean to start doing the
accent, but I found I couldn't help doing Scots because when you
say 'the crème de la crème' it sounds much better if you say it as a
Scotswoman than if you give it a very French pronunciation.

Then I found that it was inhibiting me, totally. I was tense anyway with not knowing what I was doing, feverish with not being
able to be still because there was nothing I was satisfied enough to
be still with. However, I plugged away with the Scots because what
with my chiffon scarves and my Scots accent, it was all I'd got to
show for Brodie. So I had to hang on to them. Then we got to
Torquay and I still had a completely different wig; I had a sort of

Sybil Thorndike St Joan wig, a short, cropped, free kind of hair-do; but we still had another smooth wig hanging by which had been rejected. One night I suddenly thought, I'm going to put the other wig on. I thought of Anna Pavlova making up in her dressing-room, and thinking of that, I was Brodie, because that was all that Brodie could want to be like. So I did my hair trying to be as near to the classical ballerina line as I could. That was when I got nearest to Brodie. But I was still doing her in English, because suddenly one night in the feverish conferences of 'Why Haven't We Found Brodie', someone said why don't you try to do it in English. I think it was Donald Albery or maybe old Peter Wood, I can't remember who. So by then I was the classical ballerina, I had dropped my chiffon scarves, and I was talking in English. Suddenly at Brighton some friends came round and said, why don't you try the Scots now; I hear you did have a good Scots voice. There's something so marvellous about the paradox you find in Scots history and literature – and in the Scots nature; a difference between a certain tightness and a certain prudence, a marvellous bawdiness, richness and exuberance: it is these paradoxes that make something very particular and delicious. So I went back to Scots and by then it was kind of OK.

*Was this an anxious period for you, making all these discoveries on the tour, or were you quite calm about them?*

Oh no, I was far from calm. It's the first time I've ever – I didn't throw a temperament or anything like that because we were all in the same boat, but I had a good weep on Peter's shoulder. I was actually driven to say I couldn't make head or tail of the beastly play, you know, ridiculous, paltry little words. I was in the depths of agony. It's sort of funny for me to remember that I had all this trouble; but even now, I don't quite know if Brodie's still there.

*Vanessa, how did you prepare yourself for the part of Isadora when you played in the film?*

It was slightly different from the usual way because I had to contribute almost as an author, as well as an actress. I had to contribute dialogue and monologues, as Karel Reisz, the director, wanted me to do this – it was lucky that I had read everything. I don't always read lots and lots of books before I work on a part, but with this I did because it was that kind of work.

*I believe you tackled different scenes in different ways?*

In the drawing-room scene when Isadora first came to London, I was improvising all the time, in every shot that we did. We never wrote down the text. Karel said, 'I want you to be telling some story to the people in the drawing-room, that keeps them fascinated and amused and makes you enjoy yourself.' Because I'd read so much about it, I knew her history, all the people she'd met when

1968 Isadora

she first came to London and what happened to her. I immediately thought of the account of her meeting Mrs Pat Campbell. And I told that in different forms with different adjectives on all the takes, because you can keep people amused much better if they don't know every word you're going to say. But this is the interesting thing; had a script been written which included monologues in which the author writing knew how she talked, knew what had happened to her, then I wouldn't have needed to improvise.

*Isadora was a contemporary of Bernhardt and Duse. Were you very much aware of that period and their style of acting?*

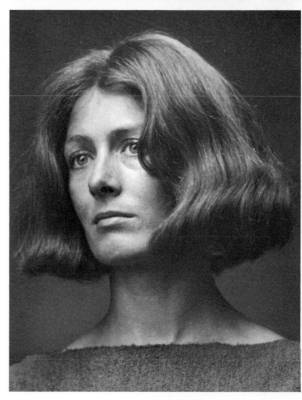

Yes, I think I probably sound stupid or arrogant, but I've got a strong feeling that I kind of know those people. I feel a very direct link, but I don't think I act like them; perhaps it's just because I'm different from a lot of people of my age, perhaps because of having a father who really is a marvellous actor, and I always thought he was. And so, I never had a reaction against the older actors' work. I might reject certain plays or reject a concept of doing it. I don't think there's a great difference between the old actors and the new actors; there's only a difference in material that you play, and the fashion and the taste of the times.

# Maggie Smith

HIGH-comedy actresses in Britain usually come from Kensington, or try to sound as if they do. Maggie Smith was born in Ilford, Essex; and it's illustrative of the change that has come over the English theatre in the past ten years that she has never tried to sound as if she came from anywhere else.

She went to school in Oxford, and in 1952 the University Dramatic Society co-opted her to play Viola in *Twelfth Night*. That was her theatrical début. Since then, she has acquired and consolidated two reputations. First, as a past-master of comedy, perhaps the lightweight champion of her sex in the English theatre. And second as a serious actress of extreme delicacy and pathos, capable of playing opposite Laurence Olivier in *Othello* and Ibsen's *Master Builder*. With every new role she has lengthened her stride and extended her range. For her age and weight she is arguably the most versatile girl on the English stage.

She came to the legitimate theatre by way of intimate revue. London first saw her in *Share My Lettuce* in 1957. Her co-star was Kenneth Williams. Working in revue taught her how to imply double meanings that often went far beyond what the author could ever have imagined. She learned how to use the arched eyebrow, the appalled glare, the outrageous double-take, the sour giggle, the adenoidal gurgle, the wince of disgust.

After a season of classical comedy at the Old Vic in 1959–60, she returned in triumph to the West End, playing two contrasting roles in Peter Shaffer's double bill, *The Private Ear* and *The Public Eye*. Her partner, in the second half of the programme, was once again Kenneth Williams. In 1962 she played the lead in the London production of a Broadway hit, *Mary, Mary*, by Jean Kerr. By now her conquest of Shaftesbury Avenue was decisive and complete. Where female performers are concerned, comedy usually means the battle of the sexes. Audiences love the sight of a spunky virgin cleverly outwitting masculine designs on her bed, and Maggie

1969 Margery Pinchwife, *The Country Wife*, Chichester

Smith handles such parts as Mary with a beady-eyed finesse that works just as well in Restoration comedy as it does in Broadway imports.

When Maggie Smith joined the National Theatre in 1963, she was still best known as a funny girl. She made her début with the company as Silvia in *The Recruiting Officer*, a Restoration heroine who dresses up as a soldier in order to be enlisted by the man she loves. Predictably, she had a vast and deserved success. But she began, soon afterwards, to reveal something new – an ability to play serious characters whose approach to sex was affirmative and aimed at total erotic fulfilment. The new Maggie Smith first asserted herself in *Othello*, begging the Venetian Senate for permission to accompany her husband on his wars against the Turks.

Soon afterwards, and even more significantly, she proved that she was ready to take on the role of Hilde Wangel in *The Master Builder*, one of the most forthright and aggressive young women in dramatic literature.

Can she achieve the final inch of assurance that would be necessary to play Cleopatra or Lady Macbeth? The answer depends on her own emotional development. She has the technique and the will-power; and there is no reason why she should not develop, in time, the full tragic passion.

*Kenneth Tynan*

CLIVE GOODWIN: *You recently played Beatrice in the National Theatre production of* Much Ado About Nothing. *How did you set about studying the part?*

MAGGIE SMITH: The first thing that happened was that I was rather thrown by Zeffirelli, the director, who said at the first rehearsal that he saw Beatrice as an albino. I found out later on, as the production grew, that he wanted everybody else in the play to be very dark and Beatrice to be the odd one out. She was the one girl who hadn't got married. She was strange because of her wit; she stood out in this little Sicilian family. He gave me an extraordinary blonde wig, and all the clothes were odd. His whole conception of the play was completely throwing; I think it would have been to anyone playing Beatrice, or indeed Benedick.

*But you looked marvellous, and I thought you gave a very good performance. Did you not think you were as good as you might have been?*

It took time, and I think it got better: it was so Sicilian, and so extraordinary. You see, everything in the production was visual – the coloured fairy lights, bands, lots of funny business, real live people came on and were sofas and chairs; something was going on

1965 Beatrice, *Much Ado About Nothing*, National Theatre, with Robert Stephens (Benedick)

all the time. In the middle of all that it was terribly difficult to be verbally funny. The part of Beatrice is wit, that is what they're always saying about her, she's always ready with a quick answer. It was awfully difficult to do that because the audience were very tuned to looking at things, and finding them funny; it wasn't, therefore, very easy to make them listen as well. The dress rehearsal was such a shock. You went on and suddenly found *everything* happening all over the stage and you thought, I don't know how I can just stand and talk. I longed very much to play the coffee boy, in actual fact.

*There is an enormous body of academic criticism about any Shakespeare part that you play. Do you go to people like Dover Wilson, or Jan Kott, for instance?*

Well, yes, you read them all and absorb them. But I think in the end it comes back to yourself, or the way the whole production is geared. You can't come to a rehearsal with a fixed idea of anything because it could be changed in five minutes.

*How self-critical are you about your performances?*

I think I am very self-critical. Probably damagingly so, because I get very depressed if it goes wrong. I am aware of it as a fault in myself. For example, you start off a performance and it's not going the way you want it to, and you think, I did that wrong, and I did that wrong. It's very difficult to pull yourself together and force the thing the right way round. I am permanently trying to get it better, or at least keep it on a level. Self-criticism, I suppose, can be a good thing, if you don't let it get you down, and I think I do.

*You played Silvia in the National Theatre production of John Farquhar's* The Recruiting Officer. *You had some wonderful scenes when you were dressed as a man, pretending to be an army officer. It was a play that gave you great scope for comic invention. How much of that was you, and how much was director?*

An awful lot of it was William Gaskill. He was a very important director for me. That was the first play I did at the National Theatre. The way Bill worked has always been useful to me; he would break rehearsals down; he sometimes got people to swop parts. It's a strange thing, but you forget when you're acting that the other person has probably got more problems than you have. And the moment you swop parts you immediately see their problems: Oh, I see why that bit is difficult – you know.

*How did you begin in the theatre? Did you act at school?*

Yes, the very first definite step was when I was still at school. When we had finished General School Certificate, we had about two weeks at the end of term which was a kind of dead time. And I immediately went to the Oxford Playhouse, where indeed I got a job; it was for two weeks, to play the Scots girl in *The Happiest Days of Your Life*. This was immediately trodden on, and I wasn't allowed to do it. So then I decided to go to drama school. I'd made up my mind to do that anyway, before I left school: they'd started a drama school in Oxford, where I lived. It was attached, at the time, to the Playhouse, and I went for two years. I wanted very much to go to RADA: it was everybody's dream to go to RADA. But my parents, I suppose quite rightly, didn't want me to go to London, when I was sixteen, and live on my own.

*And from drama school you went where?*

When I was at the Playhouse, I used to work in university productions, because they did an awful lot of them there. They did lots of cabarets and revues, run by Ned Sherrin, Desmond O'Donovan and people like that. I did those endlessly. You know, if you were bright enough at Oxford you could almost do weekly rep. round the colleges.

*So you were always playing light parts, comedy parts?*

Yes, always; I was always, always in revue and cabaret. I don't know why. I did do *Twelfth Night* for the OUDS, playing Viola. I suppose that was one of the first things that I did. Then the revues that I was

1963 Silvia, *The Recruiting Officer*, National Theatre, with Max Adrian (Mr Balance), Lynn Redgrave (Rose) and Colin Blakely (Kite)

in were taken to Edinburgh, as Fringe productions. I think we were about the first Fringe shows up there.

*It was through one of these late-night revues that you got the mythical break.*

*The* break. Yes, it was. We did *On the Fringe*, and they brought it down to London, to the Watergate Theatre, which doesn't exist any more. I can't remember which one it was now. I think it was Oxford Eight. It was seen by the American director who then took me to Broadway. The revue there was called *New Faces*.

*And was it successful?*

Yes, it was moderately successful. I mean, it was rather sad because everybody in it expected it to be a *huge* success, as the one before had been: and obviously it wasn't. Everybody who went into it thought, Oh, we're going to come out stars.

*Did you think that?*

I don't know what I thought. I was so overwhelmed at the idea of going. In actual fact, I didn't enjoy it at all, but I was excited by it. I mean, I thought anything could happen. Yes, I must have thought I would come back a great huge star.

*And then you came back to London?*

I came back for a holiday, actually. Then I did a television here, called *Boy Meets Girl*, which Sylvia Narizano directed. And then Michael Codron asked me to do *Share My Lettuce*, with Kenneth Williams; and I decided to stay.

*Again, more light comedy. Was this what you wanted to do?*

I didn't really want to do it. And yet it became a kind of habit. Everybody thought of me in that way. They thought of me always in revue, or as a revue artist: it became absolutely stuck. I don't think I thought about it very much; I was so overwhelmed, so carried away with myself.

*At working at all . . .*

. . . At working at all, yes. I was really rather grateful for that.

*Did you know what you did want to do?*

I knew I wanted to act. When *Lettuce* was over, Codron did want me to do another revue with Kenneth Williams, and that was really when the crunch came. I very much wanted to do it. At least, one part of me wanted to – yet I felt instinctively that it wasn't right. And so I went to do an audition for Michael Benthall at the Old Vic.

*And you got the job?*

Yes. I think, in all fairness, he was really running out of actors at the time. I must admit that. It was very odd that the play he was going to do was a Restoration comedy – comedy, comedy, comedy. And so it seemed to be right.

*The play was Congreve's* The Double Dealer, *wasn't it?*

Yes.

*Of course, you hadn't played classical parts before; your entire background and training had been in revue.*

Yes, absolutely. And the classical plays I did there! I mean, I tend to go hot and cold when I think about them. When I think of playing the Queen in *Richard II*, I would rather pass out: it was just awful. My theory about acting in *Richard II* was to stay upstage and do it very fast and very quietly and hope nobody would notice.

*You must have learnt an enormous amount in that season, 1959–60.*

Yes, oh yes, I did. Again, you see, I was lucky because we did the Scots play, the Barrie play, *What Every Woman Knows*.

*In which you played the lead with Donald Houston.*

Yes. You see, my mother is Scots, and it was a marvellous kind of part for me at that time. It had comedy, pathos, and everything else.

*You have played in a number of films. I saw you in* The Pumpkin Eater *with Anne Bancroft and Peter Finch. Do you enjoy filming?*

Not very much, no.

*Why not?*

I think you have to be a screen actress; I really don't think I am. You have to have the right outlook. By the time I get on the floor, after two and a half hours of make-up, I find it impossible. And also, the lack of contact, the fact that there isn't an audience. It's all a question of how you look. People are always worried, fussing round you all the time, trying to make you look like this, or like that; your costume isn't right. I find by the end of the day that one's morale is *so* low, with the cameras so close, that you feel you can't do anything because it will look ugly. You get so *concerned* with the fact that you are in the wrong light, or if you do *that*, it's unattractive to the camera, and you mustn't do this. You get so inhibited, at least *I* do, that I tend not to do anything. I'm *fine* in a film if I'm acting a small part, a neurotic person, or a shy person; then it's not quite so difficult.

*After the Old Vic season, you then played in a series of very successful West End comedies.*

The first one was Anouilh's *The Rehearsal*; it was only meant to be for a limited season, but actually it had quite a good run. Then I did

1959 Lady Plyant, *The Double Dealer*, Old Vic, with M Malleson (Sir Paul Plyant)

1959 Queen Anne, *Richard II*, Old Vic

1959 Lady Plyant, *The Double Dealer*, with John Justin (Mellefont)

1960 Maggie Wylie, *What Every Woman Knows*, Old Vic, with Donald Houston (John Shand)

1961 Lucille, *The Rehearsal*, Theatre Royal, Bristol, and Globe, with Alan Badel (Hero)

Peter Shaffer's double bill, *The Private Ear* and *The Public Eye*, and then *Mary, Mary*. I enjoyed them all, in a way; it seems ungrateful to say anything else. But I found the length of the run and what we were talking about earlier, the concentration, and keeping it going, overwhelmingly exhausting. I really wasn't equipped, at the time, to do it.

*Now let's go back to the National Theatre. One of the parts you played there was Hilde Wangel in Ibsen's play* The Master Builder. *Did you find Ibsen difficult or easy to play?*

Actually, we did two productions of it. The first time I played with Sir Michael Redgrave. And, I don't know really, but something went very wrong. I've tried hard to analyse it. I think I played it rather frenziedly; that was what a lot of the notices said. The second time round I found it much simpler, I calmed down, and held on to certain things which I found were very important about Hilde Wangel. I think what I did too much in the first production was to work on the mystery and strangeness of the part, which, in actual fact, it doesn't have.

*Did you perhaps get bothered by Ibsen's layers of meaning?*

No, I don't think that was so much the problem. The problem with *The Master Builder* is that there are three acts, and it's a continuous dialogue. In Ibsen, and in that play in particular, one was repeating very much the same thing. I tried to vary it and colour it as much as possible; I don't think I did *that* the first time.

*How big a gap was there between the two productions?*

It wasn't really very long. That's another marvellous thing, you know; working in that kind of theatre. You can start again, try again, and make something work which hadn't worked before; instead of it just being a write-off.

*Hilde's often referred to as a bird of prey. Did you find this difficult to play, because it mustn't be apparent too soon that she is luring Solness to his death?*

I don't think she's aware of it at all. I found with Hilde that it's something very much that happens to you when you've just left school. You can make anything happen, if you will it hard enough. Do you know what I mean? If you go on long enough saying, 'It must happen, it will happen, it will, it will, it will,' which is, as a matter of fact, a line of Hilde's, then it will happen.

*You've played many parts at the National Theatre opposite Sir Laurence Olivier. This must have been an enormous benefit to you as an actress.*

At the beginning it was very hard. The first play was *Othello*, which absolutely terrified me. Because it was extraordinary casting. And Sir Laurence always has, well, an extraordinary sort of aura around

1963 Mary, *Mary, Mary*, Queen's, with Donald Harr

1962 Belinda, *The Public Eye*,
Globe, with Kenneth Williams
(Julian) and Richard Pearson
(Charles Sidley)

his name. I found I was very nervous of him. It's very unfair on Sir Laurence, but it's bound to happen. You know, you are in awe of him, very much.

*Are there any specific things that you, as an actress, have learnt from Sir Laurence?*

You don't learn specific things from actors. You don't learn, Oh, that is the way that you say that kind of line. I've learnt a lot from him about discipline. Or rather, I haven't learnt – but I wish I had. He has enormous self-discipline and control as an actor.

*Desdemona is a very difficult part to play because she is innocent and virtuous, and by today's values these are very boring virtues. Did you find this?*

John Dexter, the director, pointed out that she had no mother and obviously had coped with the household in Venice, and run the affairs efficiently. So she doesn't necessarily have to be a weak, withdrawn, sad, quiet creature who just sits around and sings a lot.

*And of course, she defies her father.*

Exactly, she has a mind of her own. Very much so; she defies her father even in front of the Senate.

*At the National Theatre you have played nine parts.[1] Which did you enjoy most?*

I suppose the most satisfying was Desdemona, because it was one of the most difficult. And one that, you know, everybody thought was a mistake. It wasn't satisfying at the beginning, that I would agree. But I *think* I managed to work on it and make it better.

*It was one of your first, and one of your few, tragic roles.*

It was really my very first, and it was Shakespeare, which is rather difficult for somebody who usually plays light comedy.

*Do you have ambitions to play other tragic parts?*

Frequently you get actors or actresses who have a great passion to play one part. I don't at all. I'd far rather rely on other people's judgement. You know, other people can see things in you that you can't. For example, why should John Dexter see me as Desdemona? I doubt if many other people would. I didn't see myself in it.

1964 Hilde Wangel, *The Master Builder*, Natic Theatre, with Michael Redgrave and Laurc Olivier, both as Halvard Solness

[1] This interview took place in July 1966.

National Theatre.

Left, 1964 Myra, *Hay Fever*, with Derek Jacobi (Simon Bliss); above, 1966 Clea, *Black Comedy*, with Derek Jacobi (Brin) and Louise Purnell (Carol)

Opposite: top, 1964 Desdemona, *Othello*, with Laurence Olivier as Othello; bottom, 1965 Avonia Bunn, *Trelawny of the 'Wells'*, with Pauline Taylor (Imogen Parrott) and Edward Petherbridge (Ferdinand Gadd)

*It's as a comedienne that you are best known, so let's talk specifically about the playing of comedy, and to help us do that we've asked an old friend of yours, Kenneth Williams, to come and join us. Now you two have worked together, how often, and in what?*

KENNETH WILLIAMS: Well, we first worked together in a revue, the Bamber Gascoigne one, *Share My Lettuce*. That was in 1957. Then we didn't work again till 1962, when we did the two Shaffer plays, *Private Ear* and *Public Eye*.

MS: Yes. Kenneth phoned me up one morning and said that he'd read a marvellous play, and I ought to get in touch with my agent straightaway, because there was a great part in it for me. He thought I'd be absolutely marvellous in it. And I said, 'Oh, I'm doing it, Kenneth.' And he said, 'Ooh, you are *mean*. You might have said that you thought I'd be good in it.'

KW: Do you remember what happened after that? We decided to have a meeting to discuss it, and you came round to my flat and you said, 'What are you going to do with it?' Of course, this is one of the reasons why we're really not the sort of people to discuss comedy at all, because we both have a horror of dissecting it. We both believe in getting a technical sort of excellence, learning the part, with the moves and that kind of thing. But, with the idea that the audience alone is what's going to teach you anything about the playing of comedy. Now this is a belief we both share, isn't it?

MS: Well, yes. It happens endlessly in rehearsal when people say, 'Oh well, I think there's a laugh there,' both Ken and I will go, 'Oh, don't say it,' because the moment you decide something funny is going to happen, you've more or less killed it.

KW: I heard what you were saying earlier on about discipline. I don't think you're right at all about that. You are one of the most disciplined people to work with. That's one of your troubles, of course; you don't blow your own trumpet hard enough. There's a kind of comedy which you indulge in, particularly in the first of the Shaffer plays, which is really controlled hysteria. And without the control of that almost bubbling panic, you could never have got the kind of laughs that you did.

*Rehearsing a comedy must be twenty times more difficult than rehearsing any other kind of play. How do you know where the laughs are going to come?*

MS: Well, you don't. That is what we were saying. It really rests with the audience. Of course, you have an idea. You read the script and certain things in it make you laugh. You think, that's a funny idea and you hope it will be funny; one can work for the laugh in that way. It's not necessarily a laugh, it's a humorous passage maybe, you know that you can extract something from it and make it into a comedy situation.

*One of the extraordinary things about you as a comedienne is the way that you can take a perfectly ordinary line like 'Ooh, that's a rotten part. I assure you, Rose, as artist to artist, that part is absolutely rotten,' from Pinero's* Trelawny of the 'Wells', *and make it sound very funny.*

MS: You remember that because I suppose I found a very vivid way of saying it. That is something that Ken taught me.

*Oh really?*

MS: In one of the Shaffer plays I had a very long speech – everybody has a long speech in a Shaffer play – this was an endless speech, it seemed to me, and it did sound endless, I must say. Eventually, one day in that awful office at the Queen's Theatre, Ken said, 'Look, duckie, you're being absolutely boring.' I went through it, sentence by sentence, and he said, 'You know you would never say a sentence like *that*. You just wouldn't.' I mean I'm talking now and waving my arms around and stressing certain words. And Ken said, 'That's what you must do.' I was literally learning a speech and just saying it as a speech, thinking, Oh, how very clever, I've learned all the words. I'd never thought of colouring things as vividly as Kenneth does. I'd never thought of doing it, or I'd never had to do it. I'd never been in a modern play, I suppose. I'd never thought that one could make a speech that much alive.

*By taking it apart and making it like conversation; making it immediate?*

KW: Yes, it is *immediacy*, in actual fact, which is the greatest gift in comedy. It's what we were saying earlier on about the nightly challenge with an audience: you must make it seem as though it is coming out for the first time – make it seem as if thoughts have occurred.

MS: Yes, absolutely. You have to surprise the audience an awful lot of the time. I mean, a thought comes to *you* very quickly, and therefore it surprises the audience. It's rather like the quickness of the hand deceiving the eye. It's the same thing with comedy.

KW: The most marvellous thing about you is that electricity thing of understanding the rhythm of the dialogue, knowing how to deliver a feed line, knowing the tag's got to be played on an upward inflexion.

*And how does she do that?*

KW: In all fairness, I think it's innate, this feeling of a natural rhythm for the script, and it's got to be maintained, achieved. In all fairness, when I did say that thing about the speech in the Shaffer play, which Maggie quoted earlier on, she said, 'Yes, well, I'll get it in three weeks.' And in actual fact you *did*.

MS: Well, no. I think I was lying, Ken.

KW: But what you meant was that you had to explore.

MS: I mean, I didn't want to be told how to do it.

KW: But it was a case of exploration. The reason, for instance, that you got the great laugh on the macintosh line in the Shaffer play was the fact of its immediacy. A man did say, 'Yes, I suppose he was handsome, and debonair, and devil-may-care, a man of the world.' And she says, 'Noo, noo, he was a goofy-looking man in a white raincoat – '; it was a thought of the *moment*. It was as though you'd all of a sudden discovered what he did look like. There was another way of playing it, indeed there was. The man could have said, 'Smart, debonair.' 'No, no; he was a man in a white raincoat.'

MS: You need to have a bit of a quirk; you have to look at things from an odd angle to get the comedy out of them. You really have to see the madness. I mean, Myra in Noël Coward's *Hay Fever* is mad. She's normally a rather elegant character, but there is one point, at the end of the second act, when she just goes completely to pieces. The whole thing snaps, she goes raving mad; all composure's gone to the wind and the elegance is completely gone.

*Would you say Kenneth had been quite a big influence on you as a comedienne?*

MS: An enormous influence. I mean, I pinch from him all the time.

*Can you give us some examples?*

MS: Well, in *Black Comedy* I'm doing a complete Kenneth: it's outrageous. If he'd seen it he'd be livid. You know, that awful Mrs Panic who keeps whistling: it's pure Ken.

*What other kinds of things do you pinch?*

MS: I think I got mostly from Ken clarity and speed; incredible deftness within a line; speaking very clearly and knowing where you are, knowing the words and being able to play with them and make them do what you want them to do, not as I did, just look at a speech and think, Ugh. It's really a matter of having the speech completely under control and being able to do what you want to make it do.

KW: Do you remember in the revue where you played the very grand English lady, and I was invited by you to tea? And you said, 'Have I got a goitre?' Do you remember? It was incredible really, because she had to say to me, 'Have I got a goitre, hanging, hanging here; yes, with hairs sprouting, with hairs sprouting? Have I got a goitre hanging, with hairs sprouting?' It was the most terrible sort of manic, 'Have I got a goitre hanging, with hairs?' And I had to say, 'Yes,' you see. Then she said, 'Of course I have, but we don't discuss it.' It was a marvellous example of this sort of thing that you get in comedy, where absolute panic is put into motion and then *cut* right off. I thought that the first play in the Shaffer bill did exactly

1966 Clea, *Black Comedy*

that. There was the most wonderful opportunity there for that kind of controlled panic which was screamingly funny when you did it.

MS: Yes, being terribly nervous.

KW: And looking desperately composed every time the boy looked at you.

MS: Or when he wasn't there.

KW: Yes, precisely.

*I'm sure this is the kind of panic that you sometimes feel as a person.*

MS: Yes, one knows it and sees it. I recognise it in myself all the time. It's like saying to yourself, 'I must be controlled, I must be controlled; I won't show anything.' But underneath, one's just falling to pieces.

1969 Jean Brodie in the film version of *The Prime of Miss Jean Brodie*, for which she won a Hollywood Oscar, with Gordon Jackson (Gordon Lowther)

1969 Margery Pinchwife, *The Country Wife*, Chichester, with Gordon Gostelow (Pinchwife)

Opposite:

Top: 1970 Mrs Sullen, *The Beaux' Stratagem*, National Theatre, with Robert Stephens (Archer)

Bottom: 1970 Hedda, *Hedda Gabler*, National Theatre at the Cambridge, with Robert Stephens (Lövborg)

# Robert Stephens

I N a back-handed way, the finest tribute to Robert Stephens'
acting was paid by the first-nighters at *The Royal Hunt of the
Sun*, who came away from the Chichester Festival Theatre
in 1964 asking, 'Who is he? Where does he come from?' No
one had seen before a performance like his Atahualpa, Inca of Peru:
half-man, half-god, a strutting golden bird, draggled and choked
in the net of Spanish conquest. His voice was more than a human
voice, deep, tolling, poignant. His gestures were more than human
gestures: huge, arrogant, certain as great dancing.

But of course they had seen Robert Stephens before. He had been
active in the London theatre since 1956. He had the title role in
John Osborne's *Epitaph for George Dillon*. He'd played Dora
Bryan's one-eyed lover in the film of Shelagh Delaney's *A Taste of
Honey* and the sly young lodger in John Mortimer's *The Wrong Side
of the Park*. He had been with the National Theatre from its first
production, playing Horatio to Peter O'Toole's Hamlet; the
Dauphin to Joan Plowright's St Joan; the philandering Captain
Plume in Farquhar's comedy *The Recruiting Officer*. And he'd been
seen in countless films and television plays, nearly always in the
same role – a toothy young spiv, fawning shamelessly on those
stronger than himself, but always ready to snap at the hand that
fed him; to round, snarling with malice, on those whose success
rubbed in his own obscurity. He had become typed as a seedy,
bitter young failure. Nothing in his previous work prepared
audiences for the radiant figure he created in *The Royal Hunt*.

But, contrary to legend, actors are not made overnight. Looking
back over the line of Stephens' spivs, you can see, if you look hard
enough, the seeds of his Andean demi-god. One was that shamelessness. Each of his hang-dogs had a moment when he turned on
the world. George Dillon arrives on the Elliott's doorstep meek,
shabby and insinuating as a hungry alley-cat, but the moment he's
fed with attention and security he soars into diatribe against society,
the commercial theatre which rejects him, the poverty he comes

1969 Mark Antony, *Julius Caesar*, BBC TV

205

from and the wealth he cannot reach. Stephens seized on moments of angry self-importance with a lyricism which foreshadowed Atahualpa's chanting arrogance. In their shamelessness lay the germ of the sun-god who has never known shame.

Through his best performances runs a common thread of hatred of human limitation; of settling for the ordinary, instead of lifting oneself to extraordinariness by the bootstraps if necessary. As an actor, he obviously proceeds on the belief that there is always a physical means to success. If Atahualpa must above all be a superb body, he will acquire that physique at a gymnasium. If Zeffirelli's interpretation of *Much Ado About Nothing* is a kind of Sicilian round-dance, he will take the necessary dancing lessons to lead it as Benedick.

In his performances, he often seems to build up a whole characterisation on a physical detail of costume. His Captain Plume in *The Recruiting Officer* was most memorable for the striding swagger that set his mud-spattered red greatcoat swirling through the streets of Shrewsbury – that was what would lure the local youth after him to the colours. And Atahualpa himself – all anyone knew about the Incas was that they wore cloaks of feathers – the image behind Stephens' performance was clearly a bird: some exotic, golden pheasant, wild and vulnerable, stepping as delicately as it pecked its food.

*Ronald Bryden*

CLIVE GOODWIN: *How do you set about creating a character as difficult as Atahualpa in* The Royal Hunt of the Sun?

ROBERT STEPHENS: The play had been around for a long time before the National Theatre decided to do it. Several managements had had it, but they all said it was impossible to present the conquest of Peru on the stage, that you would need a cast of about sixty or seventy actors and the most extraordinary scenic effects. When I first read the play I thought, in fact, it was impossible. You see Pizarro in Spain; he then goes to Peru where you see him go through the jungles and climb the Andes with his Spanish army. You then meet Atahualpa who believed himself to be a god. You see the Spaniards massacre the poor Peruvians in the square at Cajamarca where the two men met. You then see the bargain that Pizarro makes with Atahualpa: Pizarro promises to let him free, if Atahualpa will fill a room with gold. You then see their relationship grow. And finally, of course, Pizarro has to kill Atahualpa. When I read all that – it seemed impossible to put it on the stage. But in fact, we arrived at a very simple way of presenting it; the stage was practically bare and the audience imagined it all for themselves.

*If you play a man who believes himself to be a god, what can you take from your own life to put into the character?*

With a part like that, a lot of problems were entirely technical. I mean, you are a god, therefore you can behave in any way you like. Besides, we don't know what the Incas were like, there is no record. If I had chosen to play it standing on my head, nobody could have said I was wrong. We have sketchy records of what Atahualpa was like, but nobody really knows. So I thought that everything Atahualpa did should be against what the Spaniards did. If they spoke quickly, then I should speak slowly; if they moved rather quickly, I should move very slowly.

*You used some rather strange vowel sounds. Where did they come from?*

We made them up, really. But we do know that the Incas tended to punch consonants very hard. Mark Wilkinson, who was in charge of the music, got hold of an Inca lament, and in that they tended to hit k's and p's and b's rather hard. So that was a starting point. I then found some records of Bolivian Indian singing, and they do exactly that even today. A friend of mine, who lived in Mexico for a long time, recorded for me some Mexican cries, the sort you can hear in Mexican music, dog-bird cries which one tried to incorporate into the speaking.

*Did you have special vocal training for this part?*

Yes, I mean at the National Theatre we have a voice teacher. I went to him for a lot of help for extending vowel sounds and making

1964 Atahualpa, *The Royal Hunt of the Sun*, National Theatre

1964 Atahualpa, *The Royal Hunt of the Sun*, with Colin Blakely (Pizarro)

them sound odd. Because I felt that when the audience saw the Incas they should be startled; they should be quite different, if possible, from anything they had ever seen or heard before.

*What about the physical aspects of the part, how did you prepare for that?*

It came partly from the mime teacher. We rehearsed the play for about ten weeks, and for six weeks the Spaniards never met the Indians: we had special classes. The Spaniards would have a movement class, and then the Indians would have a movement class, so that they were totally different. The Spaniards would rehearse without the Indians, and the Indians would rehearse, but without the Spaniards. Then finally after six weeks when we all came together, we would be totally different from each other.

*Did your conception of the part develop or change much during the rehearsals?*

Yes, because I started out with no idea at all of how I was going to play the part. I hadn't an idea in my head.

*Were you very scared?*

No, I was fascinated by the idea of playing something so outlandish and I didn't think it was a part for which I was in any way ideally cast. I'm sure if a commercial management had been putting the play on they would never have thought of me for that part.

*Did you see the costume designs before you started to rehearse?*

Yes, and that was a great help because the costumes were enormously elaborate. One in particular, which was a gown made of gold coins covered with a cloak of white feathers, and I wore a mask so that you couldn't see my face, and an enormous feather head-dress. I thought, I must make the performance bigger than the costume; otherwise the costume will completely swamp the performance. I did try to tell all the other Indians to do the same. One had to do something which was much bigger than life; you couldn't play intimately in those extraordinary costumes.

*Did you have special training for the part?*

Yes. I decided the sort of shape I should be. I've worked for some years now at a gymnasium twice a week, and I told the man who runs it what I wanted to look like; for ten weeks we simply worked on the exercises that would make me look slender but very athletic.

*Did it work?*

Yes, I think so. He was very pleased with the result.

*You mean you actually succeeded in changing your physical shape inside ten weeks?*

Yes, absolutely. I had to work very hard at it, but I think it paid off.

Atahualpa

O

*Did you find it specially rewarding to play a part that had very little of yourself in the make-up?*

Yes, I think that's always exciting work for an actor to do. Because you really have to reach out for things. I read an awful lot about the conquest of Peru and became really involved; the whole concept of what the Spaniards did to those poor people is so horrendous. One became emotional about it at times, during the rehearsal period.

*What do you mean exactly?*

Well, I really hated those Spaniards at rehearsals. I mean one's friends, one absolutely loathed them, when one thought of what they had done to that extraordinary civilisation of which there is now nothing left.

*Someone once said that you made Atahualpa a glorious but achingly vulnerable near-god. Does this mean anything to you?*

Yes, that's what I was striving for. Throughout the play you see a man who is totally isolated and alone. He is illegitimate and obviously feels this very strongly. He meets another man from another culture who is also illegitimate; they strike up an extraordinary, almost father–son relationship. I mean if I've done that, that's what I set out to do. I didn't want Atahualpa to be so isolated and cold that he had no sympathetic qualities.

*Did you work on modern parallels for this, because it seems to me that there are some; in many ways Atahualpa is a political hostage who in fact succeeds in converting his jail-keeper.*

Yes, absolutely. In fact the conquered finally becomes the conqueror. But one tried to divorce oneself from our civilisation completely and, in a way, play it with enormous simplicity, as against the machinations of the Spanish politicians and the Spanish Church of the sixteenth century.

*Is it a problem to keep this kind of part consistent in each performance?*

Not as much as it would be if one were playing it every night, which we didn't, fortunately. If you play it once a week you are always a little bit nervous because you haven't played it the night before; that always gives it a slight charge and keeps it fresh: it doesn't become too mechanical.

*Would you say that this arises out of putting plays in repertory as the National Theatre do?*

Yes. But I think it depends to a great extent upon the actors you're working with. In that particular play I worked with Colin Blakely, who is probably the most marvellous actor I've ever worked with as far as that kind of thing is concerned. He's always enormously fresh and adaptable.

*You created the part of Atahualpa on the open stage at the Chichester
Festival Theatre and then you moved it to the proscenium arch theatre at the
Old Vic. Which did you prefer?*

Because of the spectacular quality of the play I think it was much
better at Chichester. It might almost have been written for an open
stage. The actors made their entrances through the auditorium and
so I always felt it pulled the audience into the play much more; they
became much more involved in it. We even relayed the strange
sounds and bird calls out into the auditorium itself so that it pushed
the audience on to the stage.

*This play is very much a* tour de force *for the director, John Dexter. Did
you get on well with him?*

Yes, I've known John for many years; in fact we both started our
careers in London at the Royal Court Theatre in 1956. I've worked
with him many times in the past. We have always been very much
in tune as actor–director – though we've had our differences as
every actor–director does.

*Could you categorise those differences?*

If a director knows you terribly well, he is constantly aware of the
things that you can do easily, and they are usually the things he
doesn't want; if he is interested in you, he wants to push you further
all the time. He will say, 'You've done that before; do something
new. You can find another way of speaking; increase the range of
your voice.' He is constantly aware of your mannerisms and the
traps that you will fall into: the easy way of doing something. He's
probably much more aware of that than the actor is himself, and
usually the director is right. But the actor sometimes gets irritable
because he feels he is being pushed a bit too far, or the demands
being put upon him are too great. I think that's very good – that's
marvellous. It's very fortunate to have a director who's that
interested in you. Some directors like you simply to reproduce your
successes because they know that's a sure thing.

*Could you give me an example of a director bringing something out of which
you didn't know was there?*

When I first asked to join the National Theatre, I was naturally not
quite sure about it, and I was told what my parts would be. I had to
commit myself for a long time, you know, and was a bit nervous
about it. Then John Dexter finally came to me and said, 'Look,
would you like to play the Dauphin in *St Joan?*' – a part for which
I was totally unsuited; he should be a tiny little man, very weak,
and I'm six foot. But the idea of that was an inspiration and I said,
'Yes, I'll join immediately, because I don't think anybody would
ever offer me that part.'

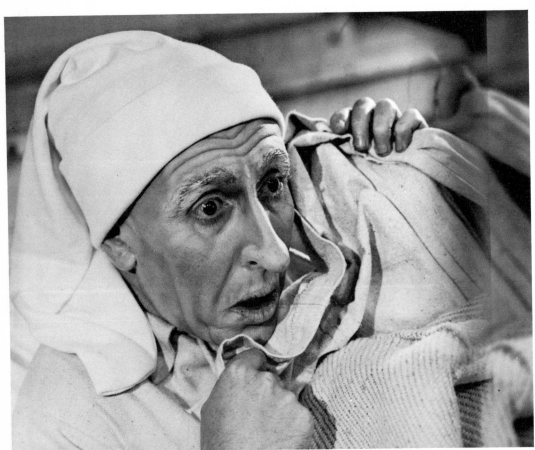

1963 Dauphin, *St Joan*, Nation[al]
Theatre, with Joan Plowright [as]
Joan

*Do you have preferences for the kind of director you work with?*

It's good for an actor to work with all sorts of directors. I like a director who makes one work very hard; I suppose those are the best directors. I don't like directors who are willing to be sold short on a performance. How can one put it? If you're in a four-week rehearsal period and at the end of the third week you feel that the director has directed the play, and that's as much as you're going to get from him – I think that is intolerable: it always makes me very unhappy. You can sense with a director when his creativity has stopped; then you know that for the next week you're just going to run through the play every day and then put it on. I think the best directors are the ones who up till the final dress rehearsal, even when you're performing it, will still come and keep pushing the play forward.

*Let's change the subject, and go right back to the beginning of your career as an actor.*

I first got into the theatre through the National Association of Boys' Clubs. I belonged to a youth club when I was about fourteen, and when I was fifteen the National Association of Boys' Clubs sent out a tour. They'd collected together a group of boy actors from youth clubs all over the country – and sent them out with a selection of one-act plays and songs to which the actors mimed; this was to show what could be done by youth clubs. I did two of their tours, and it was out of that I decided to go into the theatre. Then I went to a drama school, helped by the National Association of Boys' Clubs.

*Where was this?*

Bradford.

*And did your parents encourage you?*

Well, they were very good because they didn't discourage me. I mean they said, 'If it's what you want to do, then do it, but if it doesn't work out, don't blame us,' which was very fair.

*How old were you then?*

I was about seventeen when I went to drama school in Bradford.

*Did you learn a lot there?*

I don't know; it's difficult to tell now how much one did assimilate. I have very strong feelings about drama schools. Until you have done a lot of acting you don't value the training that you get. I remember very well that I always tried to shirk the ballet classes that we had, because I thought I would never be called upon to dance. Or I would stand at the back of the class and hope not to be noticed, because I wasn't very good. But years later, of course, you find that this is invaluable and I found that I missed it very much. Or you think, well I may never have to fence, and if I do I can learn it at the time. But if you knew then what value these things were going to be, you would take the training much more seriously.

*What you're saying is that if you ran a drama school you would emphasise the technical side of the training.*

Absolutely. All the time. Voice, movement, gymnastics, dancing, singing. Some of the courses at drama school last for three years, and at the end of that time they should be able to turn out a pretty remarkable piece of physical equipment. Someone once said, and I think it's true, that all problems are technical: it's very true for most actors. You find that they cannot play a part because, maybe, they cannot speak ten lines in one breath. That is purely technical. They cannot dance; anybody can learn to dance. You may not be able to dance perfectly, but you will be able to dance as well as you ever could be able to dance; or sing as well as possible. I don't think enough emphasis is laid on these things.

*Do you think it might be to do with the fact that, when you went to drama school, you were being trained for a theatre which has very much changed in the last ten years?*

Absolutely. I find it myself. I'm not saying that the young actors are entirely at fault. I found when I came into the National Theatre Company there were many things I simply couldn't do. I had to go back to school, as it were, and have voice lessons, movement lessons and things like that. I just wasn't equipped to cope with doing four different plays in a week: Shakespeare, Noël Coward, a Restoration comedy and a Beckett play, or something like that. But I think that the drama schools should examine their curriculum. They should be much more disciplinarian with their students, not that you want to turn out a robot, but you should be able to turn out something pretty good at the end of a three-year course. If you're a doctor and you train, when you come out you should be a pretty good doctor, there are things at which you should be skilled. But an actor, of course, is his own equipment; it's himself, he can't write it down or play it on the piano or anything like that.

*After drama school you then did five years in various reps up and down the country. This must have left its mark on you in some way or other. Do you think it's a good mark or a bad mark?*

I think it's a good mark in the way in which I was very fortunate in doing it; I didn't stay in any particular kind of repertory company too long. The first job I had in rep. was in Morecambe, I was there for sixteen months doing a different play every week. The amazing thing about it was that I was constantly being miscast, always playing old men, or parts which were not right for me. But you have to do them, and you have to do them in a week. You have to go on to the stage on Monday night with something. And I think that's very good, after a drama-school training, to be plummeted into something like that, where you are absolutely forced every week to do something different, something new, for yourself. Then I went into two-weekly, three-weekly and finally monthly repertory in Manchester; I think by that time I had assimilated all I could get out of reps.

*The kind of rep. that you were in, weekly rep., has largely disappeared now. Do you think that's a good or a bad thing?*

I think it's a bad thing for young actors because it teaches you a sense of responsibility. If you play thirty leading parts in a year, it does give you a sense of walking on to the stage and taking command of that stage, because you've just got to do it. I think that's a hard thing to learn in any other way, it's something that grows within you by constantly having to do it. But if you come out of a drama school and are plummeted straight into the West End or into television, then that's something which is difficult to learn.

*A more normal method, now, is to leave drama school and carry a spear in one of the big national companies for three or four years. You never did that, did you?*

No. Never. I once did an audition for Stratford years ago, and they said would you come and walk on and understudy, and I said no. I could see no value in it at all.

*That's not very encouraging for the spear-carriers up and down the country.*

Things have changed now, because in those days the policy of the company at Stratford was to employ so many stars and supporting players, that the walk-ons and spear-carriers had few chances of climbing up through the company; that was very rare. I remember being told, at the time, that you either had to start at the top or the bottom; you couldn't go in in the middle; I didn't like that at all. Now the policy with the Aldwych Company and the National Company is to keep a permanent company. I know very well at the National that it is possible to climb very swiftly through the company. One girl we have there, Louise Purnell, was an understudy in *Hay Fever* and the actress who was playing the part was ill and couldn't rehearse for a week; and Noël Coward took the understudy and gave her the part. The girl had originally been employed in the company as a dancer, not as an actress at all. But she played that part, then she took over the leading part in *The Crucible*, and now she is playing the name part in one of the productions. This has happened to several actors in the company; I think it's very good, very democratic and quite right.

*To go on with your history, I suppose your first really important job in London was when you joined the English Stage Company in 1956. Those years, 1956–9, for the English Stage Company, are almost legendary now, with the discovery of Wesker and Osborne, and you were very much a part of those days.*

Yes. It was very odd, because Tony Richardson, who ran the company with George Devine, had seen me years before when I was with the Morecambe rep., and he asked me to go to the Midland Hotel and have coffee with him one Sunday morning. He had just left Oxford at the time, and he said, 'George Devine and I are thinking of opening a theatre in London. Would you be interested in joining the company?' And I said of course, I would be fascinated; and I heard nothing about it for about three years. Then suddenly I got a call from Tony Richardson, when I was in Manchester, saying will you come and do an audition on Sunday for the English Stage Company. I did and I joined. But for two years I only played very minor parts.

*Your first big part was in John Osborne's* Epitaph for George Dillon.

Yes, it's a marvellous part, because it's very much John Osborne before he became a successful writer. I knew John very well at the time, so it made it easier for me to play the part, because in a way I had to play it like him, as it were. One of the critics said that I talked like him, with his nasal voice.

*Was it conscious?*

No, not conscious. In a lot of his plays he writes as he speaks, and so I tend to fall into his pattern and rhythm of speaking.

*How would you rate it in the Osborne canon?*

It's different from the plays he usually writes, because he does set up for his hero, or anti-hero, the most wonderful opposition in the character of the woman in the play. There is a long scene in the second act, a duologue; it is a real battle between the two of them – she never lets him get away with anything. It's a tough argument which I found very exciting to do.

In most of John's plays he does tend to have a spokesman, and the subsidiary characters are, for a very good reason, not given that importance, not given the strength that the leading character has. If you think of *Look Back in Anger*, the other characters are not as elaborately drawn as Jimmy Porter.

But I loved playing George Dillon, I thought it was a smashing part. I remember Joan Plowright saying that probably the part which is your greatest success is the part which is very close to you. She said that *Roots*, the Wesker play that she did, was by no means the most difficult part that she'd ever had to play, because she found herself in great sympathy with it. I suppose George Dillon was not the most difficult part that I will ever play, because at that time, knowing John Osborne and being involved with the English Stage

1958 George Dillon, *Epitaph for George Dillon*, Roy
Court

George Dillon, with Yvonne
Mitchell (Ruth Gray)

Company, one was very much in sympathy with the character. In
addition, the character of George Dillon is an unsuccessful writer
and actor, and at that time I was an unsuccessful actor.

*Let's go now from Osborne to Chekhov, the part of Trigorin in* The Seagull *which you played on BBC television. One of the impressive things
about your playing of Trigorin was the subtle way you indicated so many
of the things that he is, both as a man and as a writer. Did you feel that the
character had something in common with Chekhov himself?*

Yes, indeed I did. I read a great deal about Chekhov at the time and
did a lot of research. Some books said the actor must not make the
mistake of playing this like Chekhov, Trigorin is a mediocre writer,
which I thought was nonsense. Because, in the play, everything that
happens to Trigorin happened to Chekhov. Chekhov himself was
referred to in his short stories as a landscape writer, so was Trigorin.
Chekhov did believe that his work was not as good as Turgenev or
Tolstoy, so did Trigorin. Chekhov, in fact, did have an affair with a
young actress and he didn't marry her, but the girl had a child which
died, which happens in *The Seagull*. An actress did send him a little
medallion with a quotation from one of his short stories engraved
on it. That again happens in the play; Nina gives Trigorin a little
medallion. And so, I thought one should simply play him like
Chekhov; as an artist who is constantly questioning himself.

*What do you think is the key, if there is one, to Trigorin's character?*

1966 Trigorin, *The Seagull*, BBC TV, with Pamela Brown (Madame Arkadina)

When the Moscow Art Theatre were producing *The Seagull*, they asked Chekhov what sort of man is he, and Chekhov replied, 'All my characters are very simple, very ordinary people.' Trigorin's shoes should be rather old and battered and he wears checked trousers. I have seen productions of *The Seagull* where Trigorin is played as a very romantic-looking man, but I don't think he is at all. What is so marvellous about the scene with Nina in the first act is that the girl is praising him and saying, 'You're so wonderful; your life must be so marvellous.' But it isn't at all. He just says, 'I'm a writer, I write stories, that's all; it's frightfully tedious, distressing and upsetting. It isn't satisfactory in any way; I'm not satisfied with my work, or with my life.'

*It's true that you did knock the romanticism out of Trigorin.*

Yes, it seems to be a modern trend in acting – but I don't think it's entirely a good thing, because you can fall into traps. Actors of my age tend to fight lyricism in plays, which, of course, one shouldn't do. It's something modern actors don't trust any more, or they're embarrassed by it. But if you have a lyrical passage to speak, there is no other way of doing it. You've just got to do it, you can't not jump over the fence.

*One of the beautiful things about Chekhov is the evocation of a particular mood. Do you think this affects an actor's interpretation of his part?*

There's an awful lot of boloney talked about Chekhov. Some people say, 'But it's got to be Russian in mood and sad.' I think this is not true. I've seen many Chekhovian productions where the lines are so loaded with meaning that they become heavy, boring and melancholy. The plays are mostly comedies: he calls them comedies; and he said himself that they should be played lightly and very simply. I don't think too much weight should be given to any of the lines. What is frightening about the plays is that the characters speak their innermost thoughts, but they hardly realise they're saying them. Take the opening lines of the play: 'Why do you always wear black?' 'I'm in mourning for my life.' I mean the line is sufficient in itself, you don't need to add anything to a line like that; you just say it, very simply. If it's loaded then you know you're in for a very gloomy evening.

*But it's also quite a funny line.*

Yes it is.

*And I'm sure he meant it to be, too.*

I think that the audience must find the tragedy for themselves, and they will, if the actors just play the play through, very simply. It's interesting that Chekhov himself disapproved very strongly of the Stanislavsky productions, which were supposed to be so wonderful; you know, they were full of frogs chirruping and birds twittering; he said, the play isn't about that, it's about the people and you don't need a lot of incredibly realistic scenery, there should be no scenery at all. The audience must concentrate on the people.

*So you don't think that Chekhov requires any special technique from an actor?*

Obviously you need very gifted actors. But I think it requires from the actor, as a human being, enormous honesty to play Chekhov: he must be very honest with himself; he mustn't try to conceal any of the deficiencies in the characters. If you play Arkadina, you have got to play her as a very selfish woman. I think there are many actors who do not want to be unsympathetic to the audience; they want the audience to like them. They want the audience to feel: 'Well, of course, he's not really like that; I mean it's our old so-and-so playing that nasty man, but he's a nice chap really.' That won't do. You must show the character fully, the selfishness, the nasty parts, everything. I mean, Trigorin is not a particularly admirable man. He may be a marvellous writer, but as a human being he's not a particularly nice person–he's weak and vacillating: I think you've got to be prepared to show that. It also shows that you must be able to recognise something in yourself that is a bit like that.

*Do you enjoy working in television?*

Yes, enormously. Enormously.

*What do you enjoy about it most?*

I think it's the difference between filming and acting on the stage. In acting on the stage you could go right through the play, with one or two intervals. On film they snip it all up and you do tiny bits all the time; the performance is very much out of your control; it is very much in the director's hands. But on television, you usually do the play all the way through and you're doing it very close to the camera.

*Apart from not trying to reach the back of the stalls, do you find television requires any special technique?*

You have to check your performance down a bit. As I do so much work on the stage, I've been told that I may be doing too much; the camera's very close, I don't need to react so strongly. I think you have to use the same amount of energy as you do in a stage production, certainly the same concentration.

I do find television and films enjoyable, because there's a great camaraderie in the studios which you don't always get in the theatre. You also get a marvellous feeling that the technicians are as important as the actors. If the property man does not put that ashtray there it may ruin a bit of your performance. If the lighting man has not put that light up there it's not so good for me. If the director cuts at the wrong moment – yes, I think television is marvellous.

*Your first important film part was Shelagh Delaney's* Taste of Honey, *a play about a young Salford girl. You were her mother's boy friend. It was a very seedy part; sometimes you seem to get seedy parts. Does it bother you that you might get type-cast in this kind of role?*

Yes, that's always bothered me. I got a part about a year afterwards which was almost the same – it wasn't quite the same character but it was another very seedy part. It's very interesting about films, because I was asked to play the part of this sleazy Soho night-club owner, and I wasn't in England at the time, but I agreed to come back and play it; and when I arrived they'd already started shooting the film. So I went down to the studio to have lunch with the director. As I sat at lunch, he kept looking at me in a very odd way. And finally I said: 'What's bothering you, is something wrong?' And he said, 'Well, honestly, if you had come to see me I would never have cast you in this part.' And I said, 'But why do you say that?' And he said, 'You don't look anything like you did in *Taste of Honey*.' And I said, 'Well, of course I don't.' And he said, 'But how did you do it?' And I said, 'Well, I wore a contact lens for a glass eye and I wore a moustache, that's all.' He said, 'Didn't you wear any other make-up?' And I said, 'No, not at all.' He said,

1961 Peter in the film *Taste of Honey*, with Dora Brya (Helen)

'But you look like a country squire or something.' And I said, 'What are you paying me for? You're paying me to act in your film. Of course I'm not going to look like this on film.' He was obviously very worried about it, and he said, 'Well, go and ask them to stick a moustache on you,' which I did. He said, 'No, that's not right; it doesn't look right at all.' So we tried many different combinations, and I said, 'Well, maybe I could have all my hair cut off.' No, that wasn't right. So I said, 'Well, I do have an idea; let me try it.' So I went to the make-up room and had my hair washed, and let it set under a dryer flat back on my head. Then I went back to him in the studio and he said, 'That's absolutely right; perfect. What have you done?' And I had done nothing but change my hair style. It's a funny thing about films, they always want you to look the same and be the same.

*Are you very self-critical when you see yourself in films and on television?*

I think all actors are. They hate to see themselves on film or television – they hate it. You've seen it all in your mind, but it's never like that when it comes out.

*Do you recognise any personal mannerisms?*

Always. Always.

*Does that bother you?*

Yes. One always tries to remember next time not to do that again. It may be some little thing in one's speech, you know; fading out on the ends of words or something like that. In that way it's very good to see oneself.

*Of course, these things always look a thousand times worse to you than they do to somebody else.*

Sure. And that is what one always tells other actors who bother about watching themselves on television; it's over so quickly anyway.

*Did you enjoy playing this part in* Taste of Honey*?*

I loved it. Because it was a film shot entirely on location. We used no studio at all. I think it was probably one of the first New Wave films, over here anyway, that was shot like that. We took a house in Chelsea for all the interiors of Dora Bryan's house (she played the mother), and we used the Royal Court's workshop at World's End, Chelsea, to shoot the funny little place where Murray Melvin and Rita Tushingham finally lived. The rest of it was done on location in Blackpool and Manchester: it was a wonderful way to do it.

If you are actually in a room – I know it has great technical difficulties; you can't make every film like that – it makes an enormous difference. Whereas if you have a vast studio and one little room built in it, bells going, people shouting 'Shut up,' 'Silence' and

Peter, *Taste of Honey*, with Rita Tushingham (Josephine)

'Action,' you really feel you're responsible for the entire place, when you're shooting a scene. If you do it wrong, it's going to cost an awful lot of money.

*Let's go back now to the National Theatre. You played the leading part in Franco Zeffirelli's production of* Much Ado About Nothing. *Now, I believe that he wanted you to play Benedick in a very different way from the way that it's usually played. Did this bother you at all?*

Yes, at the beginning. I think it bothered us all because the production was so outlandish, outrageous. Zeffirelli was very funny about it, but I think he was right. It is the most Italianate of Shakespeare's plays; it fits very well into a Sicilian background; and he said the audience should feel when they go out that they have had the most marvellous holiday: I think he achieved that. But many of the actors had never been to Italy, so they didn't quite know what was wanted. They'd been to Italian restaurants, but they didn't know how to be Italian, and so it was frightfully difficult at the beginning. But Zeffirelli was very clever; he used to say, if ever one said, 'I don't know how to do this as an Italian,' 'Don't worry, when you see the sets and the costume and you put your make-up on, you'll know exactly how to do it.' Which is very bothering. But in fact he was right; when one walked on to this extraordinary set with its many colours, and the brass band arrived (which we had throughout the play), it sort of kicked it off, and you knew: suddenly everybody began to enjoy themselves.

*Did you ever find yourself playing against Shakespeare's text?*

Well, Zeffirelli wanted me to play Benedick in a way with which I didn't quite agree. He said, 'All Italian men are cowards. You must play him as a man who is always talking about women and has had lots of affairs, but he never really does; he's terrified of women.' In the famous church scene where Beatrice and Benedick are finally left alone together and they make their great declaration of love, and Beatrice asks him to revenge her cousin by killing his friend, Claudio, he said, 'This scene should be played like a farce.' And I said, 'But I don't see how you can.' And in fact we've never done it as he wanted us to do it, because I don't think it would have worked as a scene; it might be very funny, but I think at the end of the play the audience wouldn't care tuppence about Beatrice or Benedick.

But this is the way he saw the church scene and especially the character of Beatrice. When Beatrice and Benedick are left alone, there she is, wearing a great black mantilla, and she looks over and sees this poor jellybag standing over in the corner, and she thinks, 'Yes, I'll get him to revenge my cousin,' and she pretends to cry and be very upset. Finally he says, 'What's the matter, I love you, I love you, I'll do anything for you.' She says, 'Right. Kill Claudio.'

1965 Benedick, *Much Ado About Nothing*, Natio
Theatre, with Maggie Smith (Beatrice) and Fra
Finlay (Dogberry)

He says, 'No, I can't do that, I won't do that.' She then becomes Anna Magnani and screams and roars and rants. He says, 'We're in church! Shush, shush.' But finally she screams at him so much that he says, 'All right, I'll do it then, I'll do it.' Though he doesn't really mean to do it. But I think, at that point, Benedick does really mean to do it.

We didn't do it that way because I just didn't think it would work: I think Zeffirelli was a little annoyed about it.

A lot of what he wanted remained, and many people said that the play had never been so clear to them, the actual story line. There are usually some rather dull passages in the play. But because the production was so lively, and because it was played with a lot of passion and in a very Italian way, the plot came over very clearly.

*Can you tell us something about your own discipline as an actor apart from the actual rehearsals?*

Working in a company like the National Theatre one is kept incredibly busy. I don't think people would believe the hours that some of the actors have to work. A normal day starts at 10.30 and we rehearse right through until 5.30. Then we do a performance – most of the performances end at 10.30, which means you don't really get home until 11.30, if you're lucky. You then have something to eat before going to bed, and you're back again in the theatre at 10.30 the next morning.

*When do you fit in voice and movement classes?*

Usually they have a rota and you grab the lessons when you can; the movement classes are held three times a week. On those days rehearsals finish at 4.0 to enable you to have a movement class from 4.0 until 5.30. They involve tumbling, acrobatics, mime and movement.

*It must require a lot of discipline, if you've actually finished work at that time, to go on and do a movement class.*

You are not forced to go, but I think it's a very good idea to do something like that; it makes a complete break and you get tuned up for the evening performance.

*When* Much Ado About Nothing *went into production for its second season, you were put in charge of the redirection of the play. Was this your first chance of directing?*

Yes, I did direct a couple of plays ages ago when I was in rep. But that was the first serious job of directing I did, or redirecting.

*Do you want to do more of it?*

Yes, I would enjoy it enormously. It's very interesting because you see so many of your own faults as an actor; it's like looking at yourself a lot of the time. You think, 'Why is he doing that? Why doesn't

1963 Captain Plume, *The Recruiting Officer*, National Theatre, with Lynn Redgrave (Rose)

he just stand still and speak?' And you think, 'But I do that, I do that all the time.'

*So you have learned a lot from it?*

Yes, an enormous amount. It's interesting to watch how different actors develop, how actors respond to different kinds of direction, how you have to take a straightforward tack with one actor, when you may have to bully another actor. They're all different, they all need a different approach.

One of the girls in *Much Ado* had a slight problem with a particular scene, and so we swapped parts and made somebody else play her part, and made her play the other part, so that she could see what the other actress had to cope with. She could also listen to somebody else saying her lines; you see, I wanted her to play it at a very quick pace which she couldn't quite get. By doing it this way, she was able to solve the problem right away.

*Have you used improvisation much at the National?*

Yes, we used it in *The Recruiting Officer* quite a lot. I think it was very valuable. But if a director is going to use improvisation, he must have improvised an awful lot and understand it very well; otherwise it can be very destructive. When you make actors improvise you actually push them to the *n*th degree of their creativity. I think the director should say to them, 'We are doing it because the result I want is this. That is what I'm trying to achieve through improvisation, and I think we can probably get it.' Then I think it can work very well.

Captain Plume and Rose

*What kind of results would a director be wanting from improvisation?*

On the production of *The Recruiting Officer* it was an experiment. The director, William Gaskill, said, 'I want to be sure that you understand absolutely what you are talking about.' He said that in many Shakespearean productions the text went over the audience's head because the actor didn't really understand the full meaning of the words, and so he skated over them. If he made us improvise without the text, he felt he could then find out what the actor was missing. His method was to let us read a scene, then put our books down and improvise on it. We would then be told what we had missed. We then, maybe, read the scene again and improvised on it; we did this over and over again. We improvised for something like three weeks. It was extraordinary what came out of those rehearsals, and what didn't come out. When you arrive at your first rehearsal you are expected to know what the play is all about and what your character is, or at least have a jolly good idea. But I found that I'd missed lots of things which were frightfully important elements in the character and in the play.

It was interesting when we started this improvisation because,

P

when we were told, everybody was terrified of standing up and just doing things. But the director was very clever in that he made the whole company sit around in a circle, and he said, 'I want you to take an imaginary object, like a ball, and pass it to the next person.' Then the next person takes the ball, and he has to do something with it like throwing it up and down. He then turns it into something else, like a teapot. He then passes it on, so that no actor was working alone. And they all enjoyed that enormously. It was very successful; it worked frightfully well. Then he said, 'Now, we'll put a chair in the middle of the circle,' and the first actor goes up and turns it into something – like a pram. And he leaves it. The next actor comes up and pushes it around like a pram; then he must turn it into something else. So that he gradually isolated the actors and got them working on their own. Then he said, 'Now we will do a scene where an actor gets up and starts some activity, then another actor will get up and join him in his activity; he will then change the activity so that the man is mowing the lawn. The next man comes up and helps him mow the lawn. He then changes it into something else.' Finally he got them all up doing things on their own. By the end of the morning they were doing brilliant things, simply longing to get up and do something. When we came to the afternoon and we started improvising on the play, nobody minded.

*Are there any of the big classical parts you haven't yet played that you would like to play?*

I don't know; I always think this is a very difficult question to answer because what is interesting and exciting is being asked to play something; then one's imagination is fired. I would hate to say, 'I want to play Hamlet,' because then you're out on a limb and you've got to be jolly good, very good indeed. But if someone comes to you and says, 'Would you like to play Hamlet?' and they feel you can play it, you yourself may or may not think you can at the time, but I think that is more exciting. No, I can't think of any part that I would love to play, or any part that I could play better than anybody else.

*Do you think the National Theatre should do more contemporary plays than they do?*

No, I don't. I think they should do an enormous range of plays, which includes contemporary works; I think they've done pretty well with contemporary plays. When you make the National Theatre available for writers, they start with many advantages. They have an enormous company to choose from and a grant which will provide them with the very best kind of sets, costumes and everything else. I think the commercial managements would object; it would be very unfair to them.

National Theatre.
Above and top right: 1965 Tom Wrench, *Trelawny of 'Wells'*, with Doris Hare (Mrs Mossop)
Right: 1968 Frederick, *Home and Beauty*, with Laure Olivier (A.B. Raham) and Geraldine McEwan (Victo

*Do you think the National Theatre should worry about being fair to commercial managements?*

I don't think they need to worry, because there are very few plays the National Theatre have done that a commercial management couldn't have produced. I know that when we did *Trelawny of the 'Wells'* and *Hay Fever* there was quite an uproar. The commercial managements said, 'These plays should be done on Shaftesbury Avenue.' However, the plays were available for them to do, ever since they were written. They just didn't choose to do them, so they can't moan after somebody else has put them on.

*Is there any one part that you've played, with the National or the Royal Court, that's given you rather more satisfaction than any other?*

I've been very fortunate at the National in that I have been given a very varied selection of parts to play; that really is the great pleasure of working there. One is hardly ever cast twice in the same kind of role; one doesn't want to be.

*Which parts have given you most satisfaction?*

*The Recruiting Officer* I loved doing, and *The Royal Hunt* and *Hay Fever*. The marvellous thing about the National Theatre is that you can play large parts but you can also play very small parts: I played the part of a priest in Max Frisch's play, *Andorra*. That's one of the things I've enjoyed doing most. But if I'd been offered it by a commercial management I would never have taken it because the part was too small.

*Can you envisage yourself staying at the National Theatre almost indefinitely?*

Yes, in a way, because they realise that one may be offered films; and if you can give them sufficient notice they will release you. Colin Blakely, for instance, is leaving for a year to do films. He'll come back. And that's very good, because they say, 'We would rather have you here for, say, six months of the year than not at all.' I think that's a marvellous policy, because it keeps the actor happy if he knows he's not absolutely stuck there for fifty-two weeks of the year. I've also done quite a lot of television since I've been there, whenever I've been available.

1964 Father Benedict, *Andorra*, National Theatre

Opposite: 1968 Frederick, *Home and Beauty*

229

# Dorothy Tutin

OROTHY TUTIN's face – small, neat, round-eyed as a choir-boy's – is not the kind you associate with stardom. Yet, of her generation, she is probably the one actress with the personal, starry hold on audiences that managements dream about.

Partly it may be because she started so young, in the days before the English theatre found a mind of its own, distinct from the public's. Her first professional appearance, as Margaret Tudor in *The Thistle and the Rose*, was in 1949, when she was just eighteen. Her first West End lead, in Graham Greene's *The Living Room*, came four years later in 1953. The moment she walked on to that ominous, looming set, every parent in the audience yearned towards her. She was the daughter every Mrs Worthington had fought to keep from going on the stage – cheeky, off-hand, bravely trying to seem as slangy and Bohemian as the others, but under it frightened, vulnerable – obviously doomed to be let down by love, betrayed by other people's husbands, perhaps to commit suicide in a bed-sitter.

That was the quality which won her the role of Isherwood's Sally Bowles in *I Am a Camera* – the waif from the Home Counties, at large in Brecht's Berlin; of Joan in Anouilh's *The Lark*, less a saint in armour than a frightened child sleepwalking into martyrdom. It made her the perfect Ophelia at Stratford in 1958; an almost perfect Juliet; a touching Hedwig in Ibsen's *The Wild Duck*: all innocent victims of an adult world whose corruption is too much for their spirit and gaiety. It fitted less well into John Osborne's *Entertainer*. You could not imagine that slip of a thing standing alone to shout against Suez in Trafalgar Square. Defiant, yes, but independent – never.

Even in comedy – as Cecily in the film of *The Importance of Being Earnest*, as Viola in *Twelfth Night* – there was a pathos beneath her perkiness; a defencelessness which made you see why Olivia wanted to mother her, while she, herself, pined for a middle-aged

1958 Ophelia, *Hamlet*, Stratford

duke. It wasn't only mothers, but all young men of spirit, who wanted to take her away from all that and protect her from life.

A relation like that with the public can make a star, but it hasn't much to do with good acting. Still, it seems to have given her a confidence she needed to build on. In 1960 she played Cressida at Stratford; not just Shakespeare's wanton, but the girl of Chaucer's poem, Shakespeare's source. 'Sliding of courage'; hiding beneath harsh sauciness, the desperate terror of a child alone in war. The same qualities, but bigger, stronger and used with the deliberate confidence of art.

They were stronger still in her Varya, in Chekhov's *Cherry Orchard*: the adopted orphan, plain, but proud enough to choke in silence her need for the vulgarian she loves. And in John Whiting's *The Devils*, in 1962, she raised them to the strength of madness. The little, crippled prioress, out of whose racked, lonely body streamed with evil gaiety the power to mock obscenely, wound, destroy, was the finest thing she'd done, establishing her on a new level as an actress. In a sense, it was her old role – a mother's nightmares come true and worse than true. But now victim and actress rose to meet them.

The wheel came full circle in her Victoria, in *Portrait of a Queen*, making a 'star' performance of a new kind, the image of a lonely, well-brought-up young girl, beneath whose innocence and vulnerability lie an astonishing humour and strength with which to face tragedy and loss.

*Ronald Bryden*

DEREK HART: *When you embarked upon the portrayal of Queen Victoria how much research did you do in terms of reading and studying of pictures?*

DOROTHY TUTIN: At first I thought I'd do a great deal because there's much written about her, but in fact, as she was only eighteen when she came to the throne, I found that having read a book that dealt with her early life and knowing the background and how she felt at that particular age I didn't want to read any more. Perhaps it was odd but I realised that what historians had to do was precisely what we had to do – arrange, select and interpret. For instance, a letter she wrote to King Leopold of the Belgians two months after Albert's death we found, during rehearsals, worked as a soliloquy at his death bed, because it was so savage and immediate in its expression of her grief.

*What did you feel were the most important elements in her character?*

When I first started I was very objective about her. But as I grew towards the character I became less and less objective. I think this happens when you're playing a part: you forget, you accept it all, you don't criticise it any more. I find it rather difficult now to have a critical attitude about her; I grew to love her. But to answer the question, I think the qualities that probably were exceptional in her, and most extraordinary for a woman in her position, were her great honesty and her passionate nature. She also had a very uncompromising attitude about so many things. I don't think this was necessarily a virtue! But it was a very difficult thing for her to contend with, in her position as queen, and as a mother figure of a whole empire.

*Were you able to find answering echoes of these characteristics in yourself quite easily?*

I think with any part it's a question of rearranging yourself. You're quite surprised sometimes to find that you have certain characteristics that you didn't think you had – it can be very alarming! I think it's often a question of bringing things that are buried to the surface. And as I read her writings, I realised she had an extraordinary gift for expressing herself. This was a great help. I didn't feel that she was being literary or affected. She wrote naturally, in the style of the period, but she had a tremendous simplicity and directness in the way she wrote. Her letters to her daughter, for instance, are startling: very modern. I found her a most extraordinary woman, far more complicated and with a fuller range of emotion than I had imagined.

*And yet, at the same time, probably operating against a fairly simple set of standards and values.*

Oh yes, but in a very complex way. I think she had tremendous femininity, an extraordinary warmth, and a capacity for adoration which is rare today.

1965 Queen Victoria, *Portrait of a Queen*, Bristol Old Vic and Vaudeville

233

*In the play, her life span is approximately sixty years. How much did you find the ageing process which you needed to employ a purely mental one, as opposed to the physical aids, make-up and so on?*

That was really decided for me; we couldn't have physical aids because it was all consecutive; I couldn't go off and pad my cheeks or change wigs. I had a change of wig in the first interval; that was about all I had time for; and just a change of costume during the second interval, for the third act.

*Can you indicate in any way the kind of mental processes you went through to convey this vast passage of time?*

Imagination I suppose; I think you imagine it. In a way I was lucky because one went from eighteen to eighty and of course that's a great help, you can't help having *some* contrast over that span of time! You're not suddenly having to say: 'Well now I'm forty-two'; you're able to say, 'I'm gradually getting older and older and things are happening.' The grief was of great value because it aged her overnight: from a very happily married woman to a desperate woman, almost deranged – I think she herself said that she feared for her reason.

When she went into retirement the Press attacks were far more vicious than anything we know today. I was shocked when I read them, and to sit on the stage listening to them – my God, I felt for her. It was easier to understand that – with her early background, and passionate and possessive nature – the isolation of the crown, far from giving her fortitude, only emphasised her isolation as a widow.

*Did you feel a great sense of responsibility playing a real character, and a fairly recent character in terms of history?*

Yes, I did. But I tried to forget the historical aspect and think of her more as a woman, which wasn't so difficult because she had written about it. On the other hand, it was terrifying to act something that somebody had actually written themselves; I mean, for somebody to express their own grief, you feel a far greater responsibility than if it's a dramatist's idea of that person's grief – it's once removed and you're not afraid of its theatricality.

It was odd, she so desperately wanted Albert to be remembered (and he was so well worth remembering – a very remarkable man in every way, tremendously intelligent, enlightened and artistic). She was re-creating him through her letters and her diaries, and consequently through this play; by her words, and the way she felt about him, Albert was reborn perhaps more completely than Victoria.

*At the technical level, with this kind of part, is it very difficult for you to get the variations of pace and so on; or is this something that's a constant worry to you?*

Queen Victoria, with Derek Waring (Prince Albert)

You mean, when you're on the stage all the time?

*Yes, all the time.*

It's dreadful. You get a terrible feeling that, once you're on, it's never going to stop. There are some advantages: for instance, you don't have time to get out of the mood and have to pull yourself back into it. On the other hand, if you're running slow or you're not quite doing it as fully as you'd like to, you don't have that blessed moment when you can go off and say, 'God, I'm being awful, I must pull myself together, now I'll show them, now I'll be better.' You're sort of stuck with yourself on the stage throughout, which has very definite drawbacks. And, of course, it's frightfully tiring, because the concentration for three hours is tremendous. You just have to concentrate throughout.

*You're reverting now to the point that you were making earlier, that you made it very subjective after a time. Doesn't this suggest that it was even more taxing than it need be? I'm wondering, for instance, if you should have been more detached about it – there is a school of acting which says that this is an ideal circumstance.*

This happened, I think, in the play; it was both detached and involved, especially in moments at the beginning. It was a fairly detached production, it was almost Brechtian. Anyway, non-naturalistic.

*Stylistic.*

Stylistic, that's the word, yes. You were doing it and commenting on it at the same time, so that you were automatically detached. It was at later moments, the emotional moments, that one became far more involved. That wasn't so bad in fact. One wasn't desperately trying to be naturalistic all the way through.

*As a general principle, do you find that if you're studying a historical character, you tend to go in the first instance for the human qualities or for the trappings and the flavour of the period?*

I think for me it would depend entirely on the style of the play. If it was a period piece, which is more human than stylistic, well, naturally you'd go for the human qualities. And the outside trappings – I think they're terribly important too. I don't know which would come first – sometimes one and sometimes the other. But you know, if you started trying to find the motivation for certain period pieces, you'd come very, very much unstuck. They often have a convention of their own, a light touch, wit and a sort of sparkle; this is something that is almost a theatrical sense rather than a human sense. If you enjoy the style of a play, the human qualities of the character you're playing become that much richer and you can dig deeper.

236

*Going back to Victoria for a moment, you obviously felt very deeply about her and you were able to convey the feeling of emotion very powerfully. Is the expression of emotion for you a fairly straightforward and easy thing to portray, or not?*

Oh, I don't know. I think it depends on the writer. I don't think you produce it from yourself, you produce it from the script. I am, I think, easily affected; but you start with the script, and that gradually affects you. I generally try to work towards the emotion and then towards the control of it. But with *Portrait of a Queen*, because it was real and because she herself wrote of her own grief in such an extraordinary way, the emotion came all too readily, and the difficulty was to control it.

*How deep were your first theatrical longings? How did they develop?*

Well, I never thought of being an actress. It was the last thing I wanted to be. At school I was fond of painting and music and I was going to be a musician and teach music. I left school very young and I had a year studying music with a marvellous teacher but I found out, fairly quickly, thank goodness, that I just didn't have the talent. I hadn't great ambitions, I only wanted to teach, but I really wasn't talented enough; not for a career in music. It was my parents who said, 'Well, you've got a year in hand, why don't you try a drama school?' I was appalled, I thought it was a dreadful idea. I'd acted at school, but I'd never considered acting as a career and I was very shy and self-conscious; I think that was really the reason why they thought it would be good for me, you know, bring me out, sort of finish me off as it were! We got the brochure and I was attracted by all the extra things like ballet-dancing, singing and fencing, and things like that. And so I went. Of course, the thing that really made me decide that I wanted to act was the moment I found out that it was too difficult. That was a problem; I didn't get in at first, you see. I tried three times but I did get in the third time. All that was actually very lucky because I had two terms at pre-RADA. I think Sir Kenneth Barnes, the principal of RADA, had a lot of foresight really. He sent me away to find my feet; it was good because, not having done anything or thought about acting very much, it was an easier way in; doing things in a class in front of other people I found terrifying, but it prepared me for RADA proper.

It was when I was at pre-RADA that I suddenly realised how very, very difficult it was – too difficult. You see, after music I thought it was going to be easy; you know, you imagined something and then you did it – you didn't have to play scales, it would be much simpler. Then it suddenly came to me that it was more difficult because you were stuck with yourself; *you* were the instrument, there was nothing else but you. I realised that I wasn't a good enough instrument for what I wanted to express, and I came home and cried. I was desperate and I said I would give up. Then my mother was simply marvellous. She said: 'If that's how you feel, then I have confidence in you.' I don't think she'd had much confidence up till then! She had been to see me at pre-RADA and I think she was surprised that I was developing a bit and did seem to show some talent. But it was the way she said: 'If you feel like that, that is how an artist should feel; I insist you go on and do it and work hard.'

*You did this without much confidence as far as you were concerned?*

Perhaps by that time I was getting confidence; perhaps it was a kind of arrogance, that I wanted to be a really good actress, not just playing about.

*Did you feel you had talent?*

I do remember that I got a report at pre-RADA saying that they thought I was a flash in the pan, and I was terribly excited by that. I thought for anybody to think I was a flash of anything was rather marvellous; and I thought, it's *not* just momentary, perhaps it will develop.

*In the two years you spent at the Royal Academy of Dramatic Art how do you feel you did develop? Obviously you became more technically proficient. Did you feel also that you developed very much as a person?*

I adored being a student. I was very lucky to have gone there when I did. There were some very good teachers; they were tremendously varied. This was wonderful because they all had a different approach, a slightly different attitude; there wasn't one person saying the theatre is *this*, acting must be *that*. They were all very different and so one had a chance to pick, to select what one needed for one's self. There was one teacher who was really remarkable; she said: 'You cannot *think* enough, you cannot *feel* enough and you cannot have enough imagination; you cannot have too much of any of these things.' It wasn't just that she said it; anybody could say that, but she said it with such intensity and such passion, I have never forgotten it.

*There are a large number of techniques that have to be mastered. As a student, did you find particular difficulty in wrestling with any one of these, such as voice-projection, movement or fencing?*

My major problem was my voice. I lisped and I was terribly breathy, I was always gasping. I was taking breath *in* instead of letting it *out*. It was a long time before the penny dropped about that. I kept on practising exercises and getting more and more filled with breath and more and more breathy, with a hectic kind of delivery – it may sound a bit hectic now, but I hope when I'm on the stage that it calms down and I'm more controlled! I didn't learn enough, quickly

1955 Hedvig, *The Wild Duck*, Saville

enough with exercises – that was my fault. But I found that if you imagined you wanted a deeper voice you often got it – or a high voice for that matter, a child's voice. With Hedwig in *The Wild Duck*, I had a terrible fear about doing it because I was worried; I'd had trouble with my voice, I'd had nodules from wanting, and getting, a husky voice for Sally Bowles in *I Am a Camera*, and I thought: how awful to play that child Hedwig, who should be so pure and clear, with a husky voice. It was extraordinary, because when we came to rehearse I imagined what her voice *should* be, what I'd like it to be, and it wasn't husky any more. I think *sometimes* imagination and technique are interchangeable.

*When you left RADA, I think your first job was in* The Thistle and the Rose, *at the Bolton's Theatre. How did that come about?*

I was lucky, very, very lucky, because at RADA I played little boys and girls – I wasn't a leading lady type. But one teacher gave me a very good part, the young girl in *Cradle Song*, and I think it went all right. And from that I was sent as a student to The Boltons because they needed a young girl for a very small part. While I was there auditioning for that part they asked me to stay and help with the auditions for the leading part. So I read in for another character, a young princess of ten. Then they sent me away and said, 'You'll be hearing from us.' I really thought I would, you know; I didn't know then that it was a sort of a cliché, and you never hear another thing. But I was very excited. I thought, Oh, how lovely, I shall be working, I shall be working, I shall play this small part and I shall actually be in a theatre. In fact, when I got home I heard that they'd rung up to ask me to start rehearsals on Monday playing the leading part of Princess Margaret, which was the character I'd only read in for, and not the one I'd auditioned for. I was so excited I cried; it was a marvellously lucky opportunity.

*Is it possible for you to look back on that first professional performance, and remember what it was like?*

I don't think I can. I do remember that it was a beautifully written part – it was quite funny, I remember. William Douglas-Home had written it; it was a historical play, rare for him, and the rhythm of the dialogue was very helpful for a young actress, just starting off, and I enjoyed it all so much I couldn't wait for matinée days.

*Was it as a direct result of this that you went to the Bristol Old Vic where you played a large number of classical roles?*

Direct result. Lucky again.

*And what roles did you play there?*

I only played small parts, Phoebe in *As You Like It* and Lucius in *Julius Caesar*.

1949 Princess Margaret of England, *The Thistle and the Rose*, The Boltons

1953 Rose Pemberton, *The Living Room*, Wyndham's

1954 Sally Bowles, *I Am a Camera*, New Theatre

240

*Your first great success was, of course, in Graham Greene's* The Living Room. *How did this come about?*

It happened at a time when I was feeling at a low ebb; I was in a play and I didn't think I was being very good. I was talking to the friend with whom I was sharing the dressing-room, and we were both saying, 'Oh well, we must just consider doing any part that comes along.' We weren't ambitious any more, we'd just act; we'd act anywhere, we'd be jolly glad to do it without having a grand scheme. Then suddenly I was sent this play, *The Living Room* – I remember reading it in the train and arriving at Waterloo feeling different inside, completely changed. And I said to her, 'I take it all back; I've just read something I would love to play.' Of course, I never thought I'd get it. I did three auditions and I got it the last time.

*This was followed by John van Druten's adaptation of the Christopher Isherwood Berlin stories,* I Am a Camera, *wasn't it? Now this play also ran for a long time. How did you find yourself reacting to playing the same part night after night?*

I think it has great advantages when you're young because it gives you confidence – if the part is good. Donald Albery, who put on *The Living Room*, had the idea that it would be good to play a reverse type in *I Am a Camera*. So that I had two long runs in two very contrasted parts. This was extremely lucky for me because it was at a time when there weren't many good parts for young actresses.

*Presumably there's always the danger of feeling yourself getting very stale – in a long run?*

Oh, that's awful. Yes. You go through terrible phases when you get so critical of yourself, because you have *time* to be critical. You're just appalled to find that you're going on and on doing everything in the same way; you can bore yourself, and perhaps *should*, very easily. It's a question of very strong discipline. But I would like to develop a way of preparing myself to get into the best mood, so that one could put the right sort of freedom and inspiration into the part when going on to the stage. That's the problem; so that every night you're bound to be different, you're bound to vary. That's what's exciting about the theatre, the audience are seeing something that is literally an active and unique thing.

*It's like a concert, isn't it, as opposed to a recording?*

Yes. And one is immensely affected by the audiences. You're more affected by them the longer you run. This is a good thing in some ways and a bad thing in others.

*Are you sure that your performance, once set in a long run, doesn't vary as much as you think it does?*

Q

I'm sure it doesn't. It would be rather horrifying if it varied completely. Your intention is always the same, surely. But you hope you do it better, do it deeper; you hope your feelings will come more quickly, the emotion spring far stronger. During the run of *The Living Room* one went through all these phases – because one used to get depressed with one's performance. Then one would jolt one's self out of it and suddenly have a phase of rediscovery, of finding new things. The really shattering thing was that it wasn't till the last night that I ever thought I played it properly, because, suddenly, I was playing it as though – like life – it never happens again. This moment has gone, gone completely. Dead. And when you die, you're dead. You're not going to get up and do it the next day. It's finished for ever and ever. It was extraordinary to feel – not, 'Oh, I must pretend that it's happening for the first time,' which one does try to feel, but to feel the other thing, 'It's never ever going to happen again.'

*Do you feel, as an actress, very conscious of your audience in the sense that you know that they're responding well to you, but that you are able to play upon them, manipulate them?*

I don't know; I have very ambivalent feelings about audiences. Sometimes I think they help me to feel – especially if they aren't caring, perhaps, and so you must make them, then you care more. It's a difficult thing to talk about because I think I should have a more direct and simple attitude. I once spoke to somebody who said, 'Oh, it's lovely, it's the first night; I love the audience, I think the audience loves me, it's so exciting'. But I was feeling appalled and terrified; that kind of feeling is not an antagonism – it's a sort of lost feeling. No, that's not the word; it's lonely. It's lonely. Then you feel closer to the part that you are playing; you care more, so that if you feel the audience aren't caring, you hope you can make them care by caring more yourself.

*I was wondering, for instance, if you ever felt: 'They are restless tonight, something isn't getting across. By God, I'm going to make them!'*

That is what I mean. The worst thing is to be depressed, to say, 'Oh dear, it's all no good, it's dreadful, I can't, they're not listening, I'm not holding them.' No, what I was trying to explain was that if you feel all these things then it gives you more courage because it's courage that you need when you know the play is not going well. Then you've got to find a way of saying, 'This does not matter, the play is of value, it is important,' and you've got somehow to find the courage within yourself, to be still, quiet and unfussed.

*But the other thing could happen; you could feel very defeated, utterly lost, and also, presumably, very exposed.*

1963 Polly Peachum, *The Beggar's Opera*, Aldwych, v Derek Godfrey (Macheath) and Virginia McKe (Lucy Lockit)

Very exposed. That's why I think it helps you to see a performance as a triangle – I'm sure it's a triangle: it's you, the character you're playing, the audience; or the character, you, the audience; or the audience, you, the character. You're continually altering the positions of those people, because, obviously, there's part of you that's registering the audience, there's part of you that's only concentrating on the character and there's part of you that's *you*, aware of you playing the part to the audience. All that sounds much more complicated than it is.

*You must be more acutely aware of the audience in playing comedy than in a heavy drama. Because the only way in which you can measure your success is by the way they respond.*

Yes. I think the worst thing is when you've got gags to play, not lines which are unconsciously funny, but really funny jokes. My admiration for people who can stand on the stage and be funny, tell a funny story and make the people laugh is terrific; it's marvellous because it's very difficult. Sometimes, if there's no reaction, it doesn't necessarily mean that the audience aren't enjoying it – they may be smiling! When we did *The Beggar's Opera* at the Aldwych, it had very bad notices and, of course, we didn't have a very large audience. But we were thrilled that anybody had come, we were so delighted, that we thought, 'We'll jolly well entertain them and forget what the Press said, we'll be better than we were told we were; and, you never know, we may surprise them.'

*It's approximately fifteen years since you made your first film playing Cecily in* The Importance of Being Earnest. *Looking at it now, how does it seem to you? Has it got the style you would expect? If you were doing it now, would you do it in the same way?*

Oh, I don't know. I've no idea. It was my first film, and after I'd seen the first day's shooting, I was simply horrified. It's such a marvellous play, so perfectly written, and the thought of one of the big scenes being done for ever and ever in one day absolutely appalled me, I couldn't get over it; I kept on asking for retakes. Eventually the producer came up to me and said, did I know how much it cost to have these retakes? And I said no, and he said, 'It costs about £200 a minute,' so I had to shut up. Every time you see something, every time you do something, you'd want to do it again. I don't think you would ever say, 'That's it, oh yes, that's just as it should be, I think I did that perfectly'; I wish I could, it would make me very happy.

*Do you enjoy this style of comedy playing? Is it something which you feel to be a great challenge, requiring more discipline than an emotional part?*

I enjoy both. I love parts with unconscious humour, where you find the humour in it without *having* to be, as it were, funny. Having to be funny is rather a burden because you can get rather frightened and put off if the audience don't laugh. When the humour is unconscious, it doesn't really matter if people laugh or not – the wit is not necessarily laughing wit, the audience is smiling perhaps, only you don't hear smiles.

*The wit and humour of Oscar Wilde is very much a verbal thing, isn't it? Do you find your knowledge of music is of any relevance to the speaking of his lines?*

Oh yes, yes. I think it has a lot of relevance. In fact, his dialogue is written like music, perfectly phrased and beautifully orchestrated.

*Does it affect the way you approach a part, particularly if it's something like Shakespeare?*

Oh yes, but the terrible thing is that you can start to sing. And I have sung – I mean I've sung when I shouldn't have been singing! I've sung speeches; it's awful. You can take off and it doesn't sound like words; it sounds like some dreadful sung aria, but without music. That's very bad. You have to prevent that. I remember John Gielgud saying once that playing a long speech in Shakespeare *is* like music in that it has a beginning, a middle and an end. You mustn't think when you start the speech that it's all line by line. It has a natural shape, and if you play the whole shape from the very beginning, this isn't false, this isn't wrong, this gives the impetus to the speech, this makes it much, much better. You're not concentrating on yourself, trying to think every thought, but on

1951 Cecily, *The Importance of being Earnest* (film)

the whole speech having a complete shape of its own. This he can do; this I'd like to be able to do, but I can't, yet.

*I remember seeing you in a play by John Whiting called* The Devils, *in which you played a prioress possessed by the evil spirit of the prelate, Grandier. There was a scene where the witch-hunting priest tries to extract the evidence from you and you actually became possessed. Now, that is a situation which must be wildly outside your own experience. When you're doing something of that kind, is it a particularly difficult thing for you to do?*

That part was impossible really, impossible. It was a marvellous play, absolutely marvellous. But when I read it I said to Peter Hall who was producing it, 'The play is so wonderful – it would be too awful if I played it and couldn't do it at all; I must audition for it.' I had done another play of John Whiting's before and he said it would be all right and I wasn't to be nervous about it and just do it. The awful thing was whenever we came at rehearsals to the possession scene, I kept on saying, 'Well do you mind if I don't do that today? You know, I'll do it tomorrow, can we skip that bit?' I was terrified of doing it, I was balking it. Then one of the nuns came up to me and said, 'Dotty, aren't you going to do that scene, because until you do it, we can't get started either?' I was appalled to think that I had been stopping them from acting. And so that day at rehearsal, when we came to the possession scene, instead of saying, 'Sorry I can't, I'll do it later,' I did it and we started off. I didn't know what would happen, I just made my mind a blank and tried to imagine possession. The extraordinary thing was that the other nuns picked it up and in fact we had the experience that happened in the actual play, in that nunnery, a sort of catching hysteria. We all got it; we never did it again like that. The problem about hysteria of that kind is that you can't portray it in any manner that is acceptable. The audience can imagine it for themselves far better than you could ever show it. In fact it was best when it wasn't seen, when it was either talked about or when you only saw a little bit of it.

*I suppose it becomes a purely technical problem as to how you project that kind of mad, out-of-control state.*

Yes. Once you're in it, it's all right. It's a bit like a drunk scene in a way, you lose control. You must abandon yourself, it's a sort of release. The really exhausting and difficult part is making a transition from being perfectly controlled and nun-like to a completely abandoned wild creature.

*You had a humped back, didn't you, in that play? Do you find that you are enormously sensitive to your physical accoutrements when you're acting?*

Very much. Very much so. The texture, material, colour. It can affect you a lot. Yes, I had a hump in *The Devils*. It certainly helped at first. They made it into the smock underneath. But really, by the time you'd acted in it and felt it, you didn't really need it. It was jolly heavy. Sometimes you just mustn't let yourself be affected by your clothes, if you happen to have to wear costumes that you don't like and are not happy in; you've got to try not to be put off by them, which is difficult. But when we did the *Beggar's Opera* at the Aldwych Theatre, Leslie Harry designed such perfect costumes for all of us, they were simply wonderful, made from old materials, made up correctly and then tatted down – as soon as you put them on you felt, oh this is it.

*Once rehearsals have been completed and you've started to play to audiences, do you find that you establish total control of your performance fairly quickly?*

I doubt if one could ever say that one has total control. I don't know whether one should, because if you're absolutely controlled, it sounds a bit rigid. I'd have thought that the main advantage in the theatre is to be dangerous, not to be quite sure that something startling isn't going to happen. When you feel in good acting form, which doesn't, unfortunately, happen every night, then certain things will come better and suddenly a door will open. And there comes a moment when, if you are only wanting to be in control, you wouldn't go forward, you wouldn't take the step into the abyss, you'd go back and say, 'Oh no, I must be in control.' The exciting thing is to be dangerous, to say, 'If I go this far it might be dreadful and embarrassing, but at this particular moment I feel I could do it.' Ideally, I suppose, this is what should happen in rehearsals; but in three weeks you're not always able to do that, and it would be stupid if it could happen to you on the stage and you didn't let it happen. The exciting things should always happen on the stage, because of the audience.

*You played in Anouilh's* The Lark, *a play about St Joan. This wasn't Shaw's St Joan, but let's consider Anouilh's play for a moment. Was this a character that you'd always thought that you would like to play?*

No, never. I think most people at drama school either play it or want to play it; I never thought I'd be right for it because I thought Shaw's St Joan, anyway, should be a big, strong peasant girl, and I didn't think I was suitable. But in Anouilh's play *The Lark*, she was different. She wasn't *the* St Joan, she was an idea of St Joan. In a way, she represented France during the time of occupation. She was somebody holding out against all odds, resistance was something that she passionately believed in. She was the very spirit of this idea.

*The Lark, you mean?*

Yes. In fact, if we had played it in the context of the original version – which was a play within a play – where she was an actress acting the part of St Joan in a kind of limbo, that would have been clearer,

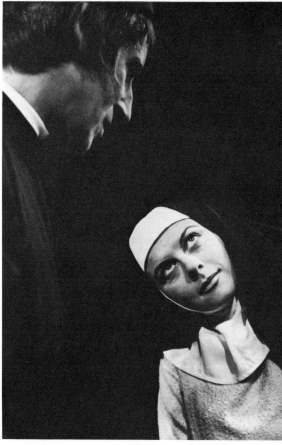

1961 Sister Jeanne, *The Devils*, Aldwych, with M Adrian (Father Barré)

246

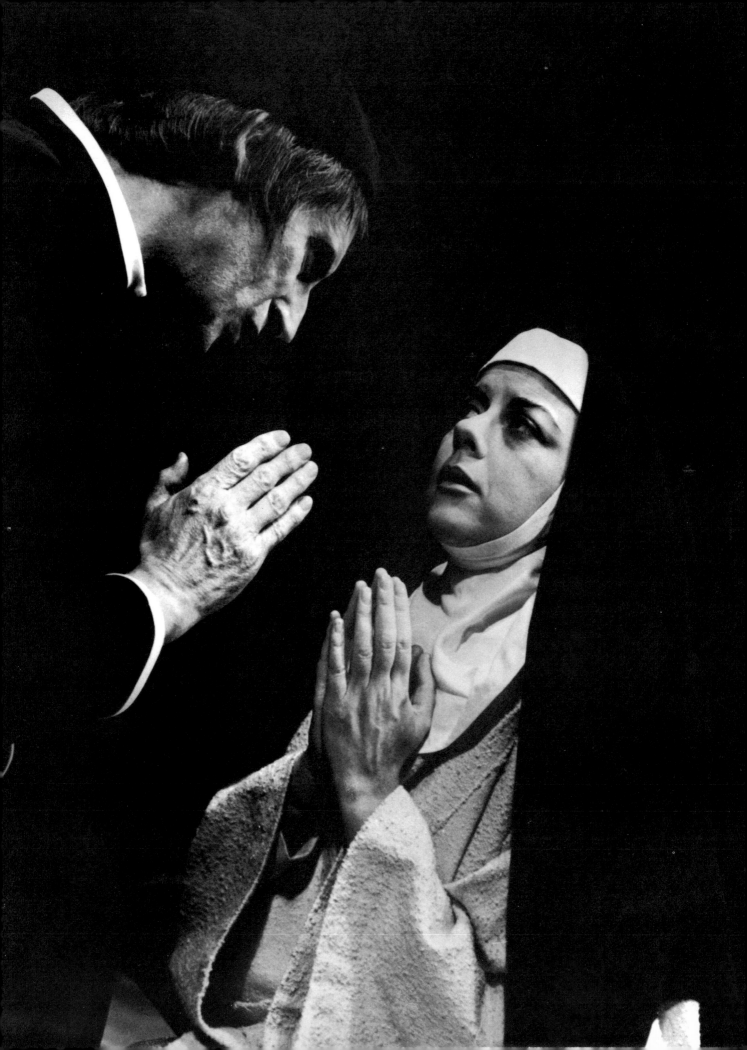

I think. Actors love being players within a play because somehow it's another dimension, it's wonderful to be able to say, I am an actress acting a part and every now and then the part takes over completely, and I'm no longer an actress, because I am carried away by the character. We didn't, in fact, do it like that, but it would have been more exciting if we had.

*How did you approach the character of Joan, given all that you've just said about the feeling of its being an idea rather than a character?*

I can't remember how I approached it. But I do remember very much how I felt when I was doing it on stage, because it wasn't a success. Of course, I'd wanted to succeed in it, I felt very deeply about playing it. But on the first night I wasn't very good. I shouted terribly and I was very nervous. The notices were very bad and I felt very responsible. In a way, I experienced something marvellous, because it was very much her play, I had to get through this awful despair. I felt that the audiences must have read the notices and they must be thinking how bad I was: it took me a long time to get over that feeling. After about a fortnight, I was much better and I was able to use this feeling of despair. It suddenly dawned on me that half of them probably hadn't read the notices and even if they thought I was going to be bad, what did it matter, because, if I could be better than they thought, then that would be something. Anyway, I was thinking far too much about myself and far too little about the part I was playing. And so I got down to it, and as a result of this despair, because I knew I couldn't be worse, I was in fact better. There were moments when I acted that play better perhaps than I had ever acted before.

*Do you have any desire, having played Anouilh's Joan, to do the Shaw play?*

No, not really. I don't think I would be very good casting for that. I don't know. I don't think about a part until somebody offers it to me. Perhaps I'm wrong, perhaps it's cowardly to say that. I think perhaps I'd like to, yes, perhaps I would. It's such a marvellous play.

*I saw you in the BBC television production of Anouilh's Antigone. This was a performance of intensity. I noticed that you were crying quite freely, at times. Is this something that you can do to order in the theatre?*

Yes, I do cry quite easily. But you see, in that play I cried quite early on at the most awful moment. I shouldn't have been crying at all, it was stupid. I was so worked up when I actually met Haemon and he was the very person who shouldn't have seen me crying; the whole point was that she was controlling herself at that moment. But I had a terrible tear that came with the mascara, running down my cheek; and it stung my eye which made it even worse, the more noticeable. I think sometimes it's a help to cry. It helps you; but I don't think it helps the audience: it's a purely personal thing. When

1955 Joan, *The Lark*, Lyric, Hammersmith

1960 Viola, *Twelfth Night*, Stratford,
with Barbara Barnett (Olivia)

you really cry it can be very awkward, you know, your nose runs
and it's a great mess. If you can somehow have a feeling of tears that
are coming and they don't come, it means that you're controlling
them. This is a help to you, obviously, because it's a physical thing
that gives you a reaction.

*This is not a technique which you have been able to acquire. You couldn't
guarantee it every night, as it were, in the performance of the same part?*

In some parts, yes; if it once happens I think probably it would
happen every night, simply because the feeling would come back
again if you had once had that feeling. I don't think it's important,
it isn't a necessary adjunct: very nice if you can do it easily.

*What is your feeling about plays like the Anouilh* Antigone *and some of
the Giraudoux plays – for instance the updating of old stories, old Greek
stories into modern terms?*

It's very interesting playing a classical situation in modern terms:
the dichotomy is a help. But Anouilh gets away from the absolute
bare savagery of the real Greek drama. The real Greek drama is
extremely difficult to do, you have a big burden to carry. I went to
Delphi and I thought if one could have acted there, how marvellous. You have the sky, and to act on the stone with the sky above;
what a strange feeling of timelessness! It must make you feel different. The whole essence of Greece and Greek drama is so extra-

ordinary because everybody recognises it, it's in all of us to understand the Greek myths: they are so completely universal.

*Do you find television is a medium in which you can create your own effects more powerfully and more immediately than in the theatre?*

I haven't done much television *or* filming for that matter; I'm not a very good person to talk about it. I lack a nice cosy approach to a camera, you see. That camera over there has a light; I've suddenly noticed it; I can actually look at it but it horrifies me. I'm not at all pleased when these monsters come close to me.

People who enjoy doing television are very satisfied when the camera comes close; they have a rapport with the camera which I haven't got: I wish I had. The thing I like about television is that you do all sorts of things which perhaps you wouldn't ever have the chance of doing on the stage. It's nice when you do something that you haven't ever played before; but it's very difficult to convert a stage performance into a television performance. It seems to me that in the theatre you have to appear to be real. It's a sort of imaginative truth; whereas on television it's a factual truth, it is in fact reality. It's a less profound thing in a way.

The effect you have to make in the theatre is probably stronger, it has to be stronger. You have to know just what it is you have to express, and then find the means by which to express it; and be sure that you are expressing it in such a way that it will travel through the whole building. That requires a lot of effort, power, strength.

*And a totality of you in fact.*

Yes, yes. I suppose the difficulty in television is that although it's more real, you have an exactitude and a smallness that sometimes seems almost unnatural. It's only for people who are really good at it. It's their natural technique and they can do it. I know that when I first did a film, I was always being told, you mustn't move your head and you mustn't wave your arms; you know it seemed terribly inhibiting. What you were going to do was to express it all with one flicker of your eye. This is marvellous discipline and wonderful if you can do it; I'd love to do more television.

*Does the technique of performing in a film excite you?*

I'd love to be in a modern film where it didn't matter what you looked like. I think films now are more like that, aren't they? In *The Importance of Being Earnest*, I was always casting shadows with my nose or doing something to the lights. It was very inhibiting, if you're not perfectly photogenic. If I could do a film now which was modern rather than stylised, where you had every advantage of the camera being very, very close and very intimate, this I would love. I would be very excited by that.

*As a general rule, how far do you find yourself dependent upon the excellence*

1960 Cressida, *Troilus and Cressida*, Stratford, with M
Adrian (Pandarus)

1961 Desdemona, *Othello*, Stratford, with John Gielgud as Othello and Peggy Ashcroft as Emilia

*of direction? Are you an actress who works very well with certain producers and not very well with others? Or do they lean on you rather more than you lean on them?*

In films, of course, I think you're absolutely dependent on the director. I'd rather a director told me what to do because, not knowing too much about filming, it's very difficult to know what is coming out the other end.

In the theatre, it's a sort of double act. The producer has a marvellous position in the beginning, because when you come to the first rehearsal, he knows the play terribly well, he knows what he's going to do with it, he's talked with the designer about the set. You feel out of it to begin with, as though it's a sort of moving train that you've got to get on to, and fit into. But then there comes a time when you have developed in the part, and what you really value and need then is the producer to be with you, to make you go that step further. What can happen is that the producer goes back and back to his production rather than coming to the point when he could give you a great shove and say, 'Now do it; do it more, do it better.'

*But you would agree that some actors and actresses are barely affected at all by whatever direction they may get?*

You mean, they go their own way?

*They go their own way, they are absolutely established. You don't work like that?*

I don't think so, although one is always responsible for one's own performance. I like being directed, I find it very stimulating working with different directors, obviously one learns and is helped tremendously by them.

*Are there any great roles that you wish very much to play now?*

It's impossible to say. I would play anything that I was offered, I think, if I liked the part: I can't say I've ever had specific ambitions. I've been lucky you see; I was lucky at the beginning having those two big parts; I was lucky with the Royal Shakespeare to be cast in perhaps unsuitable parts, Portia, *The Devils* – I mean a commercial management wouldn't perhaps have cast me to play them. The best thing you can have as an actress is to be stretched beyond your capacity every time. It's daunting and you never feel you're ever going to succeed and play something that's absolutely you, absolutely within your range. But then the thing is to develop your range so widely that eventually you can play anything.

*You've grown up in your profession at a time when there has been, in this country, a very high standard of acting in each succeeding generation. Do you feel that you are part of a different kind of acting tradition from that, let us say, of Dame Sybil Thorndike's generation?*

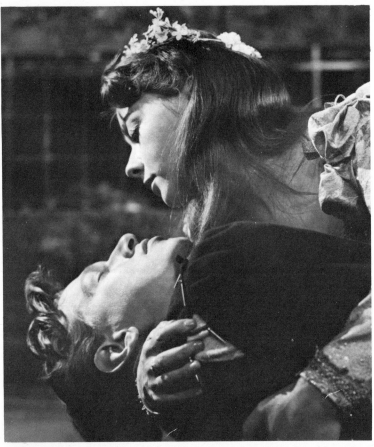

1961 Juliet, *Romeo and Juliet*, Stratford, with Brian Murray as Romeo and Edith Evans as the Nurse

I don't think so. Good acting is good acting. I think it's a very difficult question. One has heard records of very famous actors in the past and they do sound a bit unacceptable to us now. But of the actors that are living, I can't think that any of them are so different. It is the fashion of *presentation* which changes – acting problems are the same. The alarming thing is that you'd expect acting to get easier as you grow older, but it gets more difficult. I suppose it's because you know more, you're not quite so dotty, you don't rush into it. You're more aware of what should be, how it could be.

*Yes, but for instance there has been a difference of approach towards acting, hasn't there, in the last twenty years?*

You mean, it's become more naturalistic?

*Yes, more naturalistic, less of the set piece, if you like.*

There's a sort of movement against classical acting. But to me, classical acting is very exact, very beautiful, unfussed and very inspiring.

*Yes. But that's not quite what I meant. I think of classical acting and naturalistic acting, and then romantic acting coming in the middle.*

But don't actors and actresses do all three? Isn't that the ideal, to be able to do everything?

Plays are becoming more and more extraordinary, less real, more esoteric. If plays now are written for young actors, they have to find the right style for today. And this is right. But when you have a playwright like John Whiting, for instance – a remarkable writer – he wrote in a style which I imagine we never really got right. When his plays are done, probably in a few years' time, people will see them in a more objective way, and not try to make the dialogue naturalistic, but take it for what it is, a very exact, very strange almost poetic writing. Instead of trying to twist the words to make it seem natural, they will try to find the right style so that the world that he created will be doubly powerful. When you come down to it, the style of the writer is what matters. The actor is an instrument for interpreting this style.

I think probably what one hopes is that dramatists will go their own way, follow their own star, and not trends, because it seems that things that are trends don't always last, and things that are deeply personal and can only be written by that person at that particular time do last.

1961 Varya, *The Che*
*Orchard*, Aldwych, w
John Gielgud (Gae
Judi Dench (Anya) a
Peggy Ashcroft (Ma
ame Ranevsky)